Women in Pain

Women in Pain

Gender and Morbidity in Mexico

Kaja Finkler

University of Pennsylvania Press

Philadelphia

Library of Congress Cataloging-in-Publication Data

Finkler, Kaja.
    Women in pain : gender and morbidity in Mexico / Kaja Finkler.
        p.   cm.
    Includes bibliographical references and index.
        ISBN 0–8122–3243–7. — 0–8122–1527–3 (pbk.)
        1. Women—Health and hygiene—Mexico.   2. Women—Health and
hygiene—Social aspects—Mexico.   3. Women—Health and hygiene—
Mexico—Case studies.   4. Women—Health and hygiene—Social
aspects—Mexico—Case studies.   5. Sex role—Mexico.   I. Title.
RA564.85.F56   1994
614.4'272'082—dc20   93-32972
                                                                        CIP

In memory of my mother, an extraordinary woman ahead of her time, and to my father, who perished ahead of his time

Contents

Tables

Preface

In this book, I write about unknown, ordinary women in Mexico who come from the poorest strata of Mexican society. The book is about their lives and how their lives are intertwined with their experience of sickness and health. Although there are myriad books about women and women's lives, to my knowledge there are no books on the lives of women within the context of their experience of sickness.

This book emerges out of my extensive research in rural and urban Mexico on diverse anthropological concerns, including peasant economic and political activities, gender roles, sickness, and ways of healing, especially as practiced by Spiritualists and physicians.

During studies spanning twenty years, I lived with various families, participated in their daily lives, trained as a Spiritual healer, and maintained ongoing personal contacts with numerous families from many levels of Mexican society. My continuous friendship and ritual kinship relations gave me the opportunity to observe closely women's daily lives and social interactions as well as to witness their anguish and pain. I spent countless hours talking with women of all ages in different stages of their lives about issues that concerned them most—namely, how to sustain their households and feed their families. They spoke about their worries concerning their children and their futures, about their relations with mates and parents, and about their health.

During two years of intensive research on Spiritual healing (1977–1979)—as an observer and apprentice to the healers—I watched women healers at work. Some of these women were also leaders of men and women in their capacity as heads of Spiritualist temples.[1] I noted that the majority of the healers, and a majority of their patients, were women.

Later, when I carried out a two-year intensive study of biomedical practice in one of the largest hospitals in Mexico City (1986–1988),[2] I found that the majority of patients seeking treatment there were women. My findings, showing that the greater proportion of patients were women, do not identify an isolated phenomenon. In fact, in both industrializing and industrially developing nations, morbidity is more common among women than men. This situation led me to pose the question I address in this book: Why is it that women experience more sickness than men, leading more women than men to seek treatment, be it from Spiritualist healers or physicians?

Ostensibly this is a simple question, but the answers are complex. On one level we, as the inheritors of Western understandings of ourselves as biologically driven organisms, may wish to dismiss the question by saying simply that disparities in health status along sex lines are due to physiological differences between men and women, most likely related to women's reproductive capacities, and leave it at that. But the answers to this question are more complex. On a more profound level we have come to recognize that a person's health is not solely a biological event; health and sickness are embedded in social, cultural, and individual experiences. To begin to unravel the question of differential sickness among men and women is to attend not only to biological variables but to the meaning of sickness and suffering in social, cultural, and individual terms, and to ideologies and actions bearing on notions of gender and sex.

In my work on Spiritualism and biomedicine, my chief focus was on therapeutic practices, treatment outcomes, and the experience of sickness and its alleviation. In this book, my major concern is with patients' subjective experience of symptoms, and their pains within the context of the women's lived experience. I have addressed the question of differential health along sex lines previously,[3] when I examined the relationship between stress induced by life events and women's health. I identified specific life events in Mexico that impinge on women's experience of sickness, especially the death of a child. But through the years I have continued to probe further into questions concerning women's health and morbidity. In this book I add new dimensions to my analysis of differential morbidity between women and men.

The concepts I advance here flow from my close association with the people who have opened their lives to me. During the course of all my studies in Mexico, both men and women laid bare their lives to me and spoke openly about their pains.[4] When speaking about their sickness, they incessantly referred to their day-to-day experiences, which always revolved around their relationships with their mates, children, parents, and neighbors. Their discourses persuaded me that what I identify as *life's lesions*— which are embedded in existential conditions, contradictions, and moral evaluations—are as virulent as any pathogen found in nature. To isolate an individual's life's lesions we must place that person's existence in its material and ideological settings under a magnifying glass.[5] This, in fact, is the project of the book: to arrive at the totality of human sickness.

This book was difficult to write for many reasons. As I worked in the field and listened to people, I was saddened by their lives and the extraordinarily harsh conditions of their existence. At the same time, I was left with admiration for the people's resilience, good humor, limitless generosity, and forbearance. With the exception of Margarita, who lived in a well-built house situated in an elegant neighborhood, all of the women I studied existed in various gradations of abysmal poverty. Some lived in huts with permeable tin roofs, others with more resources resided in cinder block houses with asbestos roofs, and others lived in *vecindades,* old congested tenement houses.

When I reviewed the women's narratives, I relived the pain I had experienced as I listened to each woman, recalling her facial expressions as she recounted her afflictions and her life. Although my heart went out to many of the women, some women's anguish seemed less bearable than others. In Rebecca's eyes, I saw a frightened animal living in a cage. On the other hand, I always looked forward to my visits with Alicia, whose good humor made my encounters with her a delight, though her humor obscured the dilemmas she faced.

My contact with the women included in this book began during my study on biomedical practice, and patients' responses to it, in a general hospital in Mexico City. For the purposes of that project, I conducted structured interviews and open-ended discussions with patients both in the hospital and during follow-ups at their homes, all of which were tape-recorded with the participants' permission and later transcribed. The first questions I posed to all of the randomly selected patients in the study, the majority of whom turned out to be women, focused on what was wrong, what symptoms they were experiencing, and why they came to the hospital. In response to these "trigger questions" people poured out their lives and their distress through free association. They usually described their symptoms and what they thought had brought them on. Very often they would speak about the "anger they made," to which I would respond, "What had happened to make you angry?" The responses to my trigger questions revealed the underlying conflicts related to these patients' experience of sickness.

Although trigger questions stimulated people to speak about themselves without any prodding, I also queried them specifically about witchcraft, a subject people rarely raise spontaneously in unstructured discussion. I asked each patient whether witchcraft had ever been performed on him or her. I did so because in my previous research I had found that when people were unsuccessfully treated by physicians,[6] they drew on beliefs in witchcraft to explain their sickness, and that these beliefs affected their experience of sickness and recovery.

Of the 205 women I interviewed intensively at the hospital and the 161 I followed up in their homes, I introduce only ten here because of limitations of space. I selected these women because of my extensive contacts with them and because in several instances they were especially gifted narrators. Margarita, for example, spoke for eight hours in an uninterrupted flow, and Josefina needed little encouragement during the course of an eight-hour visit.

For some women, our interaction may have led them to reflect on their lives in ways they had not done before, perhaps because on an elemental level reflection on oneself and one's life is a luxury poor people can ill afford. According to a handful of women, our interaction benefited them; Rebecca and Margarita, for example, attributed improvement in their health to their association with me and my assistant.

The lives of the women, their sickness, and, in some instances, their recovery, unfolded gradually. To learn about these women is to recognize existential themes familiar to contemporary human beings. Yet their lives take on a cultural cast. Violence perpetrated against many of the women is obviously not unique to Mexico, nor are parental molestations unique to Mexican families; we constantly read about such acts occurring the world over. But such behaviors have different outcomes depending on the socio-cultural setting. In Margarita's case, her struggle to separate herself from her father and husband, and to become an autonomous individual, differs in its intricacies from women with similar biographical baggage in the United States, where individual independence is prized.

The women in this study are not movers and shakers of the world, their feats are not recorded in history books. Their heroism rests in their making it through each day. As some women themselves recognize, their lives are banal. The monotony of their daily existence is punctuated by unanticipated events such as sickness, death, arrests, and occasionally earthquakes, but also by the satisfactions they take in their children, public fiestas, and family celebrations.

Forming part of the majority of the poor of Mexico, the women we will meet shared similar rhythms of daily life, similar ideologies, and similar understandings about what constitutes a woman and a man. The resemblances dissolve, however, as we look closely at the courses of their lives, revealing the uniqueness of each woman's existence. Each woman communicated a dominant theme in her life, to which she repeatedly referred when speaking about her disorder.

In these pages I present what Arthur Kleinman (1988) calls "illness narratives," narrations that constantly reflect back on the experience of sickness. The experience of sickness dissolves the past into the present and transcends all chronological time. In this sense the life histories are not meant to be biographies, but rather they focus on aspects of a woman's life with which she associates her pain. And as I watched the women's lives change, I noted that their perceptions of their pains changed as well.

In the final analysis, we might ask, Why do we want to learn about the mundane lives of poor women? What can they teach us about women's sickness and health that contemporary biomedicine and medical academies do not already know? The afflictions of the women presented here illuminate the phenomenological nature of sickness, which is embedded in material and ideological webs and hence cannot be attributed only to the "breaking down" of the "bodily machine."

It is not my intention to deny the role of a biological substrate in human sickness. Incontrovertibly, on a most basic level pathogens and anatomical dysfunctions account for human sickness. But these do not explain all the variance in human pain and affliction. My goal is to deepen our grasp of human sickness—as has been done by others, especially Eric Cassell, George Engel, and Arthur Kleinman—and to do so I focus on what I call *life's lesions*. Nor is it my goal to disavow the achievements of biomedicine. Contemporary biomedicine has unquestionably made dazzling advances and has succeeded in treating complex medical impairments. At the same time, biomedicine often fails to alleviate patients' routinely experienced symptoms because of the limitations of the biomedical script,[7] a script that fails to comprehend life's lesions.

This book is divided into three parts. I move from general theoretical considerations in Part I, to the social and cultural contexts in Part II, and then to individual cases in Part III. Part I presents the theoretical issues that illuminate the empirical data discussed in Parts II and III. In Chapter 1, I identify the central problem addressed in the book as it relates to the differential expression of non-life threatening, sub-acute symptoms among women and men. The discussions in Chapters 2 and 3 should be regarded as the basic theoretical building blocks for our understanding of women's sickness within the context of their lives. In Chapter 2, I develop the anthropological understanding of sickness and the various nonbiological theories propounded about affliction. In addition, I elaborate on the concept of life's lesions, which I equate with anatomical lesions. In Chapter 3 my concern is with the "woman question," the various theories relevant to our understanding of gender and sex, and women's roles in developing nations. These first three chapters set the foundation for Chapter 4, in which I explore the relationship between gender and sickness.

In Part II, I present the social and cultural contexts that reverberate with the theoretical discussion in Part I and set the stage for the women we will meet. In Chapter 5, I furnish the ethnographic context of women's activities, male-female relations, and ideologies about women in Mexico from historical and contemporary perspectives. I draw on my work in rural and urban Mexico and with Spiritualist healers and patients.

In Chapter 6, I furnish an aggregate view of a large sample population from which the women we meet here were drawn; I also compare the large sample population with a healthy group along selected variables. By doing so, I situate the women discussed in Part III sociodemographically and compare them with the larger population sample along these variables. To facilitate our understanding relevant to the women's experience of their disorders, I briefly sketch Mexican cultural understandings of sickness and the differences between men and women's etiological explanations, as well as physicians' postures toward their women patients.

In Part III, I focus on individual women. In Chapters 7 through 16 we learn about each of the ten women's lives and their sickness states. To give a sense of how the women experience their sickness, I attend in some detail to the symptomatologies for which they sought treatment, to the medical diagnosis, to their health-seeking trajectories, to the history of their symptoms, and to their biographies within the context of their afflictions. I unravel the major themes in the women's lives with which they associate their disorders. Because sickness lacks a chronology[8] and the experience of pain transcends measured time, the many experiences in one's life with which sickness is associated lose their chronological order. For this reason, the women's narrations skip and jump, taking us in many different directions—to workplaces, to religious conversions, to sexual relations, to husband-wife interactions. These narratives thus become gateways to Mexican ideologies and morality, and demonstrate the ways in which society and culture interact with the personal experience of sickness and pain. From each woman we gain a glimpse of what angered her, what pained her, and most of all, her perceptions of what had made her sick. We learn about the many arenas in which affliction unfolds, and it becomes clear that at the core of these women's lives there lies a thirst for dignity, left unquenched by their existence.

In the conclusion I reflect on the contributions of my findings to the anthropology of health and sickness and the anthropology of women. This book is more an intermediary stage than an endpoint. It is meant to advance our comprehension of women's health and add another dimension to what is already known about women's physiological dysfunctions by identifying forces at work that must inform our understanding of women's health.

Although in Chapter 6 I show how the ten women represent the larger population of women from the same social strata, we may, of course, question the degree to which these women's lives are able to be generalized. My answer is that no individual life is ever generalizable. In these pages, the portrayal of a few women's pain will animate the morbidity statistics we encounter in census data. In many ways the lives of these women do not differ very much: they are all poor, they all have children; these are the sort of demographics that we easily know and about which we can easily generalize. But when we painstakingly examine the women's existence, broad generalizations melt away. Having said this, I hasten to note that any one life sheds light on the universals of human existence. In this manner, the women here speak for many worldwide.

I anticipate that medical anthropologists, scholars of women's studies, health practitioners concerned with issues of women's health, and their students will be able to draw on this work to make sense of women's symptomatologies and to help them recognize that women's sickness is not, as some would say, simply "in their heads."

Finally, it is not my intention in this book to promote any one of the competing theoretical perspectives on gender and sex or to propagate a specific ideological agenda. To repeat, the propositions I advance here arise out of the women's experiences and are informed by traditional anthropological understandings of the disposition of humans as social, cultural, and moral beings. It is, however, my hope that the data I present will improve the lives of poor women by advancing our insights into their individual suffering and their health. In this spirit, I hope that this book will furnish at least a partial reply to the question Alicia posed to me: "My old man never gets sick, there has never been anything wrong with him since I have known him for the past ten or twelve years, and why am I sick all the time?"

Notes

1. For an extensive discussion of Spiritualism see Finkler 1985b.
2. For an in-depth analysis of biomedical practice in a general hospital in Mexico see Finkler 1991.
3. See Finkler 1985a, where I focus on differential symptomatological differences between the sexes in relation to theories of life events.
4. See, for example, the candid narrative by Celsa in Tirado 1991, a biography of a Mexican peasant woman.
5. I deal in depth with men's and women's lives in relation to the effectiveness of biomedical treatment in Finkler 1991.
6. See Finkler 1985b, 1991.
7. See Finkler 1991.
8. I also discuss this point in Finkler 1991.

Acknowledgments

The gathering of the narratives was made possible by grants from the National Science Foundation #BNS8607543 and the Department of Health and Human Services #BSR1R01MH42309-1 and #BSBR01MH42309-2. I am grateful for the support I received from these institutions.

A project of this scope has accumulated debts to numerous people. First and foremost I am grateful to all the women in the study for receiving me in their homes and for offering their trust and cooperation. I am especially grateful to the ten women described in the book for their willingness to open their lives to me. I also extend my thanks to Norma Jara for her able assistance in data collection in Mexico. I gratefully appreciate the close readings of the manuscript by Terry Evens, Andrea Meier, and Tom Whitmore, and Asunción Lavrin's comments on Chapter 5. Special thanks go to Maria Correa for the excellent statistical analyses of the data presented in Chapter 6. My appreciation also goes to Dr. Fernando Martinez Cortes, convener of the seminar "Hombre en Su Totalidad," in which I participated during my stay in Mexico City.

Part I

The Problem

1. Introduction

During the past few decades there has been an explosion of scholarship concerning all aspects of women's existence in the past and present. These works address a host of theoretical issues bearing on questions such as: What is the relationship between female physiology and female thought and behavior? What is the relationship between sex, referring to the anatomical construction of males and females, and gender, defined as the culturally instituted behaviors of males and females? Are gender inequality and female subordination universal? How do engendered lives interweave with class and ethnicity in complex societies?

None of the numerous issues that have been addressed in the literature on gender and sex is more fundamental than gender differences. The question revolves around whether there are sexual differences beyond the anatomical ones, and if so, what are the nature and source of these differences? This question, like other theoretically significant issues, is now being hotly debated and will not be easily resolved. Whatever one's theoretical position regarding gender differences, there exists empirical evidence for the differential experience of morbidity between men and women. Physicians have recognized long ago that women experience pain and sickness more often than men.[1] This sexual disparity in symptomatic expression is particularly intriguing in light of the fact that, paradoxically, women's rates of mortality worldwide are lower than men's.[2]

Most recently, Lois Verbrugge (1990: 41) has written,

> In contemporary health statistics, the largest differentials in rates of illness, disability, and death are related to age. . . . Sex ranks second. Women's experience of daily symptoms, their prevalence rates for many chronic conditions, their experience of short- and long-term disability due to health problems, and their use of professional health services exceed men's within each age group. Nevertheless, women's rates of mortality are strikingly lower than men's.

After an exhaustive literature review of the subject, Verbrugge concludes that women's lives are filled with more health problems—higher incidence of acute conditions, higher prevalence of most nonfatal chronic ones, more frequent botherations by health problems. . . . Compared to men, women's symptoms are more likely to be bothersome but not life-threatening, and their limitations are mild or moderate rather than severe until advanced ages. The conjunction of more nonfatal problems and fewer fatal ones means more total years of life—and also more years of sickness and dysfunction. By contrast, men's lives are freer of illness, discomfort, and disability. But when ill health does strike, it is more likely to be via fatal chronic diseases. These abbreviate men's lives. (62)

Verbrugge identifies five reasons discussed in the literature for these differences:

(1) biological risks; these are intrinsic genetic and hormonal differences between males and females, (2) acquired risks; these are risks of illness and injury encountered in one's work and leisure activities, (3) psychosocial aspects of symptoms and care; called "illness behavior" in medical sociology, (4) health reporting behavior; this concerns how men and women talk about their health problems to others, and (5) prior health care; or how one's care for health problems affects future health (63)

Verbrugge summarizes her analysis by stating, "Biological and acquired risks determine the occurrence of disease, injury and impairment. Psychosocial factors then come into play—in perception of symptoms, evaluation of their cause and severity, choice and continuation of therapeutic actions, and short- and long-term disability" (63). She continues:

It is widely held by researchers, and increasing scientific evidence suggests, that men are disadvantaged by both biological and acquired risk for the development of fatal diseases and for experience of injuries. What lies behind women's greater tendency to develop nonfatal diseases has not been discussed and it is a real *mystery*. The diseases are so diverse, no small array of risk factors (acquired or biological) is plausible. (64; emphasis added)

Although the United States is the point of reference for Verbrugge—and by and large the evidence for the disparity in morbidity along gender lines derives from research in developed nations, especially the United States and Great Britain—a similar phenomenon exists in developing nations such as Mexico. Against this background, I found in my study of patients seeking treatment from Spiritualist healers that 58 percent were women and only 15 percent men, the remainder being infants and young children. Similarly, in my study of patients seeking treatment from physicians in an outpatient clinic for adults, in a randomly selected sample,

76.8 percent of the patients were women and 23.2 percent were men. At both sites patients sought treatment for non-lifethreatening disorders. These findings, along with data from other sources,[3] impelled me to address the obvious question: Why do women's non-lifethreatening health problems exceed those of men?

My aim here is to contribute to the unraveling of the "mystery" noted by Verbrugge by building on and expanding current explanations concerning women's health, using anthropologically informed analyses. To address the dilemma of differential morbidity between men and women is to focus on theoretical concerns about the nature of sickness and the interaction between sickness, gender, and society. From this perspective, there are important linkages between issues pertaining to gender and women's non-lifethreatening subacute morbidity. And to deal with women's morbidity from an anthropological perspective is to examine closely their lives from each patient's view of her sickness and the nuances of meaning each patient gives to her disorder within an ethnographically apprised context and personal meanings. An anthropological analysis of women's health adds new dimensions to an epidemiological and biomedical grasp of women's morbidity and provides insight into its alleviation.[4]

An anthropological study of women's morbidity must be buttressed by analysis of women's position in society and the ideologies that sustain that position, and, most important, by probing into male-female relationships. In fact, Marilyn Strathern advances the proposition that "in dealing with relations between the sexes, one is dealing with social relations at large" (1988: 35). While this proposition may be problematic because it ignores crucial relationships between people of the same sex, her assertion is certainly relevant for any consideration of women's health issues. Women's disorders are in large measure embedded in their social relations for reasons I will develop in Chapter 4.

A great deal has been written on women's lives,[5] describing women's personal histories. Although a vast literature exists devoted to women's health problems in developed nations,[6] studies in developing nations have concentrated mostly on women's health in association with their reproductive capacities. Hardly any of the literature on women's health in developing nations has explored the ways women's day-to-day existence and social interactions, coupled with the prevailing culturally produced gender ideologies, intersect with their health.[7]

On a theoretical level, generalizations are produced about women and their health. These generalizations are artifacts of the scientific enterprise that calls for the construction of universal categories. They avoid examination of women's health within the setting of the individuals' existence.[8] Not surprisingly, among the many reasons for the dearth of analyses of women's health in the context of their lived experience is the fact that the medical model has set up the agenda for the study of health issues using biological and physiological parameters, leaving little leeway for incorporation of human suffering into a model of sickness.[9] Following a scientific paradigm, earlier works with few exceptions[10] have sought to identify specific, postulated variables influencing women's health.[11] In most of the literature, the woman's subjective view is absent, her voice is not heard to help us comprehend her experience of pain and suffering. To get at women's experience of sickness I wish to eschew universalization of the category "woman" and instead situate the individual woman and her dysfunction within the context of her society, culture, and perceived existence.

In this work I weave together women's lives and women's distress, revealing aspects of women's existence that are dangerous to their health. My objective, then, is to describe women's lives in the context of their health and to provide a theoretical understanding for why women experience sickness more than men. I argue that sickness is embedded not only in physiological impairments but also, simultaneously, in conditions of life, social relations, unresolved contradictions, and moral evaluations. Women more than men are caught up in these nets of adversity (for reasons that I will explore in Chapter 4), predisposing women more than men to non-lifethreatening sickness.

To focus on conditions of human existence in tandem with their contradictions and the meanings people give to them is to attend also to the cultural context. As anthropologists, we have privileged the concept of culture to explain human thoughts and actions. Accordingly, we regard each culture as a human creation of reality, a screen for behavior and for making sense of the world in which we live. Culture guides people's behavior, their comprehension of their bodies, and their interpersonal relationships; it structures people's position in society and the realities they come to know and expect in their daily existence. In short, our culture enables us to take for granted our daily activities, our relationships, and our customary conceptions of life, including our moral footings. For example, we can expect (as we will see later) Mexican culture to define for its people what it is to be a woman or a man, and the respective roles for each. Culture defines how women and men ought to behave toward one another as husbands and wives, as parents and children.

Generally speaking, by its *naturalness,* culture smooths the course of our lives. But we must not overlook the fact that a people's culture also creates problems and contradictions, often resulting from the unintended consequences of human actions.[12] Such dilemmas may have adverse effects on the individual and the community of which he or she forms a part.[13] Having noted the singular role of culture in defining human existence, I hasten to add that when I carried out the present study in Mexico City, a mega-metropolis in a developing nation, I found the concept of a culture's uniqueness limiting. I make this assertion on the grounds that when we turn to the individual women in later chapters, we will encounter ample similarities between the lives of women in Mexico City and those of women in other contemporary societies in economically developing and developed nations, including the United States.

In fact, historically, industrialization and the contemporary global economy have structured people's lives the world over, particularly in urban areas, be it Mexico City or New York, thereby shrinking extant cultural differences. This correspondence is best seen when scrutinizing women's roles and their position in society, male-female relations, and the emergent contradictions both men and women must face. In the last decades of the twentieth century, aspects of family life, for example, have cut across cultural differences and have come to resemble one another, especially in the impoverished strata of society.

There are many preoccupations that men and women share cross-culturally when living in poverty, and women's concerns, especially in relation to economic deprivations, transcend cultural differences. As I witnessed women's daily lives in Mexico City, I noted great similarities to women from a comparable social stratum in the United States. Economically impoverished women in Mexico City and the United States must grapple with finding the means to maintain their children and their households, with disillusionment with romantic love after marriage, with abusive and exploitative husbands.[14] The similarities the women share by virtue of their sex and class overlie and conceal each woman's unique dilemma and understanding. As the stories of the Mexican women in this book unfold, some aspects of their lives will have a familiar ring to readers outside Latin America, other facets of their experience will seem culturally distant, and still others will be recognized as unique to each subject.

On these grounds, the concept of culture cannot be dismissed totally.[15] Women and men's understandings of themselves as engendered beings unquestionably have a historical, spatial, and societal context. Women in Mexico, as in most of Latin America, share distinctly Iberian comprehensions of themselves as women, wives, and mothers, although these views are overlain by notions shaped by historical forces originating in nineteenth-century Europe. But we must also remember that individuals, as thinking and evaluating beings, perceive their lives differentially within the parameters of their cultural pool of understandings.[16] A people's culture must not be construed as a straitjacket. Although each culture may limit the perceptions of possibilities, human interpretative capacities continuously shape and reshape received knowledge and understandings, as is the case of the Mexican women introduced here.

Because human beings are not passive receptacles for their culture, I take a phenomenological perspective. My point of departure is subjectively perceived experience in tandem with the actualities and the cultural and ideological templates in which daily existence is played out and which also ensnare a person in unresolvable contradictions of the kind that contribute to the onset of morbidity. But although the subject's perspective elucidates her own life, it is necessary to interject at least one caveat. Human beings themselves do not always recognize the consequences of the flow of events or the contradictions in which they are entangled. Our subjectivity restrains us from seeing our existence in its totality. There are, thus, limits of understanding to our subjective speculations. Hence, when the subjects recount their history and are unable to furnish an explanation for their sickness or make sense of their experience, the anthropological approach can be brought to bear to further our understanding of the people's subjective experience and make connections between their pain, their daily experience and cultural processes that they may not make themselves. For example, women like Margarita recognize the relationship between their sickness and their life world, whereas others, like Alicia, discern their dilemma but do not connect it with their health state; and still others, like Josefina, are just hurting. Some, like Alicia, Susana, and Carlota, recognize the economic or political injustices that impinge on their existence, while others, like Josefina, Margarita, Rebecca, Norma, or Juana, are oblivious to them. Thus although all the women discussed in this book have structurally similar positions in society, each woman's life's lesions require separate analyses.

In my analysis of individual women, I avoid the reification of each woman's anguish that is frequently undertaken by physicians and psychiatrists but rightly admonished by anthropologists.[17] These health specialists supply a label for the patient's condition, such as depression, or characterize the woman as a "somatizer," or reduce her pains to her poverty or powerlessness. Too often, however, anthropologists who criticize biomedicine and other disciplines for reifying and objectifying the subject and his or her sensibilities engage in a similar enterprise.[18] Although anthropologists, philosophers, and scholars of medicine have correctly recognized that all human paradigms are socially constructed, we often ignore the fact that our own theorizations are in themselves social constructions. Any analytic endeavor, including the one presented in this book, is perforce a socially constructed analysis of the object of study.

Tensions usually exist in human life between individual agents and the constraints imposed on them by the society and culture of which they are part. In the same vein, this dialectical tension will be reflected in my analysis of the women's lives. For while my constructed understanding regards these women as agents of their existence, impelled by their subjectivity, I recognize that they are nevertheless governed by regnant ideologies, which structure their beliefs and actions and which in turn contribute to shaping cultural beliefs and practices in an ongoing process of structuration.[19] Strathern (1988) correctly observes that much that is written about women is done to advance the interests of feminism. But she is quick to point out that feminists and anthropologists are not the same. Whereas the feminists' program is to demonstrate oppression in the abstract (Strathern 1988: 36), my intentions are to deal with women's lives in concrete terms, with their understanding of their lives within the context of sickness. My project began when I listened to women speak about their lives and the way their lives resonated with their afflictions. As I listened to individual women and watched many more women than men entering Spiritualist temples and hospitals, I questioned why women get sick more than men.

By posing this question, I was led to search for an understanding of differences in morbidity between men and women from a biological perspective. A biological view, however, is unsatisfying, because it fails to explain the phenomenon adequately. As an anthropologist, my concern is with people's existence and their embeddedness in society and culture. Therefore the social, cultural, and existential components of sickness must be identified to account for the variance. Women's health cannot be isolated from the family structure, from the men and children in their purview, from the cultural context, from gender ideologies, and from cultural comprehension of sickness. Thus, by way of background, it is necessary to furnish an anthropologically constructed understanding of sickness, the subject of the next chapter.

Notes

1. See Morris 1991, 105; also Gove and Hughes 1979; Verbrugge 1978.

2. See Nathanson 1975; Ibrahim 1980. For worldwide statistics and discussion see Weller and Bouvier 1981.

3. See Secretaria de Salud 1990; Pan American Health Organization. Health of Women Publication 524.

4. The empirical data for this study are based on a research investigation I conducted in Mexico City of the sickness experience of men and women during a two-year period, including 1986–1988 and the summer of 1991.

5. Since the initial burst of studies about women there have been a host of biographies of women including Barrios de Chungara 1978; Belenky et al. 1986; de Jesus 1962; Hemmings 1985; Jelin 1990; Patai 1988; Personal Narratives Group 1989; Tirado 1991; and many others.

6. The literature on women's health issues is obviously extensive; a good beginning bibliography can be found in Apple 1990.

7. Sayers 1982 makes a similar point.

8. See, for example, Jordanova 1980, 67.

9. Engel (1977) has long advocated an all-inclusive model of sickness, and more recently Kleinman 1988; Kleinman and Kleinman 1991; and Cassell 1991 similarly argue persuasively for an incorporation of human suffering into any analysis of sickness; See also Finkler 1991.

10. Brown and Harris 1978 were at the forefront in situating women's depression in their daily existence. See also Jack 1991, to whose work I will return in Chapter 4.

11. For example, marriage has been associated by various scholars with women's disorders, including Brown and Harris 1978; Nathanson 1975; Weissman and Klerman 1977.

12. See Giddens 1984.

13. For example, I have shown (Finkler 1986) how the unintended consequence of the Spiritualist movement in Mexico inhibits economic mobility for its members despite the fact that they decry their economic position.

14. For an excellent study of the working poor in America and the dilemmas they face, see Rubin 1976.

15. In fact, some would like to do away with the culture concept altogether. See, for example, Abu-Lughod 1991.

16. Elsewhere (Finkler 1991) I suggest that each society contains a cultural pool of understandings, not necessarily known to all its members, on which a member who requires an explanation for his or her suffering can draw.

17. See Taussig 1980.

18. Kleinman and Kleinman 1991 have recently made a similar argument.

19. See Giddens 1984.

2. The Nature of Sickness

To comprehend the impairments of the Mexican women whose lives will unfold in later chapters, it is necessary to pause to elucidate the general anthropological conceptualization of sickness. The intense interest in women's issues in the past decades has been paralleled by an outpouring of research on the social and cultural nature of sickness.[1] Whatever the individual scholar's theoretical orientation, there is broad consensus that getting sick is not just a biological fact, that symptomatologies have cultural and personal meanings.[2] This understanding has led scholars to distinguish between disease and illness, with disease referring to a biological and biochemical malfunction and illness to impaired function perceived by the patient in a cultural way.[3]

This distinction rests on the separation made in biomedicine between signs—regarded as manifestations of real disease and real pain—and symptoms—understood as patients' subjective experience, lacking objective reality. Unlike signs, which are measured objectively using various technologies, symptoms cannot be assessed by objective measures because of their very subjectivity.[4] The emphasis on objectivity, however, often ignores the fact that there is a person who is experiencing the pain.[5] As we all recognize from personal experience, physical pain cannot be extricated from our anguish or the two separated even for analytical purposes. Even when we feel sickness as an "it," disconnected from ourselves,[6] it is, nevertheless always a most intimate, personal, and solitary experience that cannot be shared,[7] or often even pinpointed in chronological time, important as it is to do so for the process of medical diagnosis.[8]

I employ the term "sickness" to signify both disease and illness. By sickness I mean an assault on the very being of the human body embedded in an inimical ecological environment, as it is played out in day-to-day existence in a given social and cultural milieu.[9] Sickness speaks to suffering, to anatomical dysfunctions expressed symptomatologically; it is usually associated with bodily pain.

Normally, as we attend to our daily activities, we take our bodies for granted. We do not experience any one part of our body more than another, nor are we especially conscious of any one part more than another until we feel it fatigued or in pain. When we start to feel discomfort in one part of our body—in a way we have not felt it before for a sustained period of time—we begin to sense we are sick, we begin to feel distress and a disorder. Sickness affects our entire being, the body and the mind, both inextricably intertwined in human experience. For this reason, scholars have argued against the prevailing distinction between body and mind, the "myth of two pains—mental and physical" (Morris 1991).[10] Although not all sickness is accompanied by pain (for example, mild hypertension), pain propelled the women in this study to seek treatment at the hospital where I first met them. Chronic pain, the kind women in this study have experienced, "is the medical term for pain that, perversely, refuses to disappear or that reappears over extended periods, in episodes" (Morris 1991: 69). Unlike acute pain, "chronic pain simply will not go away and stay away" (70), and the usual remedies are ineffective to alleviate it. A case in point are the women we will meet later who had experienced their pain for long periods of time.[11]

As a rule, in the course of our day, we do not search for causalities. But sickness begs for an explanation when it strikes because it is not solely a physiological experience. It is an experience that leads us to question its meaning,[12] or, as David Morris rightly observes, "pain is not just a biological fact but an experience in search of an interpretation" (1991, 38).

Thus, when we fall ill and the sickness lingers on, we begin to seek reasons for our new experience. We begin to ask ourselves, Why did I fall ill now? What is causing my body to feel in an odd way, in a painful way, and why does each task require undue effort? Although each person's subjective experience of pain leads him or her to define him- or herself as sick, the reasons for its occurrence are difficult to capture when the sickness is not just routine, minor discomfort.

In all cultures, at times of distress humans have sought the reasons for sickness. And each culture supplies a blueprint to explain the extraordinary—the disorder taking place in the body and in the life of the sick individual—as well as a strategy to deal with it. Sickness has been attributed to numerous causes, including punishment by deities, intrusion by evil spirits or ancestral ghosts, witchcraft, environmental assaults and imbalances, cosmological upheavals, diet, and numerous other causes.[13] Sickness is dealt with in a plethora of ways, usually commensurate with the attribution. Customarily, when routine home ministrations fail, people seek specialists to alleviate their ills and to help them make sense of their unique and personal experience.

By and large, biomedicine, contemporary Western society's predominant medical system, attributes disease to anatomical lesions, or pugnacious pathogens, independent of the human context in which the infirmity exists. Contemporary Western medicine, which has become the reigning medical system worldwide, explains sickness as having "one cause" leading to "altered structure" (Cassell 1991: 7–8). These attributions usually revolve around physical breakdown, noxious organisms attacking the body, wear and tear through aging, and environmental hazards. Eric Cassell calls attention to the shortcomings of biomedicine resulting from its search for a single source for a patient's malady or for a change in the organism. He observes that, for instance, if a patient's X-rays "showed the tumor, the patient had a disease. If they did not, it was possible to dismiss the patient's complaints as 'nerves,' or spasm—in other words, no disease" (1991: 8). Cassell rightly contends that "it is obvious that *something* is the matter or the person would not be in such pain. But no disease is present, at least according to traditional theories of disease, because there is no structural change" (8, emphasis in the original).

There is no doubt that contemporary medicine has achieved an exquisite understanding of the anatomy and physiology of the body. But despite its achievements, scientific medicine has not as yet discovered the specific etiologies for numerous diseases, including cancer, cardiovascular dysfunctions, or many others. And while contemporary medicine can delineate for the patient the complex workings of the disease process in general terms, it usually cannot explain the reason why any *one* patient experiences a sickness.

Increasingly, scholars have noted that "medicine persists in its view that symptoms result directly from the pathological processes and the objective aspects of disease" (Cassell 1991: 97), and they argue against this prevailing perspective. Cassell, in fact, emphasizes correctly that it has become apparent that "*sickness could not be completely understood apart from personal life style and the social setting in which it occurred*" (1991: 14; emphasis in the original).

Admittedly, when customary interpretations of causality fail to explain a disease, biomedicine usually relies on concepts of hereditary predisposition[14] and behavioral risk factors (alcohol and drug abuse, diet),[15] or on behavioral medicine's notion of stress. But interpretations of this kind fall short of the meaning of the affliction to the sufferer, a meaning that is intensely subjective and rooted in one's lived experience.

Stress as an etiological factor, considered as a nonspecific risk agent or cause of sickness, comes closest to a personal attribution for one's affliction.[16] It has become a free-floating justification for symptoms that lack any physical rationale. Because the stress concept is a pervasive medical and folk theory, it merits brief consideration. The assertion is that stress, usually generated by their unspecified societal pressures or by specific circumstances (for example, conditions of employment), adversely alters psychological and physiological processes in the organism.[17] The stress model of disease postulates that societal as well as emotional and psychological distress may influence the functions of the immunological system, especially through neuroendocrine mediation.[18]

Many aspects of life, including modern life itself, have been identified as stressors that produce sickness. To operationalize the stress theory, scholars have attempted to identify specific events that may be stress producing. Life events theory, a powerful extrasomatic explanation of sickness causality, is subsumed under the broader stress model of sickness. Stressful life events include exceptional events in a person's life, such as the death of a spouse or child, a divorce, the loss of a job, or moving, which are especially traumatic in an individual's life.[19] Significantly, while life events theory emerges out of academic concerns with nonmaterial sickness-producing agents, in Mexico it is commonly recognized that life experiences, such as the death of a child, produce sickness.[20]

Life events theory is closely associated with the theory of social supports. Numerous scholars have proposed that certain buffers, such as social supports, mediate the effects of stressors, such as life events.[21] "Social support" refers to networks of relationships on which individuals may rely, including kinship relationships, and the degree of perceived trust or reliance on others.

Generally speaking, life events and social supports have been studied out of context, and the meanings they hold for individual patients have usually been passed over.[22] In the final analysis, the meaning people give to the life event or the support cannot, of course, be separated from the event or the nature of the support itself. Certain life events have a great impact in human life, as will be seen in Chapter 6, where I identify specific life events associated with a sick population in Mexico.[23] But we must keep in mind that not all human beings are equally affected by divorce, separation, or a move to a new house. Nor are all social supports in one's social network equally meaningful. Subjective interpretations shape the responses to the life event as well as to the sources of support. Moreover, the role of social supports in mitigating sickness is open to question when viewed cross-culturally. For example, in my 1991 study I found that the presence or absence of social supports failed to distinguish between healthy and sick individuals in Mexico City because people are encompassed by families to whom they look for support. Families mobilize their resources and efforts on behalf of a family member in distress. Generally speaking, people normally look to their mothers for unconditional material and affective support.[24]

To expand the role of social supports in sickness, James House et al. (1988) propose that social relationships in general are a core risk factor in health. These authors assert that social relationships are the crucial under-pinnings for psychological and physiological functioning. In their words, "We now need a broader theory of the biopsychosocial mechanisms and processes linking social relationships to health than can be provided by extant concepts or theories of social support" (1988: 543).

The theories of stress and their derivatives acclaim the role of extra-somatic factors in sickness and take us beyond biomedical theories of disease causation; still, they remove the individual from his or her embodied self and the social context in which he or she is embedded. Theories of life events, social supports, or even social relationships tend to model themselves after biomedical paradigms by reducing disease etiology to a single cause.[25] By stripping the patient of his or her capacity to judge and evaluate his or her existence, the notion of stress has become just another sort of pathogen assaulting the human body.

We have all experienced stress at some point in our lives. Certainly the women in this book live under ongoing stressful environmental and economic conditions and they are frequently faced by stressful life events. But to deepen our understanding of sickness we must attend equally to the social and economic conditions of an individual's circumstances and to the nuances of meaning that she or he gives to his or her day-to-day existence in its totality. We must pay attention to life events within the context of the person's life, especially his or her social interactions, to the moral dilemmas, and to the unresolved contradictions that must be confronted in daily life, which produce what I have previously identified as *life's lesions*.[26]

By life's lesions, I mean the perceived adversities of existence, including inimical social relationships, and unresolved contradictions in which a human being is entrenched and which gnaw at the person's being. Such lesions become inscribed on the body and manifest in anguish, in generalized pain experienced in the entire body, and in non-lifethreatening symptomatologies of unspecified etiology. These symptomatologies are often untranslatable into the signs on which medical diagnoses are based, and they often go undetected by traditional biomedical technologies. Inscriptions carved by life's lesions make us painfully aware of our bodies and of being sick.

We may be tempted to set up a flowchart to display in hierarchical order the sources of life's lesions. But such a project would be unfeasible because the underpinnings of life's lesions are not amenable to diagrammatic representation; they are, in fact, fuzzy. The concept of life's lesions recognizes that human infirmities cannot be reduced to one or two factors alone. These lesions are fluid; they sum up multiple causes that are fostered by and rise out of perceived adversity, hostile social relations, stressful life events, or unresolved contradictions that corrode one's existence, take hold of the body, and carve impairments on it. Life's lesions express through the body deleterious conditions of existence, be they poverty, malnutrition, adverse life events, perceived discrepancies in our culturally shaped image of ourselves and attributes of our body, or other unreconcilable contradictions.

Most important, life's lesions develop when tacit, culturally shared understandings of moral imperatives concerning proper behavior in social relationships are contested and *remain unresolved,* especially between mates and between parents and children—the sort of encounters that make up day-to-day experiences—or when concepts of culturally defined social justice and proper human conduct are grossly violated, they forge life's lesions in an individual. Under such circumstances, unresolved contradictions and moral indignations become inscribed on the body, ensuing symptomatologically in overall discomfort, pain, and suffering.

John Dewey, whose key philosophical method focused on experience, noted that "like its congeners, life and history, it includes *what* men do and suffer, *what* they strive for, love, believe and endure, and also *how* men act and are acted upon, the ways in which they do and suffer, desire and enjoy, see, believe, imagine—in short, processes of *experiencing*" (1929: 8). Life experience has a typicality about it.[27] When the typicality of experience becomes *atypical* under conditions of perceived adversity, it becomes inscribed on our bodies, felt as pain and expressed symptomatologically.

To refute that the life one lives, embedded in society and in social relations, can become the equivalent of a "virus" is to deny the meaning of existence. Human beings are not solitary creatures, and the life of the individual "makes no sense if the structural bases of practice are not kept in view" (Connell 1987: 221). B. W. Connell astutely observes that "complexities of personal life arise from structural contradictions that go far beyond the particular person" (221).

Unreconcilable incongruities in human life grate on the body, in the same way as do adversities of existence and moral indignations. To say that human beings must face contradictions is to state the obvious. Contradictions form part of social processes[28] and each generation must confront new incongruities. According to Anthony Giddens (1984), contradictions become prominent in human life under conditions of social flux. In Giddens's words, "The consequences of intended acts are contradictory when those consequences are perverse in such a way that the very activity of pursuing an objective diminishes the possibility of reaching it" (313). Giddens situates the concept of emerging contradictions in potential "cracks" in the broader social system.

On an individual level, historical events and historical changes that emerge as unreconcilable contradictions are absorbed by the body and expressed in idiosyncratic or culturally typified symptomatology. Unresolved contradictions, contingent and changing, emanate from historical processes and become inscribed on the body.[29] In Cassell's words, memory of the past and present "exists in the nostrils and the hands as well as in other body parts" (1991: 38). Against this background, it can be said that life's lesions are the personal analogue of historical processes. On a subjective level, the cracks that occur in the broader social system resonate with our daily experience and the fault lines in our lives to bring about life's lesions; "trouble" thus becomes embodied and expressed symptomatologically and felt as pain. Not uncommonly, the actors themselves are cognizant of the unreconcilable contradictions, and their practical consciousness gives shape to the "pathogen."

Not surprisingly, it has been frequently said that social change is experienced as stressful. Clearly, not all social changes are stressful,[30] but changes that defy our perceptions of the way life *ought* to be assault our moral sensibilities and become transformed into life's lesions and expressed symptomatologically. Historical changes confront us with contradictions that grind on our sense of coherence, of how things ought to be but are not. Consider Aaron Antonovsky's (1980) notion that sickness is associated with a loss of our sense of coherence. I postulate that life's lesions are fostered by such a loss, often accompanied by historical changes that bring forth not only unreconcilable contradictions but also changes in the moral order.

Moral indignation is often expressed in anger (thus intensifying the experience of life's lesions) which in Mexico is culturally recognized as sickness producing. I will return to this point in later chapters. Generally speaking, one experiences emotions through the body.[31] In the words of one sick woman, "I feel anger in my body." Emotions such as anger are interpretations of the world involving social relationships that have gone awry, and as Rom Harré (1986) observes, to understand anger we must attend to the moral order of a given society.

The concept of life's lesions is anchored in the theory of the social causality of sickness, which derives from many different sources in Western thought including phenomenology and public health, Marxist theory, and other social sciences.[32] The theory of social causation of sickness incorporates in its model of affliction diverse societal pressures, including contemporary life itself[33] as well as poverty and hunger, which are associated by many with the workings of the extant global economy. The theory of life's lesions is also grounded in the fundamental assumption that intrinsic to being human is to engage in moral evaluations of the rightness and wrongness of the social environment that envelops us.

Major components of sickness everywhere are economic scarcity, malnutrition, and the public health deficits. Numerous scholars have given recognition to this fact, which has by now attained the status of common knowledge.[34] But notwithstanding the role of these crucial factors in people's sickness, human beings are structurally situated in a society. They exist in a social and moral universe, which forms part of their physiology, and act in tandem with poverty and malnutrition to produce life's lesions and sickness.

Consider, for a moment, contemporary theories of human evolution, which inform us that in the course of the evolutionary process humans were molded not only by the physical but also by the social and cultural environments. In human evolution, the sociocultural environment became an extension of human anatomy and physiology. Our interactions with and within the social, cultural, and physical environments have transformed us as much as we have transformed them. Our knowledge of the social and cultural setting is channeled through our bodies, and an acute impairment to our social environment, to our social relations, and to the coherence of our moral universe becomes known to our bodies and expressed symptomatologically.[35]

Informed by M. Merleau-Ponty (1963), who proposed that the body communicates to the world and the world becomes expressed by the body,

Arthur Kleinman (1986) observed, "The body feels and expresses social problems. . . . The body mediates structure and cultural meaning making them part of the physiology" (194, 195). We know the world through our bodies (Merleau-Ponty 1963), and we grasp the contradictions through our bodies, before they even enter our consciousness, resulting in the experience of pain and suffering.

Life's lesions are not fatal, as heart attacks or cancer are; rather they grind at the body and register on it non-lifethreatening symptomatologies. They intrude on the body in much the same way as any pathogen or anatomical lesion; they become fused with anatomical lesions and are felt as pain and suffering. Of course, anatomical and life's lesions reflect back on each other. To recognize the cyclical fusion between them is not to dichotomize the human being or to privilege the body, the mind, or even the environment. From the perspective proposed here, sickness is seeded by pathogens—by anatomical and life's lesions.

I must emphasize that the notion of life's lesions is not to be viewed in terms of an analogue of psychosomatic illness (defined as "any illness in which physical symptoms, produced by the action of the unconscious mind, are defined by the individual as evidence of organic disease and for which medical help is sought" (Shorter 1992: x). Psychosomatic medicine's understanding of illness rests firmly on the dualistic model of sickness, the separation of the body and mind, and the notion that the mind, wittingly or unwittingly is "dangerous" to the body.[36] To repeat, to attend to life's lesions is not to ignore or minimize the role of anatomical lesions, of biology and the physical environment, but rather to avoid dichotomies between biology and mind and biology and culture and to examine a life in the context of its totality and the meaning the subject gives to it.

The concept of life's lesions illuminates our understanding of non-lifethreatening sickness in ways that the general concept of psychosocial stress fails to do. It avoids reductionism and refines the concept of stress by attending to the minutiae of meaning and by calling for the identification of specific atypical life circumstances and contradictions that an individual confronts when experiencing a sickness episode. To be human is to feel adversity and to perceive contradictions produced by incongruities in the moral order, by competing norms, and by discrepancies between actualities and regnant cultural ideologies. For this reason, I postulate that human beings in all societies and of all social classes experience life's lesions at any given moment in history and in any particular cultural space. It must be stressed, however, that the stuff of which adversity and contradictions are comprised will vary within time and space and between subjects. As we will see in Chapters 7 through 16, the constituent elements of each woman's life's lesions differ.

Generally speaking, researchers studying stress, life events, social supports, and social relations have attempted to adhere to scientific paradigms by using quantitative measures to demonstrate the role of these constructs in human sickness. However, as David Mechanic (1979) has rightfully argued, quantitative measures fail to illuminate fully all the dimensions of sickness; they frustrate our grasp of the meanings and perceptions that define a person's life. Discrete measures using prepackaged variables are inadequate for comprehending life's lesions. To be sure, a carefully constructed life event interview schedule that also elicits the degree to which a person was affected by a given life event is a helpful initial step.[37] However, in view of the fact that these lesions are multidimensional and fester, they cannot be easily measured quantitatively. To discover them, elements of the person's life must be placed under a microscope in much the same way as pathogens are, because neither are readily observable by the naked eye. The anthropological microscope requires "thick description," careful listening, and reading between the lines.[38]

As a rule, life and sickness histories and the individual's evaluation of his or her life, often reflected as a recurring motif in the narrative, reveal the cracks in the individual's life. The ways in which the tensions along these fault lines are resolved, or fail to be resolved, open an avenue to the source of the individual's life's lesions. We must also search for recurrent paramount concerns in the narrative with which a sickness episode is associated. As we will see in the cases I present in Chapters 7 through 16, each woman, sometimes unknowingly, wove through her narrative a dominant theme with which she also associated the sickness episode.

Along with elicitations of life and sickness histories and dominant themes in the person's life, sickness attributions are crucial to our understanding of life's lesions. A person's etiological explanation of his or her sickness furnishes critical insights into the person's individual and cultural comprehensions that locate the nucleus of a life's lesion. In Mexico, anger is a core etiological explanation for sickness, and it is important to establish the circumstances that brought on a specific episode of anger to comprehend the moral indignations experienced by the person.

One last point must be made. To attend to women's life's lesions is not to ignore women's health as it relates to their reproductive capacities. In contemporary times, women's health has become a medical specialty, largely because of the medicalization of reproduction, menstruation, and menopause[39]—attributes of a woman's body that were usually relegated to the symbolic aspects of culture and not within a society's medical domain.[40] Moreover, menstruation was once probably a rare phenomenon because of a woman's numerous pregnancies during her lifetime. This was still the case for some of the women in my study, who could not recall their last menstruation because they were perpetually pregnant. Similarly, women have begun to experience menopause owing to prolongation of women's life expectancy in the twentieth century.

Not surprisingly, women's reproduction became a concern of medical practice, especially with medicine's appropriation of birth control methods and with the wider societal concerns of population control. In contemporary times, control of women's fertility through development of modern contraceptive technologies has brought women under the purview of bio-medicine and has affected their health state[41] in various ways. I will return to this point in Chapter 4.

At this juncture, I must emphasize that my concern here is with women's health outside the life cycle, with symptomatologies not directly related to a woman's reproductive capacities, while keeping in mind that life's lesions may grow from infirmities resulting from contemporary contraceptive technologies, birth complications, and induced abortions.

In this chapter I have presented an anthropological understanding of sickness and how it relates to human existence to enable us to comprehend the impairments of the women we will meet later. I have emphasized that to understand human sickness we must not only probe into the patient's anatomy and physiology, but also scrutinize the sociocultural arena to explain sickness. In keeping with this perspective, in the next chapter I explore theoretical issues bearing on gender and sex that will shed light on Mexican women's predicaments within the context of their pains.

Notes

1. For a recent overview of the field see, for example, Johnson and Sargent 1990; others include Landy 1977; Romanucci-Ross et al. 1983; see also Engel 1977; Helman 1984; Kleinman 1980; the classical work by Zborowski 1952.

2. See especially Good and Good 1981b for an excellent presentation of the meaning of sickness; and also Kleinman 1988. In a psychological vein, Groddeck 1977, a contemporary of Freud, sought, I believe erroneously, *all* etiology of sickness in symbolic meanings. Not all impairments necessarily carry symbolic meanings, as for example parasitosis.

3. Eisenberg 1977; Finkler 1985b; Kleinman 1980; Young 1983.

4. The differentiation between signs and symptoms is a phenomenon of the new clinical medicine that came into existence in the nineteenth century. See Finkler 1991 for elaboration and bibliographic references pertaining to this distinction; see also an excellent discussion by Kirmayer 1988.

5. Morris 1991 explores the cultural nature of pain and affliction.

6. See Cassell 1991; Gadow 1980; Morris 1991.

7. See Morris 1991, 38; Scarry 1985.

8. My study of physicians and patients in a Mexico City hospital (Finkler 1991) revealed that, in order to make a proper diagnosis, physicians often insisted that patients pinpoint the exact time they began to experience the symptoms, but the patients were unable to do so, to the physicians' consternation.

9. See Finkler 1991, 10; Kleinman 1988; Young 1982, 1983. For a discussion of the problematics of the distinction between disease and illness see Hahn 1983.

10. See also Engel 1977; Finkler 1991; Groddeck 1977; Kleinman 1980; Osherson and Amara Singham 1981. There has been a movement in medicine, as attested to by pain clinics, to eschew the duality of body and mind and to regard at least chronic pain as a "perception rather than sensation and understand the unity of body and mind" (Morris 1991: 76).

11. On average, they had experienced chronic pain for 2.5 years.

12. See Cassell 1991.

13. The literature on illness etiologies is extensive: see Foster and Anderson 1978; Helman 1984; and in Mexico, Finkler 1985b, 1991.

14. For a discussion of how and when the concept of heredity entered the Western medical paradigm, see Rosenberg 1974.

15. See McKeown (1979) for a detailed analysis of this perspective. For a discussion of biomedical causality, see Finkler 1991.

16. See Amkraut and Solomon 1975; for a fine review of the literature on the stress model, see Dressler 1990; also Finkler 1985a in relation to life events.

17. For example, see Birley and Connolly 1976.

18. One of the earliest exponents of this view was Selye (1956/1978).

19. There are various unresolved issues concerning the kind of role life events play in sickness and its meaning. The question is raised whether life events simply trigger the onset of a sickness that would have occurred anyway (see some of the earliest studies on this subject, Hinkle et al. 1960; 1974; Rabkin and Struening 1976) or whether life events are instrumental in producing sickness. The latter view suggests that life events produce impairments in general which would not have occurred in the absence of a stressful event. But, while the question of the kind of role life events play may not be easily resolved, many scholars assert that life events are associated with a variety of conditions in general and depressive disorders in particular. See Brown and Harris 1978; Brown 1974a, b; Paykel 1974a, b, 1979. Some scholars, including Mechanic (1974) and Bebbington (1978), are skeptical about the etiological significance of life events because, they argue, in many instances an ailment has not been preceded by identifiable experiential stressors. Some have argued that it is necessary to demonstrate the pathways by which life events produce sickness or physiological changes; see, for example, Cobb 1974.

20. See Finkler 1985b.

21. See Antonovsky 1979; Berkman 1984; Berkman and Breslow 1983; Cassell 1974, 1976; Dean and Lin 1977; Eckenrode and Gore 1981; Hyman 1972; Kaplan et al. 1979; Morgan et al. 1984.

22. Jacobson 1987 also provides a good review of the literature on this topic.

23. In this study I have employed Patrick's (1982) scale of life events. It has been suggested that any change, including happy events such as a marriage, can be stressful on the grounds that any alteration to the organism can introduce a psychological and physical disequilibrium.

24. The notion of social support emerges out of American society, where human beings function as individual entities rather than as intrinsic parts of the family in which social supports are embedded. Undoubtedly within the context of American society the presence of social supports cannot be taken for granted.

25. Engel 1977 makes a compelling argument for this position, as docs McKeown (1979).

26. I initially suggested this concept in Finkler 1991 and develop it in greater depth here.

27. See Abrahams 1986. Also see de Lauretis 1984; she states: "I use the term [experience] not in the individualistic, idiosyncratic sense of something belonging to one and exclusively her own even though others might have 'similar' experiences; but rather in the general sense of a *process* by which, for all social beings, subjectivity is constructed. Through that process one places oneself or is placed in social reality, and so perceives and comprehends as subjective . . . those relations—material, economic and interpersonal—which are in fact social and, in a larger perspective, historical. The process is continuous, its achievement unending or daily renewed. For each person, therefore, subjectivity is an ongoing construction, not a fixed point of departure or arrival from which one then interacts with the world. On the contrary, it is the effect of that interaction—which I call experience" (159).

28. Giddens 1984 provides a cogent discussion of contradictions in society.

29. Pandolfi 1990, for example, argues that all history is inscribed on the body.

30. See Finkler 1983.

31. See Rosaldo 1984; Solomon 1984, who rightly regards emotions as ways human beings interpret the world; Levy 1984 and Harré 1986, who argue convincingly that emotions express moral evaluations. See also Travis 1982 on anger and morality. For a more detailed discussion of the role of emotions in Mexico, see also Finkler 1991.

32. Many scholars have written on the social origins of sickness: see Doyal 1979; Morsy 1990; Navarro 1974; Tuckett 1976; Virchov 1958; Waitzkin 1983; and, of course, Durkheim 1951. The proponents of the phenomenological perspective include Berger and Luckmann (1967); Merleau-Ponty (1951); Schütz (1967).

33. See Durkheim 1951.

34. McKeown 1979 cogently demonstrates how changes in nutrition and public health have been the chief instruments in decreasing morbidity and mortality in the twentieth century.

35. Merleau-Ponty 1963; see also Leder 1985, 1990.

36. Life's lesions must also not be confused with the concept of somatization. I eschew the concept of somatization because I seek to avoid the notions of mind-

body dualism on which this concept is based. Somatization suggests that psychological difficulties become converted into somatic dysfunctions. The concept of somatization is a medically defined concept. By this I mean that a patient is assessed as a somatizer when biomedicine cannot find any physiological dysfunction. In the final analysis, the concept of somatization blames the victim.

Additionally, the notion of somatization is rooted in psychological distress rather than in the lived world, whereas the concept of life's lesions shows the ways in which humans are embedded in the social, cultural, and ideological world of day-to-day experience that affects their health. Using an evolutionary perspective, the concept of life's lesions emphasizes that human beings as social beings are embedded in society and culture of our own making and are vulnerable to social pathogens in much the same way as we are to pathogens such as viruses and bacteria.

37. To get at the subjective experience of these life events, to each event I added to Patrick's (1982) life events scale a question about how the subject felt when experiencing the event.

38. See Geertz 1983.

39. See Martin 1987.

40. See Buckley and Gottlieb 1988; Douglas 1966; Kaufert 1982.

41. See Travis 1988 for an overall discussion of women's health issues.

3. The Nature of Gender

In keeping with an anthropological perspective on sickness in its totality, we need to explore the sociocultural underpinnings of women's morbidity in ideology and practice. To do so, we must attend to the "woman question," because to understand women's health is to understand not only physiological processes but also women's position in society, ideologies about sex and gender, and male-female relations. For this reason, I turn here to some of the debates that scholars have raised with respect to the "woman question." The various contentions are important to comprehend (and I only raise them briefly here) because they illuminate the complexity of the issues and are pertinent to Mexican women's daily existence as well as to their health. The relevance of these debates to Mexican ideologies and practices are compelling because Western (specifically Iberian) traditions mediate women's lives.

Of the numerous matters regarding women, there are several that especially require our attention and must be addressed before we can discuss women's morbidity. The broader concerns applicable to our project include problems such as the similarities and dissimilarities of men and women. Are there universal gender inequalities? That is, are women universally subordinate to men and treated unequally? If so, why? Or is female subordination historically and culturally contingent? How is male dominance expressed in social relations? In addition, does a woman's position in the class structure influence gender relations? Lastly, and most important for us, in what ways, if any, do the economic changes in developing nations impinge on women's lives and health? To address these questions is also to access the contradictions that encroach on women's existence and, consequently, on their health.

Although we must not lose sight of the fact that, as with all human phenomena, concepts about gender and sex are cultural creations[1] rooted in a particular time and space, we must also bear in mind that a people's conception about gender and sex influence their actions and understandings of themselves and others.

To be sure, we confront the world we live in by negotiating our perceptions of ourselves and by giving individual meanings to our lived experience. George Herbert Mead (1964) advanced our understanding of this process when he observed that the "self" is a social self. In Mead's words,

> The self is something which has a development; it is not initially there at birth but arises in the process of social experience and activity, that is, develops in the given individual as a result of his relations to that process as a whole and to other individuals within that process. . . . The self understands itself by taking on the attitudes of other individuals toward himself. (1964: 199, 203)

Mead's insights on the social and cultural embeddedness of "human nature" are especially pertinent for understanding women's actions vis-à-vis men and women's comprehensions of themselves because they resonate with the unexplained differences between women's and men's morbidity.

Keeping in mind that human beings evolved as social, cultural beings and that the understandings we form of ourselves are contingent on and shaped by a cultural mirror, I briefly explore here, by way of background, some of the issues relating to the "woman question" that are especially pertinent to our project. However, I must caution that all issues bearing on gender and sex are contested in the literature, including the very common distinction we make between gender and sex. Generally speaking, sex, understood as a biological category, refers to the anatomical differences between males and females, while gender is understood as the ways in which biological differences are culturally construed and expressed in thoughts and actions. One's sex is determined at birth, but gender thoughts and actions are learned. Whereas sex as a biological category transcends culture, gender is contingent on and shaped by a people's culture and history.

Historically, the prevailing view in Western society as to whether men and women, as sexual and engendered beings, are the same or different has swung back and forth like a pendulum. According to the historian Thomas Walter Laqueur (1990), until the eighteenth century only a one-sex model of men and women existed. Viewed physiologically, women were simply a corrupt form of men. A woman's reproductive organs were a transposed version of the male genitals, a concept that is traced by Laqueur to ancient Greece and the writings of Galen. During the eighteenth century a two-sex model emerged: women were seen as totally different from men, and metaphysical musings on sex became transformed into biological and medical truths.[2]

The twentieth-century inheritors of this historical conceptual shift developed a dominant ideology of difference between the sexes, as espoused, for example, by Sigmund Freud in his theories of sexuality. Freud's theory of the difference between the sexes was remarkably influential in guiding Western cultural beliefs on gender differences for several generations, and it also permeated the Mexican medical profession and the ideologies it transmits to its patients.[3] Freud attributed gender difference to the singular anatomical difference of the genitalia (presence or absence of a penis).[4] Owing to this anatomical disparity, men and women inexorably develop separate modes of thought and behavior. In Freud's words, "After all, the anatomical distinction [between the sexes] must express itself in psychical consequences. It was, however, a surprise to learn from analyses that girls hold their mother responsible for their lack of a penis and do not forgive her for their being thus put at a disadvantage" (quoted in Young-Bruehl 1990: 353). Consequently, women possess less desirable mental characteristics than men. According to Freud, women showed less sense of justice and were more influenced in their judgments by feelings of affection or hostility than were men. The nurturing role of women affected their rationality and capacity to think abstractly.[5] In Freud's words, women's super ego "is never so inexorable, so impersonal, so independent of its emotional origins as we require it to be in men" (quoted in Young-Bruehl 1990: 314).

Freudian theory hinges on gender disparities determined by anatomy; nevertheless, Freud stressed the role of developmental forces in shaping gender differences. Biological essentialists, however, reduce all differences between the sexes to biological difference.[6] Embellishing on the Freudian assumption that "biology is destiny," biological essentialists attribute differences between the sexes to hormone levels. By extending this reasoning, there are those scholars who posit that a woman's biological constitution and hormonal changes determine her role as childbearer and child rearer,[7] giving rise to the division of labor in society and the "second sex,"[8] a reference to Simone de Beauvoir's compelling argument concerning the subordination of women. De Beauvoir accepted the premise of the biological differences between men and women,[9] but contrary to Freud, she challenged the inevitable consequences of these differences. She concluded instead that men purposefully exploited the anatomical difference and fashioned women into the "other," a being inferior to men and therefore rightfully subjugated by them.

De Beauvoir's pioneering work opened the way for other theorists to ponder the question of gender difference. By the 1970s the pendulum had swung back to an androgynous model of the sexes. Feminists in particular emphasized androgyny and minimized gender differences. Catherine Mac-Kinnon (1989), for one, argues persuasively that "considering gender a matter of sameness and difference covers up the reality of gender as a system of social hierarchy, as an inequality. The differences attributed to sex become lines that inequality draws, not any kind of basis for it" (1989: 218).

Recently the pendulum has swung again. There are those who wish to reclaim "sexual difference—and the category woman—in a way that avoids the construction of domination-subordination hierarchies" (Offen 1990: 20). Concurrently, there are those who advance theories that celebrate femaleness and gender differences.[10] Carol Gilligan (1982), a major proponent of this view, emphasizes the differences between men and women, notably with regard to their relational and emotional life, which she associates with differences in moral development. And unlike Freud, Gilligan celebrates the dissimilarities between the sexes. She asserts that men distance themselves from relationships with others, whereas women savor them. For women, morality connotes connection, care, and responsibility, whereas for men it implies independence and individual achievement. Building on theories of male-female differences derived from Freudian paradigms, Gilligan asserts that women never completely separate from their mothers; consequently their central concern with close personal relationships replicates their intense relations with their mothers. It is noteworthy that Gilligan's perspective on women's superiority by virtue of their presumed connectedness has its detractors.[11]

Linda Alcoff, for example, correctly points out that the "innateness of gender differences in personality and character is at this point factually and philosophically indefensible" (1989: 303). Mary Hawkesworth (1989) also argues against the view that women are somehow different from men, for there is no uniform experience common to all women to generate this single vision. She rightly contends that it is necessary to search for the "multiplicity and diversity of women's experiences, and to the powerful ways in which race, class, ethnicity, culture, and language structure individuals' understandings of the world" (340).

Nevertheless, for many scholars the notion of gender difference suggests, unproblematically, inequalities and subordination.[12] A major scholarly project has been to elucidate the reasons for female subordination and male dominance. In order to avoid blanket generalizations about gender subordination and inequality, Peggy Reeves Sanday (1981) advances a useful distinction between what she calls "mythical dominance," the tacitly accepted belief of male superiority and real male dominance (which Sanday defines as physical coercion of women, as in wife beating or rape), and the exclusion of women from political and economic activities.

Sherry Ortner (1974)—proceeding from de Beauvoir and combining psychological, structural, and symbolic analysis—elegantly argues that women, because of their reproductive capacities, were associated with nature in contrast to men, who were universally associated with producing and reproducing culture. Women were universally subjected to both mythical and real domination and devaluation because nature was subordinate to culture. Ortner's assertions have been challenged on various grounds by anthropologists who reject the assumption of the universality of female subjugation and devaluation. Some have attempted to demonstrate an association between a society's prevailing kinship ideologies and women's subordination. For example, in American Indian societies where kinship and inheritance rules emphasized the female line,[13] women were not powerless or subjugated by men.

Other researchers show that female subordination and male dominance covary with access to scarce resources. Using data from hunting and gathering societies, Ernestine Friedl (1978) attempts to demonstrate that male dominance correlates with the availability of meat, which was controlled by men and to which women lacked access. In the final analysis, this theory of female subordination supposes that women's lack of access to scarce resources is due to the sexual division of labor, resulting from woman's inexorable fate of having to care for her offspring because of her unique reproductive capacities.

In fact, the sexual division of labor is regarded by some as the primary cause of domination by men and subordination of women. Women's confinement to domestic work became the economic expression of the fundamental inequality of the marriage contract.[14] In this view, marriage itself is intrinsically problematic for women. This is an important point and I will return to it later in Chapter 5.

Arguing against any assumptions of the universal subordination of women, some scholars[15] have pursued a Marxist perspective which propounds that male domination and female subordination are a direct result of the historical transformation of societies to capitalism and male control of private property. With the transition to capitalism, understood as the commodification of land, labor, and social relations and the production of commodities for exchange, men expropriated control of productive goods. From this vantage point, women's subordination and the inequality between the sexes derives not from a biological imperative for women to bear children, but rather from economic requisites requiring surplus production and wealth, concomitant with undisputed paternity, and thus sexual fidelity in women.[16] From a Marxist perspective, with the historical transition to capitalism women were relegated to devalued domestic activities[17] and separated from economic and political institutions, or the public sphere. This separation further promoted women's degradation and powerlessness, because the important work and rewards derived from the public sphere.

Jean Bethke Elshstain (1981), however, demonstrates that the separation between the public and private spheres predates capitalism and has a long tradition in Western history. The Greeks distinguished the *polis* (polity) from the *oikos* (the household), dividing human existence between the public world of politics and a private world of familial and economic relations.[18] The public was open and revealed and the private was hidden and concealed; neither women nor slaves were admitted into the public spheres.[19]

Recently scholars have argued persuasively against making sweeping generalizations about women's subordination and for the elimination of all dichotomies, including the concept of the public and private spheres, on the grounds that any dichotomies are Western fabrications.[20] These scholars, as I do, promote the view that women's lives must be contextualized rather than artificially dichotomized.

Whereas most dichotomies are indeed analytical constructs of limited usefulness in illuminating women's reality as it is lived, some analytic constructs reflect daily life. None is more germane for bringing Mexican women's lives into focus than the distinction between the domestic and public spheres of women's lives. The separation between the public and private realms of existence is expressed architecturally by the walls that surround each household in which women carry out their daily activities and ideologically by the culturally shared understandings that a woman's place is in the home.

Whether women became separated from the public arena in Western societies before or after capitalist transformation may be moot. More to the point for our understanding of women's position in contemporary society, especially in Mexico, are insights gained from analysis of historical processes after industrialization. The separation between the private and public spheres intensified with industrialization in the nineteenth century and ushered in what Francesca Cancian (1985) identifies as the "feminization of love," when women and men preferred "different styles of love that are consistent with their gender role" (253).[21]

According to Cancian, during the nineteenth century love became feminized as economic production became separated from the home and from personal relationships. The increased divergence of men's and women's daily activities produced a polarization of gender roles. "Wives became economically dependent on their husbands, and an ideology of separate spheres developed that exaggerated the differences between women and men and between the loving home and the ruthless work place" (1985: 257). When love became feminized, women began to seek "emotional closeness and verbal expression," whereas men favored "giving instrumental help and sex, forms of love that permit men to deny their dependency on women" (253). Cancian argues that this understanding of love "bolsters the power of men over women in close relationships, but it also suggests that men's power advantage in the private sphere is quite limited. It is primarily in the public sphere that feminized love promotes inequality in power" because it suggests that "men are independent individuals and by so doing obscures relations of dependency and exploitation in the work place and the community" (253). MacKinnon would add to Cancian's compelling argument that women's "pervasive powerlessness to men [is] expressed and reconstituted daily as sexuality" (1981: 21).

Cancian's insights are especially relevant in the Mexican context and illuminate the lives of the women we will meet later. The realities of women's economic dependence on men, together with the idealization of love in the private realm of existence, shed light on Mexican women's understandings of themselves as dependent on the love of men to support them and to define their existence as women. In the ideology of the feminization of love, a young woman's major goal in life is to "entrap a man" into a marriage relationship, and a happy marriage at that,[22] whereas a young man's aim is to escape from it. The ostensibly opposing goals of men and women predictably generate conflicts after marriage.[23]

As I noted earlier in my discussion of George Herbert Mead, human beings' understandings of themselves arise out of society's beliefs about them. People's subjective perceptions are shaped in the context of the situation in which they find themselves,[24] including their particular stage of life. Thus human existence and the constituted self are not fixed entities. Within the family context, women act in response to fathers and husbands in much the same way that men's actions are constructed by mothers, sisters, and buddies.[25]

Against this background, in the final analysis men do not exclusively set the agenda. Recognizing that male-female relations are at the core of all social relations, Marilyn Strathern properly argues that "In no simple sense is it the case that men and women have separate models of their lives" (1988: 318). Such models change when the values of one person are constantly pitted against those of another. A woman acts not in terms of being a woman, but in response to a man. In Strathern's view we cannot simply bracket a category called "woman." Strathern, in fact, eschews the question of female subordination altogether and persuasively disputes any blanket categorizations of female subordination. She correctly propounds the situational character of extant male-female interactions: in some circumstances men are dominant but in others they are not. As we will see in Chapter 5, contradictory conceptions of women prevail in Mexico, as they do elsewhere, such as in New Guinea, where there exist concurrent gender ideologies that are "brutally chauvinistic, envious of female reproductive power and also egalitarian" (Meigs 1990: 102).

Although mythical male dominance has its variations within any given society, including Mexico, real dominance as expressed by physical coercion is a not uncommon, but certainly not universal, practice among Mexico's impoverished classes, as it is the world over. In day-to-day experience "brutal chauvinism," coupled with aspects of ideological dominance, lays down a template for a woman to develop life's lesions and sickness.

Gender and Class

In complex societies, a significant situational dimension that crafts gender relationships is, of course, class. One of the many conditions that contribute to defining a woman's existence is her socioeconomic position. Women's dilemmas and subordination cannot be attributed solely to class inequalities, however, as Marxists are wont to do.[26]

Undoubtedly, both men and women forming the poor sector of class societies are as subordinate with regard to the rest of society in Mexico as they are in the United States.[27] Elite and middle class men exert power and authority in the public domain in ways not accessible to poor people living in shantytowns. The economic resources available to women in poor segments of society create constraints on the entire family, including the men, and the duress equally affects men and women in their social interactions, their marriage, and their familial relationships.

Among the poor, the daily central concern of both men and women is to eke out a livelihood. The globalization of the market economy in the twentieth century has contributed to the impoverishment of economically developing nations, especially in the sphere of low-wage jobs, putting inordinate strains on poor men and women alike. Thus burdens emerging from economic development reverberate variously along class lines and for women of different classes. In Sayer's words, "This is borne out by the fact that although both working- and middle-class women are often understandably dissatisfied with their role as housewives . . . their dissatisfactions often vary as a function of class" (1982: 200).

Of course, there are crucial differences in the day-to-day experiences of women from different classes. Most assuredly, the typical activities of women from disparate classes vary, as do their daily concerns. For example, the vexations of economically well situated women may revolve around their desire to free themselves from daily household chores and around management of their households and maids, in contrast to most of the women in my study whose predominant preoccupation is to feed their families and manage their meager resources. Nevertheless, there is a culturally constituted ideological canopy that overlies gender relations, irrespective of class, which bears on the daily interactions between men and women. Gender ideologies that legitimate male authority cut across class lines. Ideologies supporting notions of proper male and female behavior, of defining women's and men's tasks, of obligations of spouses and of parents and children, override the dissimilarities between economically advantaged and disadvantaged women.

Women's definition of themselves in all classes is guided by the regnant ideologies relating to gender roles and gender behaviors. On the level of familial relations, both poor and elite men and women define themselves similarly in relation to each other, legitimately allocating power and authority to the men.[29] To comprehend life's lesions and sickness is to recognize that in our daily experience gender relations are prior to all other relations, including class. We live our lives *first* within the context of our immediate family, the stage on which male-female relations are played out, be they between mates, parents and children, or siblings. For this reason I assert that women's dilemmas arise out of gender relations and gender ideologies legitimating male dominance, as much as out of poverty, lack of access to jobs, and the banality of their existence. The suffering and afflictions of women living in miserable poverty are as much connected with economic scarcity as they are with inimical social relationships with mates, family, and neighbors, which also, in Mexico, lead to "making angers" and sickness.

Industrialization and Gender

The transformative nature of human beings has produced changes in men's and women's existence from our beginnings as *Homo sapiens*. However, while we have experienced change throughout our history, there have been periods in human existence that arguably have witnessed modifications of mammoth proportions. Among these are the political revolutions in Europe of the eighteenth century, industrialization in the nineteenth century, and the intensified globalization of the market economy in contemporary times, which have all wrought societal changes affecting both men and women everywhere. As we have already seen, on the level of male-female relations, one outcome of these phenomena has been the feminization of love. Viewed historically, women in the Western world from any class were in a better position prior to the eighteenth century than following the great social revolutions in Europe. Elaine Marks and Isabelle de Courtivron observe: "The startling conclusion is that women were in a stronger position in society before the French Revolution and, indeed, before the French Renaissance" (1980: 8). Moreover, with colonialism and Western penetration into all corners of the world, women's position worsened not only in Western societies but the world over.[30] Even when women were confined to the private domain, as they were in traditional societies, and were subordinate to men, men's and women's tasks were usually complementary, albeit with unequal distribution of power.[31] Generally speaking, women exercised power and authority in the private domain because they were the reproducers of the household unit, because they were in charge of home industries, and because men usually recognized that the work of the women in the home was indispensable to them. Furthermore, in some societies women exercised power through the mystery of their sexuality, be it menstruation or childbirth.[32] In their mature years, women enjoyed informal power and authority as mothers of powerful sons and as dominant forces in the extended family.

As developing nations become industrialized and capitalized, men became the major economic supporters of the household by their wage-earning work, and the best jobs usually became available only to men. Home industries lost their importance and the unpaid work of the household became devalued. More important still, in traditional societies, a woman's contribution to the household was by reproducing children (because of the value placed on them). As industrialization progressed, children lost their paramount importance, along with women's reproductive capacities and their associated mysteries. Contrary to the household logic of traditional societies, in industrialized societies children become devalued, a burden rather than an asset to the household—they must be maintained and supported in the absence of productive roles for them until they reach adulthood. In fact, with the devaluation of children, the *one* activity men could not carry out—having babies—became devalued and thereby dissolved women's self-esteem. Ironically, in contemporary developed nations it has become dysfunctional to have many children. Instead a woman may derive self-esteem and a sense of coherence from her accomplishments as *an individual* through profession or workplace. In developing nations, women are losing an important source of self-esteem as reproducers and nurturers of children without having attained any new avenues for gaining self-worth and a sense of meaning in their lives.

With the changes in social and economic conditions emerging out of industrialization, women have tended to lose their position of power in the home by becoming increasingly dependent on men. The low-paying jobs that are open to women in developing societies last until marriage and afford them little opportunities for advancement in the workplace.[33]

Most important, with the shift from extended to nuclear families, as is the case in Mexico,[34] women have lost support from other women in the household. In extended families, the daughter-in-law was commonly a major "workhorse" in the household and the mother-in-law depended on her assistance. With the move to nuclear families, the mothers-in-law are no longer aided by their daughters-in-law in fulfilling their daily chores. Living apart from their sons, mothers often make demands for financial help that the sons cannot meet, creating friction between both the husband and wife and the mother-in-law and daughter-in-law.

In extended families, marital conflicts are often cushioned by the presence of senior members of the household—a woman is often protected from her husband's physical abuse by senior members of the family, if for no other reason than because her labors contribute to the smooth operation of the household. Moreover, in extended families the married pair are not solely dependent on one another for companionship or for making important decisions, and there are various people present to diffuse conflicts between husband and wife. In a nuclear family, the couple are left to their own devices to settle marital disputes, which often lead to physical mistreatment. A woman is thus left to the forbearance of her husband, without the patriarchal protection of the family, until her sons reach adulthood and can protect her.

We must also not forget that the expansion of the industrialized economy is accompanied by a globalization of ideologies, including beliefs about progress (meaning economic progress) and equality of opportunity.[35] These ideological substrata contradict the actualities of daily experience and add to people's frustrations. Both men and women need, but often are unable, to reconcile the paradoxes that the ideology produces, such as when people fail to realize economic rewards and so do not progress as they expect they ought to in light of their hard work.

The existing contradiction in contemporary society between notions of economic progress and poor people's failure to improve their economic situation presents dilemmas for both men and women; however, the women in developing nations are less likely than the men to advance economically by their own efforts, leaving them at an impasse in relation to the ideology. And in the event that women acquire financial resources by their own efforts, as Margarita (see Chapter 7) has done, their devalued position in society or the household is not altered vis-à-vis men.

Furthermore, in the case of married women, in addition to having to fulfill their household obligations and work a full shift, as they enter the industrialized labor force in deskilled work they are placed in a subordinate position to men both on the job as well as in their homes. Unlike the men in the impoverished class who must face subordination only at the workplace, working women experience subordination in the workplace and in the home.[36]

Not only have aspirations been raised for economic advancement worldwide, but traditional Western medical ideas about sex and gender have spread as well. These ideas, transmitted routinely through biomedical practice, reinforce notions about the domestic role and social status of women's inferiority. While psychiatry may not have made inroads in Mexico, for example, the Freudian concept of women's inferiority permeates the medical profession at large there.[37] The medical conception of "genitals determine gender" (Smith-Rosenberg 1985, 23) and belief in the "Cult of True Womanhood" were turned into medical and scientific dogma in Western society, including Mexico. As Carroll Smith-Rosenberg notes, "The True Woman was emotional, dependent, and gentle—a born follower. The Ideal Mother, then and now, was expected to be strong, self-reliant, protective, an efficient caretaker in relation to children and home" (1985: 199).

Beliefs that women's unique physiology, with respect to menstruation, menopause, and pregnancy, determined all other physical and mental problems of women have formed part of the popular consciousness. The scientific biomedical model has promoted and legitimized a conception of women as emotional, hysterical, and irrational[38]—traits dysfunctional in industrial society.

In sum, as developing nations move to replicate themselves in the image of contemporary industrialized societies, women tend to lose the power and authority they may have enjoyed in the household before, yet they fail to gain access to positions in the public domain. Women's changing social position has moved them from a complementary relationship with their spouses, and from the bulwark of the household as reproducers, to dependence: from protected but respected to unshielded and degraded.

The transitions I have discussed here are not mere romantizations of an idyllic past, as we are wont to do, or mere theorizing. The historical changes that have occurred in Mexican gender relations will be discussed in Chapter 5 and our understanding of them will shed light on the present. The degree to which individual women experience any or all of these changes is associated in large measure with their actions and appraisals at different points in their life cycle; for example, young women on the "marriage track" are less likely to experience many of the changes I have discussed. They are protected by their natal families before marriage, in contrast to the young women who embarked on careers and were unable to find jobs or those who married and established nuclear families, as is the case for the majority of the women introduced here, who were dependent on their spouses materially and ideologically.

The issues I explored in this chapter regarding gender difference, inequality, and subordination in the context of class and cultural ideologies bring into bold relief the problems influencing women's lives. Their social position and the contradictions with which women may be confronted set the stage for life's lesions to deepen. Some theorists have suggested that to be a woman is to be inherently enveloped by contradictions. De Beauvoir, for example, perceives an existential paradox in being a woman when she states, "The drama of woman lies in this conflict between the fundamental aspirations of every subject (ego)—who always regards the self as the essential—and the compulsions of a situation in which she is the inessential" (1980b: 56). According to de Beauvoir, a woman's intrinsic secondary position in the world, necessitates that she cannot ever actualize her nature as a person.

From another vantage point, Gilligan (1990) asks how women can be true to themselves and yet live in a world governed by men. We should recall that according to Gilligan, a woman is true to herself when she seeks attachment rather than independence.

> The deeply-knotted dilemma, then, which lies at the center of women's development is how can girls both enter and stay outside of, be educated in and then change, what has been for centuries a man's world? And yet . . . if we live in one world and cannot dissociate ourselves from one another, and if the psychology of fathers which has ruled the private house is writ large in legal codes and moral order and supported by the ever-present threat of what is considered to be a legitimate use of force or violence, how can daughters be anywhere other than inside and outside of these structures? (509)

We could legitimately question the degree to which every woman is conscious of the paradoxes de Beauvoir and Gilligan identify.[39] Arguably, Gilligan's fundamental assumptions, based as they are on culturally bound developmental theories of women, may be questioned. Nevertheless, both these scholars demarcate dilemmas unique to being a woman.

Whether we accept de Beauvoir's or Gilligan's postulated paradoxes, and whether women may or may not be conscious of them, are subjects for debate. Decidedly, incongruities exist for women in daily experience, fostered by their immediate relationships and suffused ideologies, which may adversely affect their health. These contradictions illuminate the empirical reality of the difference in morbidity between men and women in contemporary times. It is my thesis that the *unexplained* differences in morbidity between the sexes emerge out of a difference in women's and men's lived experience, concomitant with the contradictions constructed by society on the levels of both ideology and practice, in which women and men are differentially embedded. This contention is explored further in the next chapter.

Notes

1. See Berger and Luckmann 1967; see also Ehrenreich and English 1979 on medical views of women.
2. See Foucault 1980.
3. See Finkler 1991.
4. Sayers 1982 contends that Freud's thinking on this matter subsequently evolved.
5. See Freud [1925] 1990.
6. See Hubbard 1990; Sayers 1982.
7. See Rosaldo 1974; Sanday 1974.
8. See Rosaldo 1974 on this point.

9. See Tong's (1989) discussion of de Beauvoir.

10. See Alcoff 1989.

11. For an incisive criticism of Gilligan's book see Grosskurth 1991. This is not the place to critique Gilligan's relational theory, but it must be noted that from an anthropological perspective it is culture bound. For example, in Mexico both men and women value close social relationships especially with their mothers, as we will see in Chapter 5.

12. See Warren and Bourque 1991, 301.

13. See for example Sanday 1981; also Martin and Voorhies 1975.

14. MacKintosh 1981.

15. Notably Leacock 1981; Sacks 1974.

16. For a detailed examination of these issues, see Sayers 1982.

17. Leacock 1981.

18. Elshtain 1981, 12.

19. Elshtain 1981, 14.

20. Yanagisako and Collier 1990.

21. What Gilligan regards as an ontological difference between men and women is shown by Cancian 1985 in its historical guise.

22. See Cancian 1985.

23. See Cancian 1985.

24. See Alcoff 1989.

25. To argue otherwise is to promote a separate feminist agenda that subscribes to a single perspective of women's interests. See Strathern 1988: 23.

26. See Benería and Roldán 1987, for example. These authors argue against the view that women's subordination can only be explained by class inequalities. In their view, production of goods and the reproduction of gender are interconnected and mutually reinforcing.

27. See Coles 1978; Rubin 1976.

28. There is a dearth of empirical data on middle and upper class gender relations in Mexico.

29. I make this assertion based on my extensive contacts and observations of middle and upper class women over a twenty-five-year period; however, much more empirical data, collected systematically, are required in this regard.

30. See Bossen 1975; Warren and Bourque 1991.

31. See, for example, Devereaux 1987; Finkler 1974; Paul 1974.

32. See Paul 1974.

33. See Warren and Bourque 1991.

34. See Finkler 1974.

35. See Finkler 1983.

36. See Warren and Bourque 1991.

37. See Finkler 1991.

38. See Smith-Rosenberg 1985.

39. It could, of course, be argued along with MacKinnon that "Women's bondage, degradation, damage, complicity and inferiority, operate as barriers to consciousness" (1981: 21).

4. Gender and the Nature of Sickness

In this chapter I attempt to demystify the mystery of the differences in morbidity between the sexes, against the background of my discussions in the previous chapters relating to sickness, gender roles, and ideologies, and the contradictions women must confront as women.

The literature on the differences in morbidity between men and women in developed nations is extensive[1] and supports the idea that women more than men experience non-lifethreatening impairments. Much of this literature seeks to explain the disparity in health status between men and women. There have been two separate avenues of research dealing specifically with women's health in developed nations, and they mirror the Western dualistic model of the separation between body and mind. One area of study has dealt with women's health as related to women's biological constitution and reproductive capacities,[2] and the second major concern has been with women's mental health, ranging from the work of Sigmund Freud to the numerous investigations of depression[3] and other mental illnesses among women. For example, women outnumber men by two to one in diagnoses of psychological disorders, especially depression.

Generally speaking, women's impaired health, and particularly ill mental health, has been attributed to biological factors or to women's social role. In order to set the stage for my discussion of the reasons for differential morbidity between the sexes, it is important to note that historically, medical beliefs about women's health in the Western tradition were anchored in the view of women as sickly and biologically weak,[4] which was usually ascribed to female physiology and reproduction.

Current extensive historical scholarship of women's health reveals that women's complaints, be they mental or physical, were usually associated with the uterus and the ovaries. This view, with its antecedents in Greek philosophy and medicine, left its imprint on nineteenth-century medical beliefs. At that time most women's maladies were attributed to the woman's constitution[5] or to the physical stresses of pregnancy that were regarded as a threat to female health.

Most women's dysfunctions were ascribed to malfunctions of the womb and were diagnosed as hysteria. Carroll Smith-Rosenberg convincingly shows that by the last third of the nineteenth century, physicians had cataloged "hysterical symptoms that included virtually every known human ill" (1985: 202). The diagnosis of hysteria was made especially when no other cause of a woman's malady could be found,[6] and not uncommonly gynecological surgery was sought as a way of curing such ailments.[7] In the words of historian Ellen Dwyer, "while most male insanity resulted from lesions in the brain, in women disturbances of the brain were primarily sympathetic responses to irritations in the reproductive system that appeared first at puberty and persisted until after menopause" (1989: 27). It is important to stress that not all physicians at the time held that women's reproductive systems and female physiology were the direct cause of insanity, or of hysteria with its concomitant ills, or that these were uniquely women's maladies (Dwyer 1984). In fact many, including Jean-Martin Charcot, regarded hysteria as an affliction of the central nervous system, but women experienced it more because their nervous system was more sensitive than men's and the disease was caused by excessive sensitivity of the nervous system.[8] But, although many doctors may have "initially stressed the importance of the differing environments in which men and women operated, such moral theorists were eventually overwhelmed by the somatists, who stressed the significance of female uterine disorders as the major source of female emotional instability" (Dwyer 1989: 42).

Nineteenth-century notions of the womb as the cause of women's sickness have been discarded. In the twentieth century, however, women's normal physiological processes, especially menstruation and menopause, are still regarded as hazards to women's health. In fact, as I noted in Chapter 2, most of women's normal physiological functions, including menstruation, menopause, and pregnancy, have become medicalized and brought into the orbit of the medical profession. Consider, for example, the current preoccupation with premenstrual syndrome, or with the consequences of the cessation of the menses that is usually held responsible for mood alterations and any other unexplained symptomatologies.[9] In developed nations, medical indications for estrogen replacement therapy following menopause[10] have brought women into the medical domain for treatment of this transitional condition as a disease.

Women have, of course, benefited from scientific medical advances, as is evident by the decrease in mortality at childbirth, especially the reduction in puerperal infections, and also improved nutrition and public health practices.[11] Concurrently, as I noted in Chapter 2, the proliferation of contraceptive technologies has adversely affected women's health.[12] Women in developing nations have been experiencing health complications ensuing from the use of intrauterine devices (IUDs) and from poorly performed or self-induced abortions.[13] All these factors have contributed to women's sickness (see the cases of Julia and Josefina in this volume), requiring them to seek medical services. But even when we set aside problems related to women's reproductive capacities, women still have greater rates of morbidity than men.[14] Among the various reasons given to account for this phenomenon, it has been suggested that many complaints women present to physicians are dismissed as "feminine hysteria," or, in modern parlance, as psychosomatic, or that women simply speak more about their health than men. Doctors may medicate women who are free of any problems, which may in turn lead to addiction, concomitant with iatrogenic effects of overmedication.[15] All such factors no doubt contribute to differences in morbidity between the sexes, but in the final analysis they fail to delineate the difference between male and female morbidity.

The earliest explanations for the sexual disparity in morbidity in developed nations were grounded in biological and hormonal differences between the sexes, but biological explanations have been disputed by many scholars.[16] Roughly corresponding to Lois Verbrugge's classification of psychosocial and health-reporting behavior (cited in Chapter 1), the view of these scholars favors social structural and psychosocial explanations that revolve around three complementary propositions: (1) women are culturally permitted to express illness, whereas the sick role is unmasculine; (b) women's social roles are more stressful than men's, resulting in more illness among women; and (c) women's roles are more compatible with the sick role than men's roles because women have more time to be sick. The first two propositions assume that women's status and role in the social hierarchy produce stresses that are expressed in physical and psychological disorders. Thus Constance Nathanson (1975) observes that gainfully employed women reported fewer illnesses than housewives; she maintains that the number and character of the women's role obligations must be considered.

Indeed, some aspects of women's status and role have been the most important explanation for the disparity in health between men and women. For example, Smith-Rosenberg (1985) attributes women's experience of hysteria in the nineteenth century to women's role conflicts and psychic discontinuities, emanating from their isolation, loneliness, and ill-preparedness for the changes that took place during that period. And

Nancy Tomes's review of the history of mental illness among women contends that "When women with low self-esteem and limited access to social resources face stressful situations, especially ones that contradict their expected sex roles, they are likely to respond with emotional distress" (1990: 151).

Significantly, Freud recognized that for women marriage was a conflicting institution.[17] He asserted that the "spiritual disillusionment and bodily depravation to which most marriages are thus doomed puts both partners back in the state they were in before their marriage, except for being the poorer by the loss of an illusion, and they must once more have recourse to their fortitude in mastering and deflecting their sexual instinct" (cited in Young-Bruehl 1990: 173). Freud claimed that the sexual frustration women experienced in marriage, resulting in large measure from a "'*double*' sexual morality which is valid for men in our society" (174; emphasis added), led to their nervous disorders. He realized that men, unlike women, have "the sexual freedom which is allowed them" (173). He quickly added, however:

> But experience shows as well that women, who, as being the actual vehicle of the sexual interests of mankind, are only endowed in a small measure with the gift of sublimating their instincts, and who, though they may find a sufficient substitute for the sexual object in an infant at the breast, do not find one in a growing child—experience shows, I repeat, that women, when they are subjected to the disillusionments of marriage, fall ill of severe neuroses which permanently darken their lives. (174)

Freud's attribution of women's mental disorders to their inability to sublimate their sexual instincts in marriage arguably has lost its validity. But Freud's recognition of the role of the double standard set by society is significant and I will return to this point shortly.

In her exploration of depression in women, Dana Crowley Jack (1991) explains the differences in morbidity by probing into the conundrums women must confront in contemporary times. She concentrates on the conflicts women face in marriage relationships and as moral beings; for instance, she notes that a woman may be afraid to express anger because she fears her husband's retaliation, and this inability to express her anger leads to depression. According to Jack, the institutionalized inequality between women and men contributes to the pattern of "compliant relatedness and loss of self associated with women's depression" (43). Jack regards the ideals of romantic love, which as we have seen earlier became exalted in the nineteenth century, as pathogenic. Romantic love, according to Jack, "portrays a selfless transcendence and a union of mutuality. It obscures the problem of inequality" (1991: 66). This ideology fostered a view of women as morally superior because it was "based on love, family loyalty, and unselfishness" (86). Concurrently women must reshape this image of intimacy and superiority to conform with their subordination in marriage, and this process leads to their experience of depression.

Jack's analysis is significant because she locates a woman's disorder in moral imperatives that gnaw at her depression. Jack observes that depressed women "consistently use moral language—words such as 'should' 'ought' 'good' 'bad' 'selfish'—as they assess themselves and their role in causing the problems in their relationships" (1991: 89). A depressed woman's voice tells her "of how one *should* be or behave in order to be loved" (108; emphasis in the original). "Thus, the link between the female social role and women's vulnerability to depression lies in a set of moral imperatives that dictate how a woman *should* care for another—that is, how she should relate interpersonally, particularly to the male world" (120; emphasis in the original). Jack argues that "if events in the interpersonal sphere are especially critical to the definition and evaluation of women's core sense of self, then analysis of a woman's images of a 'good' self in relation is essential for understanding her depression" (93).

Jack's work deepens our understanding of depression in women, but her analysis reflects Western sensibilities and bias with her focus on the individual. Her explorations of women's sickness attend to the individual's self-absorption and reflexivity; her center of concern is how women judge themselves. I believe, however, that her focus on how women evaluate *themselves* limits her analysis of sickness. Her analysis must be broadened to incorporate the *circumstances* of the lived world. Indeed, as we saw in the last chapter, human beings exist in and apprehend themselves as members of a society, and in so doing they are engaged in an ongoing process of negotiation with and evaluation of the world in which they live.

Jack's focus rests on how women evaluate *themselves* and how they *ought* to have behaved, rather than on how women judge the *situations* in which they exist and how *others* ought to have acted. For example, in Mexico, where "making an anger" is widely believed to produce numerous illnesses, women "make angers" not because of the ways *they* "should" behave but because of how *others* "ought" to behave, including their husbands and children. Jack speaks to the cultural context that creates the moral dilemmas for women, but she neglects to incorporate the contradictions arising out of the *circumstances* that create these moral dilemmas for women. She disregards the situations that bring on a breach of moral values by *others,* especially those with whom a woman must interact on a daily basis. She emphasizes a woman's perceived inadequacies rather than the conduct of others who define her existence and her "self," influences which create life's lesions and which may be expressed later as depression or other ills.

In Mexico the circumstances that lead women to "make angers" and are culturally perceived to be sickness-producing abound: when children who ought to obey their parents do not; when husbands who ought to be faithful betray their wives; when husbands get drunk but ought not to; when husbands dissipate their meager earnings on drink and other women and the wife is left with no money for her daily expenses; when siblings who ought to share in taking care of their elderly parents leave one with the entire burden. Most important, women "make angers" that lead to life's lesions when tacitly accepted ideologies are violated, such as when a woman, conceding to the prevailing standards of male dominance and female submission, fails to realize the reward of that submission, as when her spouse spurns her, or beats her.

Angers leading to life's lesions are made and embodied when human beings are caught in contradictions between the realities of daily existence and prevailing cultural ideologies. In Mexico a powerful ideology of monogamy and romantic love exists; however, the realities of the double standard recognized by Freud are such that men maintain more than one woman and often support more than one household, as Alicia's lover has done (see Chapter 8). While women usually endorse the culturally prevailing view that men are inherently sexual beings and women are not, a woman will "make angers" provoking sickness when she learns that her husband has failed to give her money to meet her daily expenditures because he cohabits with "another woman." The "other woman" experiences dilemmas, as well, of the kind described by Smith-Rosenberg (1985), when she must deal with herself as a True Woman and Ideal Mother, as Alicia and Margarita must do.

Additionally, more and more parents and particularly mothers are confronted with the contradiction that, though children ought to obey them, they fail to do so. The conflicts are aggravated by the fact that people demand obedience from their children, but in the absence of the availability of any transmittable property all they can transmit to them are their moral precepts of right and wrong behaviors, which children may reject, especially at a time of accelerated societal changes. In the face of such paradoxes provoked by the immediate context of a woman's life, angers are made and sickness ensues.

Many of the theorists discussed in the previous chapter call attention to the inherent contradictions of women's existence, and Smith-Rosenberg (1985) and Tomes (1990) specifically perceive that women are enmeshed in discontinuities that lead to affliction.[18] Whereas men and women are faced with similar existential conditions, the differences in morbidity between the sexes can best be explained when we consider that *women, more than men,* are enmeshed in contradictions, eliciting angers and moral indignations that make them sick. Women more than men are placed in contradictory positions are exposed to unresolvable paradoxes that lead to differential experiences of life's lesions, resulting in diverse symptomatologies.

How could it be otherwise? Men and women from the lower social strata are similarly subject to environmental insults and adverse existential conditions, poverty, and malnutrition. If these conditions alone could explain sickness, then we could rightfully expect morbidity of the sort associated with life's lesions to be distributed equally among men and women. This is clearly not the case. In Mexico more women than men find themselves in untenable situations and are faced with contradictions that produce life's lesions; not surprisingly, then, almost four times more women than men comprise my randomly selected sample of sick individuals with non-lifethreatening, subacute ailments who seek treatment from Spiritualist healers, and three times more women than men seek help from physicians.[19]

It must be emphasized that I do not claim that men are not placed in situations that produce sickness. They certainly are, as I have shown elsewhere.[20] Undisputably, poor men and women must both endure insults in the public sphere. In Mexico men from the poor social strata experience affronts to their person by the police and by the demeaning conditions of employment. And, in light of the predominant ideology of economic "progress," men also are encompassed by unresolvable contradictions, because of their failure to provide in some instances even minimal subsistence for their families. Men are shielded from sickness, however, in ways that women are not, even in the face of such circumstances. The unresolvable contradictions men must face become attenuated or obliterated by the coherence they encounter at home as the rightful heads of the household. In their households men are protected from external assaults, while women suffer sickness-producing affronts to their beings above and beyond those incurred by the world outside the home, owing to the dominant ideology of male superiority and the culturally accepted rights men have over them. Men's hegemonic superiority by virtue of their sex cushions them against assaults on their beings in the private and public domains. The ruling ideology supports male superiority and privilege, mitigating against life's lesions and protecting them from sickness.

Moreover, for poor women like Rebecca (see Chapter 10), in the absence of relationships outside the private sphere, women's interactions, confined to the private arena, are intense and continuous, unlike those of their spouses. Women more than men are confronted by situations of highly charged relationships of the kind that produce angers and sickness. Women are placed in daily relationships with children and neighbors, whereas men are removed from similar interactions by working outside the home.

This point brings me back to a point made earlier regarding Freud's theory of neuroses in women. Freud's claim that women's sickness is related to marriage is significant, although arguably his explanation that the reasons for it are rooted in sexual frustration is flawed. More to the point, the marital relation is problematic for women in Mexico, as it is in the United States, for many reasons, not the least of which is the fact that many women in my sample have experienced male dominance through physical coercion and abuse. Undoubtedly, physical force insults the body on many levels—it leaves the body with temporary abrasions and permanent life's lesions, especially since the practice is uniformally condemned and considered evil;[21] thus it carries a moral load.

A double standard is significant in women's sickness, too, albeit for reasons other than those cited by Freud. In Mexico, the double standard ideology may promote health for men but is certainly inimical to women. The very characteristics that emphasize a man's self-esteem, that make him a macho male when he establishes a household with a mistress, produce in the wife life's lesions, when she must face the fact that her husband has another woman. In Mexico, for men to have many women is a mark of status, reaffirming their perceptions of themselves as men, *whereas for the wife the very act that affirms her husband's manhood creates suffering and pain.* Aside from the fact that a philandering husband in the poor social strata syphons off scarce economic resources from his household and deprives his wife and children of a livelihood, a woman's culturally idealized concept of love is shattered, leaving her morally incensed.

It is important to repeat a point made previously, that situations

problematic for women with their attendant symptomatologies are historically contingent. As we saw earlier, the changes in women's lives produced
by industrialization and its attendant discordances, in addition to the
previously existing patterns, take their toll on women. In economically
developing nations women have lost sources of livelihood and sources of
power in the private domain,[22] as well as the sense of self-worth that ensued
from the complementarity of the marital relationship, without having as yet
achieved the commensurate gains that have appeared in Western economically advanced societies. Consequently, we should anticipate high rates of
life's lesions resulting in morbidity among women in economically developing nations such as Mexico.[23]

A further point needs to be made before I turn in the next chapter to
the social and ideological settings in which the women in this study are
embedded. It is not my intention here to portray women as victims or in a
stereotypical way. To the contrary, as I have repeatedly stressed, human
beings' evaluations of their lives open the way for a variety of understandings of their existence, and the two bases for interpretation—the social and
ideological setting and its phenomenological expression—are in dynamic
tension. But we cannot escape the fact that women, more than men, find
themselves within sickness-promoting situations.

In conclusion, I note that, while my entire endeavor here is to address
the question of differential morbidity, it is perhaps relevant to stand the
question on its head and ask why so many women stay healthy. Although
we might be tempted to furnish a facile response—"because they are
biologically stronger"—it is my belief (as I have demonstrated empirically
elsewhere) that as long as a woman's life moves along *as it ought to be,* that
is, when she is not physically abused by her mate, when her mate meets his
obligations, when her children behave as they ought, as long as her life
retains a sense of coherence, then she is less likely to develop life's lesions.[24]

Notes

1. Briscoe 1987; Brown and Harris 1978; Celentano et al. 1990; Dohrenwend
and Dohrenwend 1976; Gove 1978; Hinkle et al. 1960; Jack 1991; Lieban 1978;
Mechanic 1978; Murphy 1978; Nathanson 1975, 1979; Rosenfield 1980; Roskies 1978;
Weissman and Klerman 1977.
2. See Browner and Sargent 1990; Martin 1987; Travis 1988. There are very
few data, however, on women's morbidity unrelated to women's reproduction.

3. Brown and Harris 1978; Jack 1991; Weissman and Klerman 1977. For other mental disorders see Jordanova 1980; Tomes 1990.

4. See Doyal 1979; Ehrenreich and English 1979.

5. Ehrenreich and English 1979; Rosenberg 1961; Sheehan 1981; Shorter 1992.

6. See Morris 1991; Sheehan 1981; Smith-Rosenberg 1985.

7. See Sheehan 1981; Shorter 1992. Morris 1991 remarks that "Feminists divide over whether to commend the hysteric as a protofeminist, a woman valiantly resisting oppression without the resources of feminism, or to criticize the hysteric as the passive victim of a repressive social order" (122). Morris's observation assumes that hysteria, like any other sickness experienced by women, is experienced by choice, having a secondary gain—that women have to act in defiance, in resistance or to cry for help by getting sick, as if hysteria were not a "real sickness." The diagnosis of hysteria has gone out of fashion, but the experience of pain that comes with it, as with any sickness, is not a matter of choice, it is a matter of being rather than choosing to become sick.

8. See Shorter 1992: 212; Dwyer 1984.

9. See Johnson 1987; Martin 1987.

10. See Kaufert 1982; Lock 1986.

11. McKeown 1979.

12. See Browner 1989; Marieskind 1980.

13. Many women I studied had had IUDs inserted, but they were unaware that these devices required checking. Consequently, after a number of years they experienced heavy bleeding and other complications, which propelled them to seek medical treatment (as was the case of Josefina, Chapter 13). See also Nomi's case in Finkler 1991. Many women complained that the contraceptive pills they had been prescribed made them sick.

14. See Travis 1988.

15. A fine review of the biological, behavioral, and artifactual hypotheses to explain the differential health status of men and women is provided in Travis 1988.

16. Gove 1978; Nathanson 1975; Rosenfield 1980; Weissman and Klerman 1977.

17. See Young-Bruehl 1990, chapter entitled "Civilized Sexual Morality and Modern Nervous Illness."

18. See Turner 1984 for anorexia nervosa, and Dressler 1990, who found that high blood pressure is associated in the general population with incongruities related to education.

19. See Finkler 1985b, 1991, and this volume, Chapter 6, note 1.

20. See Finkler 1991.

21. The anthropological literature provides ample evidence that wife beating is pervasive in many societies, as for example, among the Yanomamo of Venezuela (Chagnon 1983) and some groups in New Guinea (Counts 1992). The ethnographic record suggests that in these societies wife beating may be endemic and anticipated by the wife. In Mexico among the poor, wife beating is not endemic, but it occurs in epidemic proportions (under the epidemiological definition of epidemic to denote "excessive prevalence"). I make the distinction between endemic and epidemic not

because of an academic propensity for nitpicking, but because in societies where wife beating is endemic people may consider it a "natural" aspect of male-female relations. In Mexico, while some women may consider it "normal," the society at large condemns the practice.

22. An exception is when women become religious leaders, as they do among Spiritualists. See Finkler 1981, 1985b.

23. This hypothesis requires further testing in other developing nations.

24. In an earlier study (Finkler 1985a), I showed that a control group of healthy women had led a more peaceful existence than the sick subjects, less punctuated by tumultuous interpersonal relationships.

Part II

The Context

5. Gender, Culture, and Society in Mexico

In the previous chapters I focused on theoretical considerations regarding women's roles in societies, including examples from Mexico. In this chapter my concern is with furnishing a panoramic view of the actualities and norms of contemporary life that reflect back on the theoretical issues I raised in Chapter 2.

In writing about Mexican women, my reference point is women from the poor social strata, but I hasten to repeat that prevailing gender ideologies, if not day-to-day concerns, extend across class lines.[1] The ideologies ushered in by the Spaniards during the colonial period coupled with those introduced in the nineteenth century from the rest of Europe,[2] permeate contemporary Mexican society's comprehensions of gender and gender relations. Our understanding of women's position along historical and cultural dimensions, therefore, will elucidate their daily lives and their life's lesions when we encounter the individual women in subsequent chapters. The burdens borne by contemporary women in Mexico, the inheritors of ideological changes and industrialization with its attendant contradictions, become expressed in their sickness.

In colonial times, contradictory demands were made on women in terms of asceticism and womanhood (Franco 1989: 57). Women were either mystics or mothers; the only other category available to them was "prostitute." To be neither a virgin nor a mother was to be a whore (Franco 1989: 60). The paradigm Jean Franco presents for the only legitimate categories are virgin/not mother (nun, unmarried woman), or mother/not virgin (married woman) (60).

The Iberian colonists brought to the New World their ideologies and practices, including notions about marriage and male and female roles. According to Asunción Lavrin, "Home and family life were aspirations of all colonial peoples" (1989: 16), and marriage represented an alliance between families and established the home as an economic and reproductive unit with the wife as its manager. In Iberia "The status of a woman in comparison with that of her husband is a lowly one" (de Leon [1584] 1943, 70). The "perfect wife" must never "transgress the rule laid down by her husband, but obey and serve him in every particular" (45). A wife owed her husband total obedience (Arrom 1985).

Canon law recognized divorces only under the gravest circumstances, if a spouse was cruel or physically abusive or threatened murder (Arrom 1985: 208).[3] Under these conditions the community and the church provided the woman with an alternative in the event of an unbearable situation. As Silvia Arrom notes, such a woman "was taken from her home and placed in a *deposito,* literally, 'deposited' in the trust of a respected member of the community for the duration of the trial" (1985: 212). The depository "controlled women at the same time that it protected them" (212). "In practice, the rigidity of the *deposito* varied considerably from case to case. The depository was often chosen by the litigants from among their friends and relatives. Most women took their children with them" (214). In fact, Arrom points out that some women even lived quite happily in their depositos (214). This kind of alternative may have been used only by a few women in extreme cases, but it is not available to women today. While elite and middle class women in colonial Latin America were subject to the pervasive ideology of male hegemony, women of these classes, unlike poor women, were usually better treated and often pampered, because they were supported and protected by the members of their families.[4]

Among the poor classes during this period, women were under men's domination, which included physical coercion. Husbands had the right to administer physical punishment (Lavrin 1989): "In the sexual dialogue of power within marriage, the woman's position was weakened by the circumstances of her economic dependence, lesser physical strength, legal and social subordination to her husband, not the least, by her obligation to fulfill the physical demands of matrimony" (78). Women who could not or would not become mothers had the option of joining a nunnery and devoting themselves to the spiritual life" (Franco 1989: 103).[5]

Lower-class women, of course, always worked, although they did not seek employment in search of personal fulfillment or freedom but for survival (Arrom 1985). Working as servants circumscribed their physical and social mobility then as it does now. Moreover, women's work opportunities fluctuated with changes in the broader economy: by the nineteenth century the percentage of women working as housemaids had decreased by 24 percent (Arrom 1985: 161).[6] During the late colonial period Mexico City's economy began to expand and diversify. Consequently, lower class women had greater job opportunities and the growing economy also removed legal, educational, and ideological barriers to their work. But after independence (1821) a recession followed and the stagnant economy no longer required women's work. "Women retreated from the artisanal trades they had begun to enter and, even in the traditional female crafts like cigar making, and spinning, they lost ground in the fact of factory production and mechanization" (Arrom 1985: 204).

With the transition to Mexico's independence, nationhood, and industrialization in the nineteenth century, the nature of women's subordination changed, with important consequences for the present. The development of commerce and economic mobility for men meant that the trend toward greater independence of the conjugal pair left the woman without as much close support from and protection by her extended family as she had received in colonial times. In aristocratic families women had exercised power through inheritance,[7] but the new bourgeois home brought together love and marriage, and led to women's greater dependence on men than before.

Among the many changes in the nineteenth century was an important shift that began to take place within the family as a result of the greater economic mobility that was available to men. Whereas during the colonial period both young men and women were subjugated to the family patriarch,[8] with incipient industrialization following independence[9] men found greater opportunities for employment independent of the extended family. Consequently the property a woman brought to a marriage became less relevant. Women in Mexico, as elsewhere in the Western world, became more dependent economically on their husbands, and they lost their position of power in the private domain. With the decline of the need for property, the marital relationship became transformed into a personal relationship and the woman became more economically dependent on her husband than before. In fact, contrary to common assertions, modernization "did not necessarily mean that women's status improved; quite the contrary, due to their exclusion from the sophisticated technological tools, women have been marginalized in the schemes" (Lavrin 1987: 115).

With the rise of the bourgeois family, the wife lost her role as manager of the household and reproducer of the family, whose task it was to satisfy her husband's comforts; instead the household became predominantly a reproductive unit oriented toward the labor market.[10] In fact, in response to commercialization and industrialization, the "household size in Latin

America increased significantly in both the rural and urban areas during the 19th century (Kuznesof 1989).

When Mexico became independent from Spain in 1821 and the new nation began to industrialize,[11] European and especially French society and culture became a model for the Mexican intelligentsia. The French philosophies introduced a new definition of the family based on love and benevolence rather than coercion (Franco 1989: 84) and glorified motherhood and the family. Concurrently, the feminization of love and the glorification of motherhood took hold in Mexico as in Europe, having been imported from Europe along with numerous other cultural influences.[12] The nineteenth-century Mexican intelligentsia "set out to educate mothers so that they would instill in the new generation patriotism, the work ethic and belief in progress" (Franco 1989: 81). With nationhood "women were now to be persuaded to 'mother' their children by breast-feeding, and educating them in early childhood in order to guarantee the future well-being of the nation" (82). "The burden of nationhood was thus placed on the family, which was responsible not only for internalizing Christian morality but also for developing the virtues necessary for the smooth functioning of a society that could no longer be policed by the Spanish imperial bureaucracy, the Inquisition, and the Church" (84).

As we learned in Chapter 3, societies harbor conflicting views about women, and Mexico is no exception; there women are viewed as both subordinate and powerful. On the one hand, and this point cannot be overstated enough, woman as Mother is idealized by both male and female children, in the fashion of what Smith-Rosenberg (1985) identified as the Cult of True Motherhood. Woman in the personnage of the Virgin Mary and her many guises is worshiped. An often heard remark in Mexico is that the Virgin is the "Mother of us all" and the repository of all moral rectitude.[13] She is the universal Mother, as well as the intermediary between the awesome father and his children.[14]

The universal Virgin Mother is also the suffering mother. In Mexico, as in some other Latin societies, such as Italy, the pervasive belief in the suffering mother permeates women's lives.[15] In Mexico there is a collective conviction that women must suffer: it is their destiny. The culturally legitimated ideology of the suffering woman pervades Mexican society and is continuously reinforced by women's experience in their daily life. In fact, the ideology of sacrifice sustains women in their daily lives, even in the face of physical abuse by their husbands. They may remain with the men because, they say, "my children need a father." Indeed women do make great sacrifices for their children in many other ways as well, when, for example, the mother sends her daughters to school, and she is then left with all the housework, a daunting task for poor women.

The veneration of the Virgin Mary reveals the irony of the ideal Woman having power most when she is sexually impotent, distant, and worshiped; but when a woman is near, and potentially sexual, she is beaten and abused. Thus on the one hand, Woman, in the guise of the Virgin of Guadalupe, is the patron saint and the very symbol of Mexico[16]—the mediator between God and men and between God and the Mexicans[17]— whereas on the other hand, women are immoral, lascivious, seducers of men and therefore also dangerous.[18] In this view, Woman is a seducer of men, a being whose power men cannot resist.[19] Although Elaine Marks and Isabelle de Courtivron write about France, they could also be speaking about Mexico when they remark that Woman "is simultaneously an insatiable cunt and the charming, gracious, virgin mother of God" (1980: 5).

On the level of historical experience, Woman, in the guise of the Virgin Mary, is the national symbol of Mexico's past, of the country's subjugation by the Conquest. Her passivity, residing in her sex, equates the Woman with Mexico as the conquered and the violated (*chingada*). Mexico, like Woman, is the *chingada,* or the female "who is pure passivity, defenseless against the exterior world. The relationship between them [men and women] is violent and it is determined by the [man's] cynical power and the [woman's] impotence" (Paz 1961: 77).

The passive woman is confronted by the macho man, usually defined by people as meaning a seducer of many women, the man who drinks a lot and does not let himself be bossed around.[20] As characterized by Octavio Paz, "The macho is the *gran chingón.* One word sums up the aggressiveness, insensitivity, invulnerability and other attributes of the macho: power. It is force without the discipline of any notion of order: arbitrary power, the will without reins and without a set course" (1961: 81). In Mexico's gender ideology the father is not a caring creature, but rather a powerful being in whom "power almost always reveals itself as a capacity for wounding, humiliating, annihilating" (82). Echoing Simone de Beauvoir, Paz maintains that Woman in Mexican sensibilities *is* the image that men create of her. "She never expresses her femininity because it always manifests itself in forms men have invented for her" (197). Since women are men's creation, women are forestalled from becoming actors. Woman has always been for man the "other," his opposite; she is never her own mistress. "If one part of our being longs to unite itself with her, another part—equally imperious— rejects and excludes her" (197).

It must be stressed that men also are apprehended in ambiguous ways.

Just as Woman is regarded as both seductive and passive, so too Man regards himself and is seen by others as the predator and protector of women and also helpless in the face of women's allure. In fact, in all the cases of infidelity or abandonment of a fiancée or wife, the woman almost invariably blames "the other woman"'s wiles for the man's defection. In such instances, there was never any question that a man could act on his own volition.[21] Thus both sexes must resolve ambiguities about their manhood and womanhood. In concrete terms, however, a woman suffers from these ambiguities because any transgression on her part will quickly transform her from the sacred mother to the lascivious whore. A married woman who exudes her sexuality (as do Margarita and Alicia, discussed in Chapters 7 and 8) is looked on as a "whore," much as in Victorian Europe, when a woman's fecundity precluded sexual desires. Women, in fact, are aware of the precariousness of their situation (as Susana [see Chapter 14] was in the secrets she kept).

In the case of a man, the prevailing ideological inconsistencies enhance his image of the powerful man, while excusing his behaviors on the grounds of women's seductive powers. And in this context, a point I made in the previous chapters is worth repeating, that the very men's acts that give women grief, (having many women, drinking heavily) and produce life's lesions nourish the self-esteem of the macho man.[22] This is not to suggest that every woman is "under a man's thumb." Paz's depiction of Mexican notions of the macho man and the put-upon woman obviously does not represent every man or woman. Generalizations of any kind are suspect, and not all men are macho males, nor are all women always passive, *la chingona*.[23] Ideologies about gender differences form part of a cultural pool of understandings.[24] In the case of gender ideologies, beliefs about the attributes of men and women are models *of* as well as *for* behavior[25] and they give shape to our engendered beings. Obviously not every member of a culture adheres to the cultural paradigms in actual practice. Nevertheless, Paz's description of Mexican beliefs about women reflect the realities of many relationships between men and women, as we will see in Chapters 7 through 16.

Each man and woman brings into a marriage his or her interpretation of the cultural baggage each carries regarding proper male-female behavior and the roles of husbands and wives. A woman ought to be a virgin at marriage, and when she is not she may be beaten on her wedding night.[26] Of course, many women are not virgins on their wedding day. It is not uncommon for a young woman to become pregnant before marriage, and for the responsible man to escape when he learns about the pregnancy. In such instances, if the woman later marries another man, her parents may rear the child for her, willingly or unwillingly, or she may remain a *madre soltera* (a single mother).

Although common-law marriages are unexceptional, ideally a woman aspires to marry in a civil and religious ceremony. A woman announces with great pride that her husband had requested her hand in marriage. In such instances, and this is the most common form of marriage, the couple marries in a religious and civil ceremony and the woman proudly states that she was married by both laws (*por las dos leyes*).[27]

In fact, while in Mexico monogamy is the norm, de facto polygyny is very common and it is not unusual for a man to support two or more households—to have a *casa chica* (little house)—with various numbers of children.[28] In most cases when a woman finds out about the "other woman" she is unquestionably distressed, although women frequently justify the man's behavior on the grounds that, unlike women, men are highly sexual beings.[29] But among the poor what angers the woman most, and grates on her life's lesions is not when the man possesses another woman, but when the man fails to support the wife and her children by diverting to the other woman's household scarce resources that rightly are due the wife. In such instances "trouble" emerges.

The household, usually comprised of consanguineal and affinal kin and formed around a nuclear or extended three-generation family, is the basic unit of existence for the individual in Mexico in every social stratum.[30] In contrast with contemporary North American sensibilities of the independent individual actor,[31] always in control,[32] Mexican women regard themselves as embedded first in their natal and later in their conjugal families, which define them as persons. This point is important to keep in mind to make sense of the lives of the women we will meet later. Whereas in some societies the individual is embedded in a wide kinship network of people constituting a lineage or clan,[33] in Mexico the family is the all-encompassing unit of people's existence, and women form a focal part of this unit. The family is a basic building block of human existence in the present as it was in the past.[34]

As noted in the previous chapter, within the natal family the universally problematic relationships between parents and children are, of course, present in contemporary Mexico.[35] Conflicts between children and parents can become acute. In these instances the mother is left to deal with the recalcitrant offspring, causing her numerous angers and sickness. In the past, when parents transmitted their property to all their children, a woman maintained a degree of independence in a marriage, attendant with her self-esteem as the mistress of a corporate household, and the parents maintained a degree of power and control over their children because of the children's expectations that they would inherit the parental estate. This implicit contract between parents and children is still evident in rural communities where parents have land, even a meager piece, to transmit to their offspring. In such instances, parents retain their power and authority over even their married children.[36] But among the working poor in Mexico City, including the people discussed in this book, parents lack any tangible property to pass on; all that parents have of value to transmit to their children is encapsulated in parental moral values—sentiments about right and wrong behavior—and they expect their offspring to adhere to these dicta. Morals, however, unlike property, lack concreteness. Morals are ethereal, ambiguous, and difficult to get a grip on. Consequently, tensions between parents and children over interpretations of right and wrong behavior lead to conflicts and angers of the kind that produce sickness, especially in the mothers because they must deal daily with their rebellious progeny.[37]

During a couple's courtship the ideology of romantic love prevails. Cultural notions of ideal synergy between the man and woman dominate the relationship, as they do in the United States.[38] In fact, among the poor, after marriage, lower class men and women normally lead separate lives, except if they join a religious sect. While women expected affective ties with their husbands, in reality women's closest bonds are with their mothers and siblings. They look for companionship and moral support from their mothers, sisters, and adult children. In Mexico, then, a woman's strongest bonds are with her children and her siblings.

Table 5.1 displays the percentage distribution of responses by sex to the question "Who are the persons closest to you?" The data reveal that a spouse is usually not regarded by either sex as the closest person in one's life, and this seems to be true even more so for women than men. In fact, both men and women of all ages regard their parents and siblings, rather than their spouses, as the people closest to them.

A senior woman often becomes the focal point for her many children, and in her capacity as matriarch she may even have some influence over her children that she had lacked at an early age.[39]

Domestic relations are a point of departure for our understanding of life's lesions. It is on the level of the home and family life that gender relations become crucial for our comprehension of life's lesions, especially

TABLE 5.1   Responses to the Question "Who Are the People Closest to You?"

	Men (n = 62) (percent)	Women (n = 203)* (percent)
Mother	26	28
Other†	21	13
Brothers	23	14
Sisters	6	13
Mother and father	10	11
Children	6	16
Spouse	7	3
No one	1	2
Total	100	100

*2 cases missing from the total sample.
†"Other" includes other family members, ritual relatives (*compadres*), and neighbors.

because marriage and motherhood are the sine qua non for most all women. The women's narratives about themselves and their health usually revolved first around issues relating to subsistence and then around their health. Yet these narrations were laced throughout with talk of the moral indignation and pain that the women associated with social relations, particularly those with their mates. Although the women decry their poverty, their social interactions rob them of their dignity and affect them at the core of their beings, leading to life's lesions that are expressed symptomatologically.

In Mexico, conjugal relations depend on myriad factors, including individual temperament, family structure, a man's drinking behavior, class, and household economic strategies and resources. While clearly there exists individual variability in male-female relations, in broad terms a pattern of combative conjugal relationships emerges shortly after marriage,[40] not an unexpected turn, considering the historical process of the feminization of love[41] and the different expectations of marriage held by men and women.

At present, as in colonial times, one hears women speak of *la mala vida,* or what Richard Boyer (1989: 279) defines as "trouble," referring specifically to the abuse of power by a spouse. In contemporary times *la mala vida* refers to lack of financial support, overwork, and mistreatment, especially physical abuse. Boyer observes that "trouble" is "a window on the politics of marriage" and "the catalyst that moves us to order our thoughts about most matters" (279). As long as life is smooth and the way we think it *ought to be,* we rarely question it. When "norms and experience roughly coincide, one is unlikely to change course or analyze experience; the awareness of a disparity between them is what spurs thought and action" (279). When there is "trouble," beliefs and lived experience fail to coincide, producing the kind of contradictions that cannot be easily reconciled and become inscribed on the body symptomatologically.

The striking historical continuities in the sphere of domestic relations exist in sharp contrast to other, important discontinuities between the past and the present. In the past the wife, as the subordinate to the husband, was recognized as the moral and intellectual superior of the two (Arrom 1985: 260). And whereas formerly a woman was in a subordinate position and required to obey her husband, the husband had well-defined obligations toward the woman. As Friar Luis De Leon warns, "the right-minded husband must not, with ill deeds and words, oppress or put to shame the heart of his wife, of itself so ready to fail and so wanting in confidence, but, on the contrary, by loving and honoring her, upraise her so that her every thought may be conceived in rectitude" ([1584] 1943: 25). In keeping with de Leon's declaration, Boyer, writing about the colonial period in Mexico, observes: "Our cases of the *mala vida* have shown that to the degree that obligations were neglected, *the logic of obedience was undercut*. However slanted in favor of the husband, there was an aspect of marriage that insisted on a degree of reciprocity" (1989; 280; emphasis added).

Unlike in times past, when a woman whose man did not meet his obligations could be "deposited" with a member in the community and cared for, in contemporary times formal community institutions to sanction the man and remove the woman from the situation are lacking.[42] When a man mistreats his wife, or fails to meet his obligations for whatever reason, and the woman has met hers, the anger she feels (which also produces and nurtures her life's lesions) is due to the fact that she has obeyed her spouse, been the "perfect wife," and yet failed to reap the economic support justly due her. The actual economic deprivation and mistreatment coupled with the moral indignation leads to sickness. Single mothers or women in female-headed households face fewer contradictions in this regard and ironically may feel a greater sense of coherence. In the case of Josefina (see Chapter 13), however, she may be criticized by other women for being alone and even accused of eyeing their husbands.

Whether a woman forms part of a nuclear or extended family and whether she resides with her or her husband's family after marriage greatly influences domestic relations. Historically, the transition to the nuclear family led to the dependency of a woman and her offspring on the male breadwinner. When a woman, especially with small children, is dependent on her husband for support (such as Rebecca, in Chapter 10) and the support is not forthcoming, the woman is left with few choices in contemporary Mexico. Moreover, when the man has other households, a woman residing in a nuclear family is left completely isolated and in unbearable pain. In Rebecca's words as she spoke about her husband, "Many times it's not the economic problems, even though there are many, it is the problem of not getting along."

In extended families, if the man comes to reside with the woman's natal family, resources are pooled and a man's infidelities are more easily tolerated because the woman is enveloped by her parents or her siblings, and she is not left at the mercy of her husband. She is, in fact, shielded by her family from her husband's physical abuse. However, when a woman goes to reside with her husband's family after marriage, as is the accepted norm in Mexico, the husband's mother demands respect from her daughter-in-law. In a conflict the mother-in-law will usually side with her son, from whom she may also expect financial support. In fact, in Mexico kinship, especially the mother-child dyad, overrides gender affiliation. Consequently the mother-in-law invariably justifies the actions of her son in opposition to the daughter-in-law. These familial interactions cause angers and sickness for people like Josefina (see Chapter 13).

A statistical comparison of women's reports of conflicts with their mates residing in a nuclear or composite family reveals that there is a statistically significant association between the type of family and reported conflicts (p = .0094 level of significance, chi-square = 6.75). Married women living in a nuclear family were more likely to report dissension with their spouses than women residing in some type of extended family, be it three generational or a household comprised of married siblings.

The central "trouble" impinging on marital relations is a man's drinking habits. Undoubtedly a woman suffers most from her husband's bouts with alcohol. Drinking is most often accompanied by physical and psychological abuse, and in those instances women experience angers and sickness.[43] Furthermore, any consideration of domestic relations cannot ignore a couple's class position. The women described in this book originate from the underprivileged class—the people the elite usually fear. For upper class Mexicans residing in the elegant sections of Mexico City, these people are murderous thieves who live licentious lives and are dangerous and mysterious. They are, in contemporary parlance, the "other." They provide the negative image in which the elites can mirror themselves and see themselves as meritorious. While the images elites paint of the poor are not based in fact, these images serve to affirm the elites' righteousness; they provide what I call negative models of behavior that nourish elite and middle class comportments. In some measure, elite and middle class Mexicans pattern their own behaviors on the negative models the poor people provide them. That is, the elite sanction behaviors of what they ought *not* to do based on their perceptions of what the poor people do: we do not beat our wives, only poor people do so.

To what degree domestic relationships of the kind we encounter in the women's histories are recreated in elite and middle class families remains an empirical question. Whether physical abuse is practiced among elite and middle class groups cannot be ascertained with our present state of knowledge of the family life of these groups. For this reason my discussion of the lives of the women in the poor strata cannot be generalized to the upper and middle classes with respect to abusive domestic relations. In fact, using the concept of the negative model as an important sanctioning agent, I hypothesize that there is less physical abuse of women, and also less of the resulting sickness, among elite and middle class people. We can speculate further that, to the degree elite and middle class men live by concepts of male honor, it would preclude them, as honorable men, from abusing their wives physically if not psychologically.[44]

Undoubtedly, domestic relations are shaped in large part by household economic resources and men's activities.[45] In my earlier studies of rural communities, among agricultural producers, for example, where men cultivate land and women's routines of unceasing daily chores, women rarely left the household and never without prior permission from their spouses. The men were usually in charge of all decisions in both the public and the private domains, certainly until the women reached a certain age. Enterprising women opened little stores, but usually these women were without spouses. Prior to marriage, young women sought work as maids until they married.[46] One of the changes I observed that took place during the past twenty years is that all girls are now sent to high school, and with their absence from home, the mothers' work burden has been greatly increased. Armed with their high school education, these young women seek employment outside their communities, but they usually marry shortly after they graduate from high school.

On the other hand, in one community I studied where all the men illegally migrated to the United States for ten months of the year, the women depended on their own artisan work and their wits to sustain themselves and their children. Remittances from their mates in the United

States were more a windfall than a regular occurrence. Women in this community assumed the dual roles of housekeeper and provider of daily subsistence; they moved freely out of the house and participated in community activities. The decision-making process was left to the women in the men's absence. These women had more skills in planting and in supervising workers than did homemakers in agricultural communities. In fact, in several instances the women decided to plant fields to the objection of the men who, as proletarians, regarded planting as wasteful. The women in this proletarian community enjoyed greater mobility and decision-making roles, but when the men came home, the women became subservient to their mates.[47]

Yet the ideology of male domination supersedes the actualities. Only when men were absent did they lose by default whatever supremacy they might otherwise have claimed. When the men were away all decisions were made by women; the minimal income women possessed derived from their own efforts and gave them an independence that women in an agricultural village lacked. However, on their brief return visits to the community, men reclaimed their dominant position over the women.

In merchant households in rural or urban areas, in families of itinerant vendors, or in merchant households where family labor organization was interdependent and where women were involved in the selling end of the business, the marriages were less conflicting, even harmonious and stable. The women usually assisted the men in the family enterprise; for example, a woman might act as the distributor of merchandise that the man had purchased in his travels.

Aside from such situations where the men are absent, where household economies enable the husband and wife equal participation in the household enterprise by fostering complementary economic roles, or in female-headed households, limited opportunities exist for women to retain their dignity and self-esteem and elude physical abuse.[48]

Customarily men were and still are opposed to their wives working (Arrom 1985: 175). It is dubious, however, whether working women improve their position in society by increasing their independence, status, and power. Silvia Marina Arrom writes about nineteenth-century Mexico City but could easily be writing about the present situation when she points out that though employment then may have permitted some women and their families to survive, it did not normally make the women prosperous and emancipated, nor was work an avenue for upward mobility. Women, like Margarita and Julia, for example (see Chapters 7 and 9), may earn a livelihood and improve their economic positions through their work in the informal economy. By so doing they free themselves of dependency from the man. Nonetheless, the ideology of male superiority nullifies a woman's economic gains. She still remains subordinate to the man. The contradiction a woman must face is that when men gain access to resource they usually gain status and power in the public sphere, whereas women do not in either the public or private domains.[49]

In colonial times women could join a nunnery.[50] In contemporary secularized Mexico the convent is no longer an option for women in lieu of marriage and domestic strife. Although women like Margarita cannot become nuns, they can resort, as Margarita had, to contemporary options by becoming an outstanding karate master,[51] which for her was the equivalent of a mystical experience.

This is not to suggest that the spiritual life is completely unavailable to contemporary women. In fact, women can become religious leaders and healers, as is the case for those who join the Spiritualist movement[52] and become Spiritualist healers. Ironically, becoming a Spiritualist is an option more readily available to poor women than to women of the middle class, such as Margarita, because sectarian movements such as Spiritualism are often denigrated by the society at large; people who become Spiritualist healers are commonly regarded as witches.[53]

It is useful to pause for a moment on the subject of Spiritualism—one of the fastest growing religious and healing movements in contemporary Mexico[54]—to illuminate women's options for mobility. Unlike the Catholic church, Spiritualism opens positions of leadership for women and, for some, avenues for economic mobility as well. Women who become heads of Spiritualist temples have large followings and gain access to positions of authority and power. From the time of its founding in 1861 until the present, a time of great expansion for Spiritualism, the "mother temple" in Mexico City, which stands at the top of the Spiritualist hierarchy, has been headed by women. In fact, the position of headship is transmitted through the matrilineal line. The heads of the "mother temple" claim direct descent from the woman who was originally assigned by the founder, one of twelve sacerdotal positions awarded to women.[55]

Spiritualists recruit their members by curing the sick. Indeed, most if not all leaders and temple functionaries, as well as ordinary members, make their initial contact with Spiritualist temples during a sickness episode, when they come to seek treatment. At such times, they are recruited into Spiritualism to serve as functionaries or healers.

The women who head these temples play an important part in providing health care services to a multitude of individuals. A case in point is Mariana, who is now in her seventies. She established her temple in 1962. During the course of my close contact with her for eighteen years, I have watched the temple and its membership grow from a small room, accommodating about twenty people, to a large establishment that now holds about five hundred. She is the absolute ruler of the establishment, as are the women who preside over the "mother temple" in Mexico City with its thousands of parishioners.

The Mexican constitution of 1917 assigned identical rights to men and women,[56] and women from the middle strata of Mexican society have managed to achieve public recognition through the professions.[57] Similar opportunities for women from the lower social strata are lacking. By becoming a Spiritualist, however, a woman can achieve public renown and improve her economic status independent of her husband or mate. Although temple leaders cannot be regarded as wealthy by national criteria, they enjoy a relatively higher standard of living than others forming part of the same segment of society. Mariana is fond of recalling that her father prophesied she would become a leader, and she, pointing to her house and the large temple that she heads, says, "And look where I am now."

Mariana's statement crystallizes the opportunities Spiritualism has made available to some women. Not surprisingly, Mariana is extraordinarily energetic, intelligent, and self-sustaining. She has the ability to motivate people to do her bidding without undue coercion. Expanding and directing a temple of the size Mariana established requires independence, enterprise, and the ability to manipulate the social environment.

Spiritualism is not unique in attracting women to its doors. Protestantism too has grown enormously in Latin America and Mexico.[58] But inasmuch as Spiritualism attracts people through their sickness, and since more women than men experience sickness, not unexpectedly women predominate in the movement as functionaries and healers.[59] Women are drawn to alternative religions, including Protestant Evangelical groups, which have taken hold in Mexican society, especially among the women of impoverished classes.

Although Spiritualism and Evangelical groups differ greatly in religious practices (Protestants study the Bible, whereas Spiritualists depend solely on revelation through spirit possession), both movements emphasize abstention from alcohol and interactive male-female relations. A prime motivation for a woman to convert to one of these sectarian movements is that she is married to a man who drinks excessively. If the woman prevails on the man to join also, he usually abandons his drinking habits.

Conversion to Protestantism or Spiritualism alters domestic relationships to the advantage of the women. These religious movements do succeed in altering relations between the sexes. Like the Spiritualists, the Protestant movements tend to promote equality between the sexes that is reflected behaviorally in various ways. In Spiritualism a man refers to his wife as his companion rather than the usual reference to "my woman." One twenty-five-year-old man went to great lengths to explain to me that, in contrast to non-Spiritualists, he regards his wife not as his property but as his true companion. I have always been struck by the greater sharing of concerns among Spiritualist and Evangelical couples than among non-Spiritualists from the same socioeconomic strata. And while these religious groups promote among their members the traditional sexual division of labor, men usually assist their wives with the household chores when they are home, which is not a common practice in traditional Mexican families. Most important, these religious groups place great emphasis on monogamous relationships; among couples, husbands and wives usually spend their leisure time in joint activities, while in traditional Mexican society wives normally do not accompany their husbands nor do a husband and wife participate in joint leisure activities.

Conversion to Spiritualism or Evangelical Protestantism alters not only a woman's familial relations but her social relations in general. In Spiritualism and Evangelism, the central concern of converts turns from interaction with people to an interplay with God. This shift is exemplified by Norma after she converted to Evangelical Protestantism (see Chapter 15). Norma noted how serving God became more important to her than her interaction with people. The changes in daily interactions attenuate any aggravations an individual had felt in her social relations because she simply removes herself from the interactions.

Most important, these movements tend to alter the individual's notions about witchcraft. In Mexico there is a common belief that human beings can harm one another by witchcraft; Evangelical groups and Spiritualists usually vehemently deny the existence of witchcraft. With their vigorous preaching against witchcraft beliefs, these religious groups lay the foundation for smoother social interactions with neighbors, friends, and within the family. Generally speaking, when people harbor suspicion of witchcraft they are mindful of other people's evil intentions and suspicious of their actions. By repudiating the possibility of witchcraft, these movements abate mistrust. Yet as Norma's predicament will show, by abandoning their belief in witchcraft people renounce the possibility that their sickness was caused by others and so place responsibility for their affliction on themselves and on their misguided acts. Blaming oneself instead of others for one's misfortune, including sickness, may aggravate rather than alleviate life's lesions.[60]

Both Spiritualist and Evangelical movements advocate abstention from alcohol. When the man gives up drinking, the woman is shielded from his acts of violence after a drinking binge, and the resources that are usually diverted for alcohol consumption revert to the household. Not surprisingly, the usual pattern is that a woman is attracted first to a Spiritualist or evangelical group and in turn recruits her mate. The woman tends to succeed in her efforts to recruit her husband at the point when he has reached his last limits with alcohol.

While conversions to Spiritualist or Evangelical movements significantly alter the male-female relationship, these movements reaffirm traditional gender ideologies of wifehood and motherhood. The sort of changes often associated with women's "liberation" come about with profound changes at the deepest level of a woman's self-understanding as an autonomous individual, rather than as a mother and wife whose personhood is defined by the encompassment of her family. A woman's restructuring of her understanding of herself—from motherhood to personhood, from constituent member of a family unit to autonomous individual—can take place only when she can take pride in her accomplishments and in herself rather than when she is merely the bearer of many children.[61] In contemporary times, when a woman seeks individuation she may ensnare herself in a mesh of contradictions or be unable to contemplate herself as separate from her husband, despite the beatings he gives her. Although Mexico is on its way to becoming an industrialized capitalist society, the accompanying comprehensions of oneself as an autonomous individual existing outside any social unit have not as yet taken root.

For poor women in Mexico, fertility means identity and a sense of importance. Barren women are in a precarious position given the emphasis on children.[62] It is not uncommon for menopausal women to regard dysmenorrhea as a sign of pregnancy.[63] For example, Raquel, a vivacious forty-eight-year-old woman, sought a medical consultation because she stopped menstruating. For Raquel, these were symptoms of pregnancy because otherwise, in her words, "*uno vale menos,*" one is worthless.

Two points still remain. First, by discussing the plight of poor women in Mexico, I do not wish to disregard the adverse realities of the men of the economically impoverished classes. Unquestionably, men too are confronted with contradictions that affect their health.[64] The husbands and sons of the women we will meet lack power in the public domain and they similarly suffer from assaults on their dignity, as discussed earlier. Nevertheless, the woman is the one who gets the beatings while the man retains his self-esteem at least in the home, where he is in command, nurtured by the knowledge of his own superiority and buttressed by the fact that he was born a male. The abused woman lacks a similar belief to sustain her, setting the foundations for development of life's lesions. All she possesses is her moral indignation, felt as anger and experienced as sickness. In her later years her adult sons may protect her from her husband and are also a source of her self-esteem as the mother of men.[65]

The second point before closing is that momentous social forces and events in a society's history often propel women to act in concert and enter the public sphere in ways other than through work. Women became politicized following the calamitous 1985 earthquake in Mexico City. Prior to the earthquake, Raquel was employed in a garment factory, working under abysmal conditions. When the factory collapsed she reverted to maintaining her household. One of many people in her neighborhood whose house collapsed after the earthquake, she joined a citywide coalition of women who petitioned the government and private agencies to secure new housing for the displaced families.[66] Another example could be Susana, who became active in a union of street vendors to protect her rights to several square feet of sidewalk where she had her candy stand (see Chapter 14).

In this chapter I sketched in broad strokes the world of Mexican women and beliefs about them. In the next chapter we turn to a socioeconomic profile of the women in my large study sample, from which I selected the subsample of women presented in Part III.

Notes

1. There is a great need for studies of the elite in Mexico. Lomnitz's and Perez-Lizaur's study reveals no differences in ideologies and practices between the elites and the poor people, other than that the elites are richer (see Finkler 1989); see also Lavrin 1987.

2. See Arrom 1985.

3. Included too were "other conditions such as curable contagious disease, such as leprosy, or if a spouse compelled the other to perpetrate criminal acts, and other such heinous acts" (Arrom 1985: 208).

4. See, for example, Tutino 1983.

5. Ines de la Cruz (Sor Juana), the great Mexican poet and nun, even gained the begrudging admiration of the church (Franco 1989).

6. Arrom cites the following statistics. In 1811, 54 percent of the women worked as domestics, whereas before 80 percent had worked as housemaids. Twenty percent, the next largest group of those working, were involved in the retail food industry preparing finished food products at home or buying fresh produce in bulk and selling these goods from homes, street corner stands, and market stalls (Arrom 1985: 158–59). The remainder were petty merchants. In my large sample of women's occupations, 17 percent had worked as maids (see Chapter 6).

7. See Tutino 1983.

8. See Tutino 1983.

9. See Finkler 1983.

10. See Finkler 1983.

11. See Finkler 1983.

12. See Arrom 1985; Franco 1989. As in the rest of Western Europe and America, motherhood and the family became glorified with nationhood (Franco 1989). See also a similar argument by Mosse 1985 for the conceptual underpinnings of the role of the family in ideologies about nationhood.

13. See Pescatello 1976.

14. See Lafaye 1974; Paz 1961.

15. See Pandolfi 1990 for Italy.

16. See Lafaye 1974; Wolf 1958.

17. See Lafaye 1974: 288.

18. See Paz 1961.

19. In his analysis of Spanish male ideology Brandes (1981) could have been describing Mexico as well.

20. See Finkler 1974, 1981.

21. In fact, a fiancée or wife may attempt to perform witchcraft on the "other woman" because it is the other woman's fault, not the boyfriend's or husband's.

22. It is noteworthy that macho men also have difficulties handling all the women they woo, who may interfere with their daily activities, but at no time in the large sample of males did they associate their problems with women as sickness-producing in the manner women did when speaking about their own sickness.

23. Stevens 1973 argues that the cult of womanhood gave women leverage, allowing them to manipulate their husbands. There is merit to this contention; however, the constant manipulation women must engage in may in itself be debilitating. On the other hand, see Margarita's depiction (Chapter 7) of how her husband and father have manipulated her.

24. Differential concepts about women and men are extended to the fetus. Some say that male fetuses are formed fully forty days after conception and begin moving within that time, whereas female fetuses are not formed until three months of pregnancy and up until that time are just pieces of flesh.

25. Geertz 1965.

26. See the case of Nomi in Finkler 1991.

27. While it is common for couples to marry in a civil ceremony only, when a

couple is married in church but not in a civil ceremony this may suggest that the man is already married to another woman in a civil ceremony.

28. See Finkler 1974.

29. See the discussion in Finkler 1991 of a doctor teaching his students that though men cannot exist without sex for even a short period of time, women may be harmed by too frequent sexual intercourse.

30. See Kuznesof 1989; Lomnitz and Perez-Lizaur 1987.

31. See Bellah et al. 1985.

32. See Finkler 1985b; also Jack 1991.

33. This situation is found in primitive societies, such as Melanesia (Strathern 1988).

34. Boyer 1989; Lavrin 1989.

35. Generational conflicts are common, especially in societies with a historical consciousness where people tend to compare the past and the present—the way "it was and ought to be, and the way it is now. I wonder whether we would find parental conflict in societies where consciousness of historicity was absent.

36. Finkler 1974; see also Tutino 1983.

37. Rubin 1976 makes a similar point.

38. See Jack 1991. The contradictions between ideal romantic love and the reality were jarring to the young women I met.

39. Sundays are usually spent with one's natal family and thus several generations may spend the day together. It is when a woman is isolated from her natal family and mother that she recognizes her loneliness. Not uncommonly, one hears of an adult woman, the mother of adults, deeply longing for her dead mother.

40. See Finkler 1991: 24; see also Ehlers 1990 for Guatemala.

41. In cases where there is a good marital relationship the woman may be subject to envy. For example, one woman had told me that she, like some others she knew, had been accused of having a lover by her neighbors, who wanted to create discord between her and her husband because she had a good life with him.

42. Women can petition the local police delegation to sanction the husband when they are mistreated. On occasion the authorities successfully intervene; but seeking assistance from the authorities is an extreme measure that most women attempt to avoid.

43. In the control group of my earlier study (Finkler 1985a) women whose husbands did not drink were "trouble"-free and suffered fewer sickness episodes. The fact that, when drunk, a man might beat his wife but not his mother or even his children, suggests that drinking and the concomitant aggressive behavior reflects the ideology of mate coercion rather than uncensored aggression due to the action of alcohol on the psyche.

44. This assertion is based on my personal contact with numerous families during all my years in Mexico. However, to repeat a point made earlier, there is great need for anthropological studies of elite women and their health. Historically, while there are instances of elite men physically abusing their wives, this behavior was not common (see Arrom 1985).

45. Finkler 1974.

46. For a detailed analysis of women's lives in rural communities, see Finkler 1974.

47. See Finkler 1974.

48. In his study of elite Mexican women during the colonial period, Tutino (1983) demonstrates persuasively that in the absence of male heirs a woman could inherit property and become the head of the family. Widows were also privileged in this way.

49. See Benería and Roldán 1987.

50. See Franco 1989.

51. See de Beauvoir's 1980 statement about this; see also Chapter 7.

52. See Finkler 1981.

53. See Finkler 1983.

54. See Finkler 1983, 1985b; Sylvia Ortiz, personal communication 1980.

55. See Finkler 1981.

56. See Signorelli de Marti 1967.

57. See Macias 1973.

58. See Stoll 1990; Willems 1975.

59. There are numerous explanations for the preponderance of women in dissident religious movements of the Spiritualist kind, in which voluntary spirit possession plays a central role in ritual and healing. Lewis argued convincingly that "it is in terms of the exclusion of women from full participation in social and political affairs and their final subjugation to men that we should seek to understand their marked prominence in peripheral possession" (1989: 88). According to Lewis, women who lack power in society resort to possession as a form of domination of their superiors without overtly threatening them. Movements such as Spiritualism clearly attract the disadvantaged and the powerless. But the fact that women are the heads of Spiritualist temples also adds to the appeal as well, as does the emphasis on social equality (Finkler 1983).

60. Spiritualists, unlike Evangelicals, blame impersonal spirits for sickness rather than a person's misguided actions. By so doing, Spiritualism eliminates potential conflicts with oneself that may be associated with self-blame.

61. See Handwerker (1986) who rightly asserts that population control is accompanied by changes in concepts of the individual.

62. For example, a woman's sister and mother-in-law taunted her because she was infertile and useless. The woman agreed that her husband had every right to divorce her for this reason. In this case the man refused to do so, claiming that he had not married her solely to have children.

63. Several physicians commented to me on this phenomenon. As we will see in Chapter 14, later, Susana came to her physician to establish whether she was pregnant.

64. See Finkler 1991 for cases of men.

65. See MacKinnon 1981: 7.

66. The movement was known as MUDI, or Movimiento Unidad de Indem-nificados.

6. An Aggregate Profile of a Sick Population of Women

Each human life represents itself and speaks for all humanity. We may, nevertheless, question the degree to which the women I write about in this book represent a larger population of Mexicans. For this reason I present an aggregate overview of a large (n = 205) sick population sample (SPS) from which I drew a subsample of the ten women we will meet in Chapters 7 through 16. I compare the SPS with the ten women along several sociodemographic variables. I also compare the SPS with a randomly selected healthy population sample from the same social strata along several sociodemographic dimensions and their experience of life events in order to assess the association between life events and the experience of sickness.

I consider the differences between men's and women's etiological explanations of sickness and emotional states on the aggregate level, using the Cornell Medical Index (CMI). These comparisons are instructive for our understanding of differences between men's and women's attributions of sickness because they reflect the differences in women's and men's lives. I present broad measures of men's and women's differences in "emotional states" to deepen our insight into life's lesions. I conclude the chapter with my findings about the ways men and women are generally treated by physicians, which may influence women's experience of life's lesions.[1]

A Sociodemographic Profile of a Sick Population

The average age of the women in the SPS was 33. Fifty-five percent were married, 29 percent were single, and the remaining 16 percent were widowed, separated, or divorced. Of those who were married, 49 percent were married both in church and in a civil ceremony, 27 percent lived in common-law marriage, 17 percent were married in a civil ceremony only, 4 percent of the women were married in church only, and 3 percent identified themselves as single mothers.

The women had on the average three children (ranging from 0 to 14)[2] and they resided in households with an average of seven people (ranging from 1 to 23). The overwhelming majority of the women in this group (66 percent) identified themselves as housewives, while 17 percent were employed for the most part as maids; some were students (12 percent) and the remainder were self-employed (2 percent). Only 43 percent of the women in the SPS group were born in the capital, whereas the majority came to Mexico City as children and had lived in the city for extensive periods of time. Most of the women (56 percent) had completed elementary school, and 27 percent had finished high school; 9 percent also had at least one year of preparatory schooling.[3] The overwhelming majority of the people in the SPS group identified themselves as Catholic (88 percent), while the remainder of the sick population were either Evangelical Protestant or Spiritualist (6 percent), and 6 percent lacked religious affiliation.

I compared the SPS group along identical variables with a healthy population (54 women) residing in the same neighborhoods.[4] This comparison revealed that there were no statistically significant differences between the healthy and sick sample of women along these variables, except the husband's occupation, a point to which I will return shortly. The comparison between the SPS group and the healthy population suggests that the two groups are comparable and that they probably come from the same population. Hence, I conclude that the women in the SPS group are representative of the poor population residing in the same area of Mexico City (10-mile radius of the hospital).

Interestingly, the SPS and the healthy group differed on a statistically significant level, ($p \leq 0.05$) in relation to the husband's occupation. In the healthy group the husbands of 72 percent of the women were employed by others, 21 percent were self-employed, and the remaining 2 percent were unemployed. In the SPS group the husbands of 62 percent of the women were self-employed, 34 percent were employed in factories and other commercial enterprises, and 4 percent were unemployed. Among the poor in Mexico City, self-employment usually refers to a precarious existence of ambulatory petty commerce that provides a less predictable, if not a lesser, source of livelihood than wage labor. Within the general framework of my discussion, the finding suggests that the *nature* of the man's employment may influence his disposition and overall domestic relations. We can speculate that when husbands are permanently employed the pressures on them may be diminished, as compared with those who are occasionally employed. The lack of predictability ensuing from a transient source of livelihood surely reverberates adversely on family economic resources and marital interactions, in turn resonating on the wives' life's lesions.

Live Events Comparison: Healthy and Sick

I compared experiences of life events between the SPS group and the healthy population. As we saw in Chapter 2, various theories of life events have been advanced to explain morbidity. Undoubtedly, the concept of life events as a traditional measure of association with illness must be incorporated into our understanding of life's lesions. From the Mexican point of view, life events play a crucial role in perceived sickness, but people do not regard a life event as a discrete occurrence that they bracket within a definitive time frame. A life event becomes an ongoing experience and, like sickness, transcends temporal dimensions.[5]

To assess the role of life events in people's expression of symptomatologies, I used an adjusted life events scale developed by Donald Patrick (1982). With modifications, the final instrument focused on life events including failure in school, change of domicile, death of spouse, divorce, separation, abortion, injury to loved one, business failure, lay-off, a child leaving home, being a victim of crime, unemployment lasting over two months, a jail term, illness in the family, the 1985 earthquake, sudden fright, or being a victim of witchcraft.[6] When the SPS and healthy populations were compared a statistically significant difference was found[7] between the healthy and the sick group for the following life events: change of residence, unemployment for more than two months, being a victim of crime, illness in the family, the earthquake, and being a victim of witchcraft.[8] Table 6.1 displays the life events that differentially affected the sick and healthy populations on a statistically significant basis. The differences in experience of life events between the two sample populations flag important occurrences to consider in exploring life's lesions, but it is important to bear in mind that discrete life events fail to explain all of life's lesions. Life's lesions are fluid, and life events are but one important component of human existence associated with sickness.

TABLE 6.1   Statistically Significant Differences in Life Events Between Healthy Women and Sick Population Sample (SPS) of Women*

Life event	Sick population ($n = 205$) (percent)	Healthy population ($n = 54$) (percent)
Serious illness (other than respondent's)	55.1	33.3
Earthquake	54.0	37.0
Crime victim	43.0	28.0
Unemployed within last two months	34.0	18.0
Change of residence	30.2	13.0
Victim of witchcraft	18.0	4.0

$p \leq 0.5$

Comparison Between Ten Women and the Sick Population Sample

The ten women I have selected to place under an anthropological microscope[9] do not differ from the entire population sample. The average age of the ten women is 36.4 years as compared with 33.5 years for the sample population. The highest percentage in both groups were married in civil and religious ceremonies, resided in nuclear families, and had lived in Mexico City since their childhood.[10] The women in both groups ranked their mothers, siblings, and children, respectively, as the people they regarded as closest to them. In both groups an equal percentage of women had children between the ages of newborn to 5; 5 to 10; and 16 and older. However, whereas 60 percent of the women in the small sample had children between 11 and 16 in the home, only 32 percent of the women in the larger sample had children of the same age in the home. This may be due to the three-year average age difference between the two sample populations.

Because the comparison between the SPS group and the healthy population is similar along major sociodemographic variables, and the ten women were drawn from the SPS sample, I conclude that the ten women tend to represent the population at large along sociodemographic dimensions. Each woman's life's lesions, however, were uniquely experienced by her within the context of her existence.

Etiological Beliefs

Differences in etiological beliefs between men and women disclose an important dimension of contrast between the sexes in Mexico. Culturally constituted etiological beliefs render critical clues to a person's sickness. They tell us about human preoccupations with causality and they help us make sense of the person's suffering. Moreover, when sickness is attributed to emotional discharges, etiological beliefs become assertions about human behavior and human interactions, about moral failures, and about social relations gone sour.

I have discussed Mexican etiological beliefs in great detail elsewhere.[11] At this juncture, it is noteworthy that while both men and women share a cultural pool of sickness attributions, each group draws on this pool diversely. A comparison between men and women in the SPS group showed the most common attributions of sickness (Table 6.2). The comparison between etiological beliefs of men and women from the larger sample population reveal their different concerns.

Although the percentage differences shown in Table 6.2 are not statistically significant, they illuminate the different experiences and considerations of men and women. A higher percentage of men than women attributed sickness to environmental causes. This is explained by the fact that men are usually exposed to pollution and smog more than women because their activities take them outside the house where there is most exposure to environmental assaults. Women, on the other hand, are sheltered from environmental adversities because they spend their lives predominantly in the domestic sphere.

Twice the percentage of men as compared with women attribute their sickness to diet. Close inspection of this finding discloses that while more women expressed the belief that they became sick because of eating the wrong foods (for example, pork or spicy foods) and inadequate food, men tended to attribute their sickness to eating food sold by street vendors. Eating "in the street," as the Mexicans say, is commonly recognized as the central reason for stomach disorders of all kinds. Women, on the other hand, were more aware of dietary deficiencies because they often had less access to money for food.

Both men and women similarly attribute sickness to "work," although the nature of the work obviously differs. Most often when women refer to work they speak of washing and ironing, and invariably when they say they have pain in the lungs (*pulmon*) they refer to pain in the upper back which

TABLE 6.2   Most Common Sickness Attributions

Sickness attribution	Males (n = 67) (percent)	Females (n = 205) (percent)
Environment	8.0	5.3
Diet	12.9	6.3
Work	12.9	12.6
Don't know	22.5	24.0
Emotional discharges (include nerves, anger, fright, overall adversity)	43.7	51.8
Total	100	100

they attribute to the hard work. Both men and women associate their pains in the *cintura* (lower back) to hard work of any kind, and women often link pain in the "ovaries" or "fallen womb" with lower back aches (*cintura*).[12]

Both men and women attribute their health state to emotional discharges, referring to anger, nerves, and fright.[13] Not surprisingly, a higher percentage of women than men ascribe their sickness to anger and nerves, ranking nerves first as the cause of their sickness. As I discussed earlier, women find themselves in many more anger-producing situations and anger-producing contradictions.

Within the Mexican context, anger is singled out as sickness-producing, and "making an anger" is sufficient to produce a variety of conditions and impairments. Anger is probably the most widely attributed general explanation for sickness, and a common admonition is "do not make an anger and you will not get sick." Anger provokes sickness in general, but it can also cause facial paralysis, stomach pains, bloating, heart palpitations, jabbing in the heart, shortness of breath, and diabetes. Pain in the back of the head (referred to as the *cerebro*) is almost always associated with anger, as are pain in the gall bladder and high or low blood pressure.[14]

Anger is felt in the entire body and is often accompanied by "nerves." Nerves pertains to a state of being, associated with anger and a variety of physical symptomatologies. Nerves is when "the entire body trembles and aches," with a jabbing pain in the heart, and it is associated with most all other symptomatologies. People may experience nerves before they experience a sickness condition. Nerves and anger are so closely associated that either one may trigger the other. Nerves, like anger, produce a wide variety of symptomatologies experienced in the whole physical makeup. Every conceivable symptom is aligned with nerves.[15] Women have related nerves to powerful emotions, to use of birth control measures, and to child rearing.

Along with anger and nerves, fright (*susto*) is etiologically significant. Sudden fright produces jabbing in the heart or chest, fainting, bloating, dry mouth, high sugar levels or diabetes, miscarriages, and a variety of other symptoms. "Overall adversity" refers to an unhappy life in both the present and the past, and especially to *la mala vida,* the troubled life, and to poor social relations.

Poor social relations, when they grow sour, may become transformed into accusations of witchcraft. Witchcraft, like anger, reflects social intercourse "gone rotten." Witchcraft is not an uncommon explanation for sickness when medical treatment fails. In fact, it is common for people to conclude that their condition was due to witchcraft because biomedicine failed to remove their sickness. Belief in witchcraft is problematic for Mexicans, placing them in profound contradictions. To admit to beliefs in witchcraft is to admit to being ignorant, because the society at large condemns such beliefs as marks of ignorance[16] and frowns on them. On the other hand, to deny witchcraft as an assignation of affliction is to renounce blame on another for one's misfortune and assume culpability for the sickness, which may have adverse repercussions for one's health.

Differences Between Men and Women in the Experience of Emotions

Inasmuch as women in the SPS group more than men tended to attribute sickness to emotional discharges, I compared emotional states of men and women in this group, as measured by the CMI.[17] This section of the CMI, divided into seven subsections, purports to measure fatiguability and feelings of inadequacy, depression, anxiety, sensitivity, anger, and tension. I compared men's and women's responses to each individual question within the eight subsections of the instrument measuring emotional states. This comparison discloses important similarities and dissimilarities between the sexes, chiefly concentrated within the subsection measuring feelings of inadequacy. The subsection measuring inadequacy is comprised of eleven questions. Of these men and women responded differently on a statistically significant level ($P \leq .05$) to the following questions: (1) Are you afraid when you are near a boss or superior? (2) Are your thoughts confused when you have to do something rapidly? (3) Are you afraid of strange people and situations? (4) Are you afraid when you are alone and have no friends nearby? (5) Is it always hard to decide something?

Not surprisingly, women tended to experience feelings of inadequacy (as measured by the CMI) vis-à-vis higher ranked individuals, including their husbands. This is not unexpected considering the structure of gender relations within the household and the fact that frequently women are deprecated by their spouses.

Men and women responded on a statistically significant level of difference to only one question out of ten in the subsection measuring depression ("Do you cry easily?") and to one out of six measuring sensitivity ("Are you extremely sensitive?"). The fact that women tended to feel more vulnerable and experience more crying episodes affirms their experience of pain.

Four out of eight questions measuring tension were answered differently by men and women on a statistically significant level. These questions were: (1) Do you tremble at minor things? (2) Does it frighten you to hear movements at night? (3) Do you wake up from frightening dreams? (4) Is it difficult for you to stop having thoughts that frighten you? The fact that women tended to indicate that they frightened more easily probably reflects their lesser exposure to the outside world and confinement to the home. One might expect that a difference would exist between the sexes for the variable "anger" in light of the predominant Western assumption that women are by "nature" more emotional than men. The most interesting finding of this analysis is that there is no statistically significant difference between men and women on this variable, as measured by the CMI. This finding supports my contention that women are not inherently more angry than men. Although men and women may have similar propensities for anger, *women's anger emerges in response to specific circumstances and to moral indignations and actualities that provoke their anger.*

Doctor-Patient Encounters

The final area of comparison on an aggregate level still remains: physicians' responses to women compared to men. Studies have shown that in the United States men and women are treated differently by physicians; for example, it has been asserted that physicians tend to treat men's medical problems more seriously than women's.[18]

Significantly, both men and women in the SPS group presented the same symptomatologies of pain in the abdomen, head, chest, or back,[19] and the diagnostic categories used by physicians did not differ along gender lines, except for the category of "psychological problems." The predominant diagnoses given by physicians were infections and parasites for both men and women. Yet whereas only 34 percent of the men were given a second diagnosis, all the women in the SPS group were given more than one diagnosis on their first visit to the physician.

Women tended to be diagnosed more frequently with "psychological problems" than men, however. In fact, 33 of 41 psychological diagnoses were made for women. It must be stressed that of 17 physicians, two of whom were women, only two doctors, both men, tended to diagnose their patients as having "psychological problems"[20] or attributed the problems to menopause. As I have shown before,[21] physicians tended to reinterpret a patient's complaints to fit into their standard diagnostic repertoires, irrespective of the patient's sex. In one extreme case, a physician diagnosed all of his 31 patients as having scoliosis, regardless of their sex or their complaint.

When we turn to communicative aspects of the medical encounter, for the most part my observations revealed that there were no differences in the way men and women were treated.[22] Comparative measures of physician-patient communication shows that there was no statistically significant difference in the way physicians dealt with male and female patients or the time spent with patients of either sex. Physicians did instruct women more often than men how to take their medication, with the difference being statistically significant ($p \leq .05$).

In general, during the first visit physicians gave the same indications to men and women, although the order in which they were given differed (see Table 6.3). Whereas women were first prescribed medication and then were ordered analysis, for men the sequence was reversed. Interestingly, although both men and women presented the same symptoms, the fact that women were diagnosed with more impairments may have prompted the physicians to refer them to specialists. Taken together these findings suggest that the general practitioners were possibly less prepared to deal with women's than with men's maladies. Each sex received similar orders for X ray and ultrasound examinations, but physicians usually instructed only the women to go on a diet, and only the men were admonished not to smoke or drink.

In the United States, it has been observed that physicians address male patients with greater respect than women. In my sample of 17 physicians,

TABLE 6.3   Order of Physicians' Indications to Patients by Gender

To women patients	*To men patients*
Prescribe medication	Order analysis
Order analysis	Prescribe medication
Refer to specialist	Refer to specialist
Order X-rays/ultrasound	Order X-rays/ultrasound
Recommend weight loss	Recommend no drinking or smoking

however, there was no difference in how the physician addressed male and female patients. Usually age overrode sex, because patients older than the physician were addressed in the honorific formal "you" (*usted*) while patients younger than the physician were addressed in the informal (*tú*). On the other hand, the paternalistic nature of the physician-patient encounter was most noticeable by the informal manner in which patients were addressed above and beyond the honorific "you." For example, it was not uncommon for a thirty-year-old physician of either sex to address a female patient of any age as "my daughter" (*mi hija*), a term of endearment used by a father or lover, and a female physician might address a woman patient senior in age as "my queen" (*mi reina*), a term used by mothers speaking to daughters. It is noteworthy that when I questioned patients about the paternalistic posture of physicians as reflected by their informal speech, one woman's response summed up the general consensus: "I was treated the same by my parents." She did not seem to find it offensive to be addressed or treated as a child.

In a separate analysis of the transcribed interviews of a random sample of male and female patients, I compared the frequency of physicians' questioning of men and women about their sexual activities because I was struck by how often women were questioned about their intimate lives. Every male physician questioned women patients about their sexual habits, including whether they were sexually active, the frequency of the activity, and whether intercourse was painful. But only when a male patient reported some problem with his sexual organs did the physician ask him about his sexual life.

Similarly, the two female physicians in my sample rarely questioned their female patients about their sexual relations, but they tended to inquire of their male patients about their sexual relations, and one female physician lectured her male patients about the immorality of womanizing and the importance of monogamy for health. She even mischievously warned them that excessive womanizing would render them impotent.

It is certainly true, as we will see in our case studies, that sexual relations were problematic for women.[23] Although a few women voluntarily noted during the medical consultation that their sickness was associated with their sexual experiences,[24] on the whole the doctor was the one to elicit information revolving around sexual habits.[25] The fact that male physicians tended to question only women about their intimate lives, and female physicians did not, suggests that such a line of questioning was not intrinsically necessary for assessing women's health, but was a way for both sexes to impose their privileged position on the other within the medical consultation.

Overall, weight is not a concern for women among the poor, but physicians usually labeled women obese. Physicians in this study reminded women patients that they needed to lose weight, even though the women usually failed to comprehend the connection between their weight and their symptomatology. For most of the women, the physicians' recommendations to follow special diets were distressing and a hardship on both economic and aesthetic grounds. Weight-control diets were expensive in comparison with the standard diet of tortillas and beans, and patients were unaccustomed to preparing meals in the manner prescribed by the physician. Moreover, telling women that they were too fat was an incursion on their image of their bodies, with which they previously had not felt any dissatisfaction. Physicians would resort, as Carlota's doctor had done (see Chapter 12), to the diagnosis of obesity when other diagnoses failed to explain the patient's symptomatologies to her satisfaction. The diagnosis of obesity creates for a woman new and unnecessary pain when it changes the woman's image of herself and her body. In these instances the physician would say to his female patient, "You are too fat and that is why you are sick."

To summarize this chapter, I presented my findings on an aggregate level of a sample population in order to situate the women we will meet next within the broader population. I have shown that, by and large, the ten women I discuss in detail in this book do not differ from the larger population I studied along sociodemographic dimensions of contrast. We also saw that men and women tended to attribute their sickness differently, and that women tended to experience certain emotions more than men; both variables reflect the different lived day-to-day experience of men and women. Last, we saw that on an aggregate level there were no major differences between the ways physicians treated women and men in a medical encounter, with the exception of questions about sexual habits. Thus the doctor-patient interaction neutralizes differential experiences of sickness. In the next part of the book I turn to the individual lives of ten women, which illuminate best their worlds and their life's lesions.

Notes

1. The aggregate findings are drawn from a data set that included a specially designed interview schedule to elicit a sociodemographic profile, a modified life events scale developed by Patrick 1982, sickness attribution, and other variables that I have discussed elsewhere (for a complete discussion of the methodology used in the study see Finkler 1991). I administered the Cornell Medical Index (CMI), which is an extensive questionnaire that focuses on all systems of the body and is divided between mental and physical symptomatologies. The instrument was altered to accommodate to the local population's comprehension following a pretest on ten patients. Because I had used this instrument before, I found it useful to employ it again in this study for methodological reasons. For an extensive discussion of the CMI, see Finkler 1981 and 1985b.

The participants in the study were selected from a pool of first-time patients seeking treatment in the internal/general medicine clinic for non-lifethreatening conditions. Patients residing within a ten-mile radius of the hospital were selected for the study. I interviewed and observed 205 women and 62 men. (For additional details of the sample selection see Finkler 1991.) All the patients I studied, including the women I present here, were initially interviewed in the outpatient internal/ general medicine clinic of a large public hospital in the center of Mexico City, before they saw the physician. I then sat in on the medical consultation. I saw the patient again on each return visit. All medical consultations were tape-recorded and later transcribed.

Subsequent to the hospital visits, I met with patients in their homes. I visited 161 women (the sample size shrank due to attrition). During these visits I carried out extensive follow-ups at which time I obtained sickness and life histories from each patient. In addition 85 healthy people were randomly selected from the same neighborhoods for study. Of these 54 were women. The sociodemographic variables I examined included age; marital status; city of origin; household composition, including average number of children, average number of people living in the house, and distribution of the age of the children; respondent's occupation; husband's occupation; education; people the interviewee considered close to him or her; and religion.

2. Distribution of age of children:

0–5	27%
6–10	33%
11–16	34%
17	36%

3. People who aspire to higher education usually enter preparatory school. Following preparatory school students can enter the university to embark on a specialized career.

4. The chi-square test or Fisher's exact test, when applicable, was used.

5. On the basis of the theory that life events may have triggered their present symptomatology, I queried people about a life event within the past 12 months. Invariably, however, people responded by recounting events that had taken place years earlier, and they were unable to bracket the time of the event, suggesting that it had become embedded in their daily existence.

6. The life event identified most often in 1986–88 was the earthquake of 1985. The instrument was modified to include the earthquake and culturally identified stressors, especially sudden fright (*susto*) and accusations of witchcraft.

7. I used either the chi-square or Fisher's exact test.

8. Although there was no statistically significant difference between the two groups for children's failure in school (20.4 percent in the healthy group and 33.2 percent in the sick group), the two groups of women were differentially affected by a child's school failure on a statistically significant level (using chi-square test at $p = .05$ level of significance): 18.5 percent of the women in the sick population were affected deeply by a child's failure in school, as compared with 1.9 percent in the healthy group. Similarly, though for most people the earthquake was an important life event, among the women who answered yes to the question about the earthquake, 61 percent of the sick women said that they have been extremely affected by it, as compared with 44 percent of the healthy women.

9. My research design called for ongoing contact with a small sample of families. The ten women I discuss here were individuals who were especially articulate and who recounted their stories without any prodding (see Preface).

10. Due to the small sample size of ten, no statistical analysis could be done along most of the sociodemographic variables.

11. Finkler 1985b, 1991.

12. "Fallen ovaries," however, has many meanings for women. See Chapter 8.

13. See Finkler 1991. A higher percentage of women attributed sickness to emotional discharges. When attributions were ranked along sex lines in terms of how often a particular category was used to explain any one symptom a person was experiencing, emotional discharges ranked first among women and environment ranked last; whereas among men environment was ranked first and emotional discharges last.

14. High or low blood pressure, or "pressure," is characterized by a wide variety of symptoms that incorporate the heart, eyes, head, and chest, with faintness or feelings of dizziness and tiredness. Most important, it occurs when one feels either crestfallen or agitated and angry. High or low blood pressure describes the vicissitudes in one's daily life: when one is dejected one's pressure is low, and when one is agitated and angry one's pressure is high. Thus when people speak of low pressure it is analogous to feeling depressed.

15. "Nerves" is an illness that has been widely described for Latin populations; see section I of Davis and Low 1989.

16. For a similar phenomenon in France, see Favret-Saada 1980.

17. Brodman et al. 1952.

18. See Armitage et al. 1979. With the exception of Finkler 1991 there are very few studies of the doctor-patient relationship in Mexico.

19. The percentage of complaints, including the category "other," were compared using the chi-square test; there were no statistically significant differences in the nature of complaints as verbalized by men and women.

20. Given the smaller sample size of the men (62 men as compared with 205 women), however, it is difficult to say whether these diagnoses reflect the physicians' bias or whether they are artifacts of small sample size.

21. See Finkler 1991.

22. I focused on variables (derived from the verbatim transcripts by independent observers) commonly regarded as relevant to the doctor-patient interaction. These variables centered around the doctor communicating to the patient the nature of his or her sickness, giving the diagnosis, explaining its reasons, the patient agreeing with the physician about the diagnosis, the doctor meeting the patient's expectations of treatment, providing instructions about the prescribed medication, giving reassurance, and the patient participating in the consultation by posing questions to the physician.

23. Only one male patient in the sample reported problems of impotency to a woman physician.

24. See, for example, the case of Nomi in Finkler 1991.

25. One physician impressed on his students the necessity to question women patients about their sexual habits because, he said, "Male machismo can hurt women." "To understand women's ailments better," he urged the students to inquire about their sex lives, because a man may "want to have fifteen times a day sex with his woman to exhaust her because he is afraid she might betray him." He also counseled his students to inquire about oral sex—not to pass moral judgment, but because it should not be performed for hygienic reasons. According to this physician, a doctor needs to watch for gonorrhea in children and in virgins.

Part III

Women's Lives and Women's Pains

7. Margarita: A Woman in Search of Individuation

Margarita was a thirty-seven-year-old woman whose appearance had changed during the time I knew her. When we first met she conveyed the image of a sexpot. Her dark black hair was elegantly coifed and her face was heavily made up. She wore a sparkly sweater and tight glittering jeans tucked into stylish, tall leather boots. Later her appearance changed. She often wore a karate outfit and no makeup, and when I last saw her she had on plain slacks and a loose T-shirt. The child-temptress became a plain-looking woman during the course of my contact with her. The changes in her dress and makeup evolved gradually and undoubtedly reflected the transitions she underwent during the four-year period of our association.

Margarita was the mother of a nineteen-year-old son and a three-year-old daughter. She resided with her two children, a maid, and her husband in a poorly furnished rented apartment situated in one of the finest neighborhoods in Mexico City. A single room was outfitted with expensive wallpaper, huge mirrors hanging on all the walls, a stereo, and a couch. Margarita's shabby apartment existed in distinct contrast to her very expensive Datsun Spitfire, which she took pride in and said she had bought when she "was feeling down"; at the time of our first meeting, however, her husband would not permit her to drive it.

Early on in Margarita's encounter with the hospital physician she announced that she was ready to do anything the doctor suggested because she thought of herself as "a sick person." She reported fatigue, pains in the back of her head (*cerebro*), a dry mouth, and sweating hands and feet. She said, "I couldn't breathe and I knew I had tachycardia of a nervous type. I felt anxiety and a desire to cry." She feared closing her eyes, "because I thought I would die. That is how I have been all along."

In detailing her life, Margarita revealed within the context of her symptomatology an ongoing struggle with her sexuality that also reflected the broader Mexican cultural norms pertaining to women's sexuality (discussed in Chapter 5). Margarita, born in Mexico City, was the oldest of twelve children. Her family resided in a working class neighborhood in the northern part of the city. Her father, who was unquestionably a predominant influence in Margarita's life until his death when Margarita was thirty-six years old, owned a pharmacy where Margarita spent most of her childhood working. She recalled:

> I had the life of a dog in my parents' house because I was made to work unceasingly, and because my father beat my mother and my sisters. He attacked everybody. He even beat my brothers, particularly the one who was very dark, and how could that be otherwise, my grandparents were of Arabic descent. He never hit the brother who followed me. My father wished that my brother had been [born] first because he always said that I could not study, because I had no economic future. He said that because my brother was a man who would have to maintain a family he needed to study. But I, a woman, didn't need any studies because when I got married I would be supported. I believed it should be that way. My brother studied, and he helped my father to take care of my mother and my brothers. But when my brother finished his studies, he left my father and he never returned. My father felt defrauded, and he then used me as his example of the child who helped him most, but since I was badly treated I became very depressed.

When Margarita spoke about her father's conduct her muscles tightened and she cringed in a fetal position, reminiscent of the little girl she was when he first violated her.

> When I was a child I noticed my father's strange conduct. When I was eleven years old, I was in secondary school and working in the pharmacy, my father looked at me out of the corner of his eye, and I had a terrible desire to have sex, it came suddenly, and I became very tense.

She recalled how on their way home around midnight, it took her father a long time to start his car, and she said:

> I wanted to go home but he wanted to wait. Since then whenever my father came close to me and he wanted to hug me I put my hands around my breasts. I remember that in the car I always had to sit in the middle next to him, and he always brushed around my breast with his arm. Thereafter, whenever he told me to sit in the middle, I refused. One day my mother was there and I sat in the middle. He tried to open the window, and brushed his arm against my breast even though she was present. I told my mother what he had done and my mother said "Ayy" [presumably dismissing the issue] and I never told her anything anymore. I have had an aversion to my father since that time.

Margarita's father tried repeatedly to touch her breasts, and as she spoke she covered her breasts with her arms, suggesting how she would protect herself from him. When recalling this story she was reminded of the time when they had lived in another town where her father was manager of a company.

> In this town he violated the ten-year-old peasant girl who was our maid. I remember that my father used to send me and my mother away. My mother didn't realize, until the girl told her, that my father ran after her and raped her. The girl cried not to tell my father because he threatened her. My mother returned the girl to her home and she told the girl's mother that she was afraid of my father. Since the girl's mother was ignorant—she was an Indian—she didn't do anything, but the incident remained in my mind.

Margarita was now afraid for her three-year-old daughter, especially when her husband bathed the child.

> I get overcome by thoughts that if my father could do this why not somebody else. I do not allow my husband to be alone or in bed with her, and especially to bathe her, because I once noticed that the child cried when he was bathing her and the door was closed.

When Margarita was seventeen years old, in preparatory school, she ran away with a university student, her girlfriend's boyfriend, against the wishes of her father.

> My father would never let me out of the house. I couldn't ever tell my father that I had a boyfriend. I could see him only on the sly, because if my father had found out he would have killed me. My father said that he was a student who needed to finish his studies and after he finished, he would laugh at me. He courted me for a year. He tried to talk to my father but my father insulted him. When I became pregnant, he [the boy] set me up in the basement of his grandmother's apartment, which had a bed, a stove, and a refrigerator. That's all, but I didn't care. I loved him. We married in a civil ceremony, because I was three months pregnant and my father made him marry me or he would have killed him. Yes, we loved each other, but he was an egoist. At first he did not want to marry because it would interfere with his career if he did. I told him that I preferred to face the ogre—my father—who would beat me, rather than become a mistress.

She lived with her husband for five years and gave birth to a son.

> I could not live with this man who was a professional [he had studied law]. He was very jealous. I was locked up all day until he got home around 6 or 7 P.M.

> He gave me no money and I could not leave the house. He never took me out of the house at night. My parents never stepped through the door of my home.

Margarita claimed that her husband locked her up because he was afraid she would return to her parents.

> My parents didn't like him, because we lived in a proletarian neighborhood and he lived in an elegant neighborhood; my father said he originated from another class and he thought I should have married a man of humble origins. My father said that I must marry a farmer, who worked on the land and with animals, not like this boy, who was of a class higher than ours and good looking. We lived in a neighborhood without any pavement, and my father's pharmacy was located in La Villa.[1]

As it turned out, Margarita's husband had girlfriends.

> I was eighteen years old then, or nineteen, and he went out with women thirty-five years old. I felt defrauded that he did not appreciate me. He was rich and he had a higher education, and I only had one year of preparatory. But he wanted me to stay with him because he said I would be beaten up if I went back to my father. I would not be able to take care of my son and give him a good education. He was in love with me but he wanted to marry somebody who was wealthy, and I came from a proletarian neighborhood. He was from Polanco [an old, established wealthy neighborhood] and I was from Casas Aleman.
>   I ran back to my father's house with my baby, but my husband came after me. He took me back to his house and locked me up again.

Margarita ran away again with the child, and to do so she had to employ a ruse on a passerby she saw from her window. She asked the person to send for a locksmith because supposedly the child had lost the keys. The locksmith arrived and unlocked the apartment, and Margarita returned to her father's house having no other options. She called her husband a *niño popis* [a young spoiled upper class person] and said, "He had everything." She recalled:

> I returned to my father's house but he beat me a lot. He told me that everybody was going to laugh at me now that I have a child and nobody would want to marry me except to sleep with me. He chased everybody away who talked to me. My mother never said anything. I worked for my family from ten in the morning till eleven at night. Sometimes I didn't eat, or I ate only a hot dog. I was very skinny and I was always anxious that I could not see my child who was always with my mother. I knew she took care of him well. I was very depressed, and I smoked a lot and sometimes I wanted to commit suicide.

There was a time I couldn't even see my son because I worked so many hours. When I left in the morning and by the time I returned home he was asleep. I worked on Saturdays and Sundays and holidays. And I couldn't go out by myself because my father said that I was a woman who had experience and any man would easily deceive me. He ordered my brothers to watch me. There came a time when I believed there was no reason to live, especially because I could not see my son and I did not want to live without him. Having worked in the pharmacy I knew about medicine and I read once that one could kill oneself with barbiturates. I took this medicine[2] when everybody was asleep. But when I did my child woke up and he looked at me. He was only two years old. I wondered how strange that he should have awakened at the very moment I took the medication. I repented taking the medication and I made a noise, people came to my room and started screaming when they saw all the pills, and they took me to the hospital.

On my way to the hospital I felt many hands on my body. I think it was the stretcher bearers and they put their hands in my pants, and I could not do anything. I felt very anxious. Even now I can recall how I started feeling the cold air. I was left in a cubicle where there were many people around me, asking me questions, but I could not speak. A doctor with a beard washed my stomach, made a hole in it, and put a tube in my hands. My hands trembled a lot. I was in a coma for fifteen days. When I left the hospital everything trembled in me. I went back to work after a month. My family assumed a different attitude toward me. Thank God I didn't succeed in committing suicide.

Margarita remained in her parents' home for seven years. Because her husband wanted the child, her parents decided to adopt the boy so that his father could not have access to him.

My parents made believe that it was their child; they registered him in their name and when I protested that he was registered in school in their name, my father beat me. The boy denied that I was his mother; my father said it was for my own good because otherwise nobody would marry me and this way nobody would know that I had a child. But I said that the man who would want me would have to take me with the child. My father didn't think I could marry because, he told me, all men want to marry a virgin. My father said, if I did get married next time I would have to have a civil and religious ceremony. My father blamed me for my husband's behavior.

Margarita repeatedly referred to her life in her natal home as the life of a dog. "I decided to leave my father's house with my child and build a new family. One day my father actually threw me out of the house, and I had nowhere to go; my mother was silent." Margarita recounted the odyssey after leaving her father's house—how a woman she had met by chance had offered her shelter and helped her find a job in a real estate office. She saved up some money and went back to her father's house to abduct her son. "My parents found me and they brought me back to their house and once again I had to work in that pharmacy."

When Margarita was employed in the real estate office she met a man with whom she lived for three years. She wanted to take her son with her, but her father would not permit it. The man took her to another state to forget the child but, Margarita said, "All I could do was cry, and I returned to Mexico City after six months." This man wanted Margarita to give up the child but she refused. She subsequently left him and married a different man, with whom she lived when I first met her and who was the father of her three-year-old girl. "I knew that he could not give me very much money but it didn't matter, I was earning money; he had been married and had adult children. I loved this man." He had divorced his wife, but he had two daughters, nineteen and seventeen, whom he had to support, and a girlfriend. Margarita's son, who came to live with her after she married this man, claimed that her husband deprived him of Margarita's love. Margarita added, "Gradually my son lost his egoism and he even became accustomed to my little girl, whom he now loves."

> My husband's daughters and former wife hate me. His former wife cannot marry again and she and the daughters blame me for it. This woman can work witchcraft, she even performed witchcraft on me. I never believed in this before, but I believe in it now. It influences me mentally because I now suffer from depressions and anxiety and I cannot breathe. When I was pregnant with my little girl all my pains had stopped but then the pains returned. I became pregnant three years after I married my present husband, and I have been sick for six years, from the time I got married. One doctor told me to take Valium for nerves, another prescribed pills for my headaches and for jabbings in my heart. But I stopped taking them. I could not sleep and I could not breathe at night.

In recent years Margarita worked for one of her brothers, who had an employment agency and an encyclopedia distributing service. Margarita was the billing agent for her brother's firm, working out of her home and using the telephone and messengers. She received a percentage of the commission from the sales of the encyclopedias and from employment placements. She said proudly, "I earn twice as much as my husband, who is a computer engineer, and in less time." In fact, Margarita indicated that her husband was envious and angry.[3] Yet despite financial security, Margarita's marriage was an unhappy one. On separate occasions, she recounted the same reasons for her unhappiness to me and to the hospital physician when he questioned her about her sexual life. Unlike the vast majority of patients, who had little to say about their sexual habits when questioned by the physician, the doctor's query opened a floodgate of pain for Margarita. She said:

> We get along well but there was one thing strange: even though he is a man and I am a woman, I have more desire for sex than he does.

Margarita reported that whenever she wanted to have sexual intercourse, her husband would not. She continued:

> When he wants to have sex, he does it one time and it's finished and I am left half finished. It's not that he does not love me, as many women would think. I am convinced that he is in love with me and that he is also faithful to me. Yet I recognize something strange because I have desire and he does not. And what is more, when he has desire for sex I don't, and when I do he does not. He is active, but calm. I am perhaps a bit impetuous and sometimes I feel as if I am not normal. No, because he is the man and I am the woman and supposedly the woman is supposed to be more passive and less demanding, and in this regard I am not.

The doctor followed up on Margarita's narration by asking whether she experienced orgasms, and she responded, "Sometimes; not always."

The subject of Margarita's sexuality was raised on almost all recall visits. On her second visit to the physician, Margarita noted:

> When I have desire for having sex and I don't do it I cannot sleep and I begin to itch. Sometimes my whole body itches as if something where pricking me and I must have it. If not I cannot sleep, and so for me it is very disturbing that my husband is asleep. I wake him up to tell him that it's bad for me to take pills, because I don't want to become addicted to medicines.

Several months later, Margarita reported to me:

> Then yesterday he wanted to have sex and I said I was tired. He said you don't do anything all day. And that made me very angry. The next day he told me to iron his shirts, and I told him I make more money than you, I contribute to this household more than you, you can iron your shirts yourself. He remained quiet and I told him that from now on I will do mine and you will do yours.

I asked Margarita whether she had ever told her husband such things before. She said, "Never." In fact, during the course of a few months she had changed her sexual tactics: "Whenever my husband wants to have sexual intercourse, I make believe I am asleep and instead of feeling bad about it I laugh."

Margarita was not a passive patient, as were most of the women I observed during a medical encounter. In fact, on her third visit to the doctor, she lectured the doctor about men, after telling her story. She said:

> Men are very special, people say that women are conflicted, complicated, but men are, too. They want it at the time they want it. Men like women to ask them for favors so that they can say "No" or "I am tired." When they do this the woman's dignity, her pride is gone, and she is left with a feeling of having been rejected. And then one thinks, "Does one need a man? He is not the only one." But then enter the religious and moral questions. Sometimes I thought I would sell myself in the street. But then the next day I would get over my anger because I am incapable of doing that.
>
> All such questions [referring to morality and sexuality] are vital for a human being. My husband knows that I would not go with another man. One needs to do the same thing [go with other men] so that he could see how it felt.[4] You men can say this woman will do whatever she wants, and maybe she would, but I don't depend on my husband for economic support. If I depended on my husband economically then I would probably do what my friends do. My friends say that their husbands earn a lot, and they give them everything. They pay for servants and so they have to remain on good terms with their husbands. But I have my own business. I have a sports car that cost ten million pesos and he has a Dodge that cost a million pesos.

Margarita claimed that the people closest to her were her mother and her son, but her relationship with her mother was unusually distant. Nevertheless, following the traditional Mexican pattern of living near one's natal family, Margarita was building a separate apartment for herself next to her mother's house on a piece of property left to her by her father. Once the construction was completed, she expected to vacate her rented apartment and move to her new quarters.

Margarita was alienated from her sisters, who, she claimed, always asked her for money. "They are envious because I make more money than they." But despite the fact that her sisters were, as she put it, "negative people," Margarita interacted with them "because we are tied by blood." She was close to her six brothers, however, especially to the one for whom she worked. Her strained relationship with her female siblings was revealed when she said, "I can also go to doctors, and I don't care if my siblings don't come to see me to ask about me. The doctors will care for me."

On our first meeting in the hospital, Margarita arrived with a portfolio in which she kept a well-organized record of the twenty physicians she had seen within the past seven years. These records included copies of prescriptions she had been given by physicians and the results of numerous analyses. They revealed, for example, that twenty electrocardiograms were done on Margarita by different physicians. Either the medications she had taken had made her ill[5] or medications that were prescribed to elevate her pressure had failed to alleviate her condition.

The hospital physician considered Margarita's meticulous record keeping as a sign of her compulsive character. Margarita explained to us, however, that the reason she kept these records was because physicians usually failed to believe her when she told them that she had been prescribed a particular medication. Using her portfolio she was able to substantiate her claims. In fact, Margarita's recurrent lament was that no one believed she was sick. She described how she once went to a cardiac unit, and though all the patients there described the same symptoms she was experiencing, the cardiologist told her immediately after he had taken her blood pressure[6] that she did not belong there.

Margarita narrated the extensive health-seeking efforts she had made before she sought treatment at the hospital.

> I have gone to many physicians and I have taken many medications. I took medications for the heart because many doctors believed that I had a heart problem. I feel anxiety, and I think of death, that something horrible will happen to me. I am afraid to sit down because I may have facial paralysis or a heart attack. I want to run in the street, as if I had claustrophobia.

In fact, Margarita was afraid to leave her house and she was usually accompanied by a maid. She continued:

> I went to a cardiologist who performed all kinds of tests, and he said that there was nothing wrong with me. I was then sent to a neurologist and he prescribed some pills.[7] They were antidepressants. I felt terrific for the first two weeks but then I continued to be sick. I said to myself, "I cannot be taking pills all my life" and I stopped, and then a year ago I had a terrible reaction. I had palpitations, anxiety, and I felt I was going to die. The doctor told me that it was because I stopped taking the Tofranil [an antidepressant]. I started taking it again and I began feeling sick, and I went to another neurologist who told me to continue taking the Tofranil. They were terribly expensive.
>
> The neurologist never did anything except ask me if I was nervous. He also took my pressure and he gave me pills. I went to see yet another doctor, and he told me not to take the Tofranil. He prescribed another medication. Again, I felt better at first, but later the medication didn't solve anything because I felt sick again with or without the pills. I stopped taking medications and I started

doing aerobics daily and then karate, but I still felt anxious and depressed so I decided to come here to the hospital. I have had this sickness for so long I don't think it is curable. I drink fruit punch every third day and this makes me feel better.

My mother used to say that I had low blood pressure,[8] because I felt faint. At the time I went to a local clinic and they said that I suffered from tachycardia nervosa. They injected me with Valium and from then on I started going to doctors.

The hospital physician diagnosed Margarita's condition in several ways. He, like the psychiatrist to whom she was later referred, said that she was experiencing the "counterpart to the Oedipus complex, the Electra complex," and he reassured her that nothing would happen to her. He concluded that Margarita had had a bad childhood, and he gave her a lecture on the Oedipus and Electra complexes, when "women love their fathers but don't want to admit it and they forget it, but the unconscious is unrelenting."

The doctor advised her not to worry about her husband's comportment with her daughter. When Margarita told the doctor, "I noticed recently that when my husband changed the diapers the child was red around the vagina. I checked but I came to no conclusion," the doctor advised "not to obsess about it because you may predispose him to do so." He suggested that her fears were driven by paranoia, and Margarita agreed that she was frightened when she was alone.

In addition, the physician suggested that she should not think so much about her condition because she could go mad. He told her, "And you may even think that all men are bad and abuse their women." Margarita responded that she wanted "vengeance," and the doctor pointed out that she may be doing just that to her husband and counseled her to "think positive." When he asked her if she wished to commit suicide, she responded, "When I was nineteen I did, but not anymore. Now I want to kill people."

On the basis of the results of the many previous tests performed on Margarita, the hospital doctor concluded that her body was in a disequilibrium. He diagnosed her condition as "prediabetic." The doctor meticulously explained to Margarita that though her glucose content was fine, her pancreas secreted sugar irregularly, and for this reason she was feeling sick. He emphasized that this was a hereditary condition and Margarita agreed because her maternal grandmother and her father's brother were both diabetics. Nobody before had ever told her that she was prediabetic and Margarita accepted this diagnosis with great relief. Moreover, the diagnosis was very plausible to her because she knew that "making angers" could produce diabetes, and "I make many angers," she said.

The doctor prescribed a daily dose of juice and Coca-Cola. Margarita agreed that Coca-Cola always made her feel better. He recommended that she not gain weight[9] and he even prescribed a diet for her. He advised her not to be suspicious and anxious that there was no medication he could prescribe for her condition. He encouraged Margarita to regard herself as a prediabetic who one day may develop diabetes because her pancreas functioned irregularly. Margarita concluded, "I will start thinking about my pancreas."

The doctor told me later that he purposefully warned her about becoming a diabetic to distract her from her anxieties and "imagined problems and erase her fears." He also observed that Margarita's problems with her husband reflected her emotional instability.

The hospital physician referred Margarita to the neurology department,[10] where, in the words of the nurse, "the crazies" (*loquitos*) go. The neurologist informed Margarita that there was nothing wrong with her and he ordered her to stop taking any pills she had been prescribed. He, in turn, referred her to a psychiatrist. Margarita recounted, "I spent an hour with the psychiatrist, and he told me that I had an emotional problem and a psychological problem." Margarita reported that the psychiatrist recommended to her that

> If my husband wanted to have sexual relations and I didn't, I should simply refuse because, as I told the doctor, when my husband refuses me I get so angry that I almost want to kill him and I have never told him no. That is a conflict for me. And so when he wants to be with me, I tell him I am very sleepy and very tired and I have many things to do and now he gets angry. The psychiatrist told me to take a lover.

Margarita indicated that the hospital psychiatrist's diagnosis was that "my father was in love with me." He concluded that Margarita idealized her father, and because he died at the moment when Margarita arrived at the hospital, this has caused her problems (Margarita's father died a year before she came to the hospital).

Margarita agreed with the psychiatrist's diagnosis that her father was in love with her, because

> He never let me get married or have boyfriends and he used to tell me, "If you have a friend other than me he will try to kiss you and grab your breasts. He will get excited." He told me all these details when I was eleven and twelve

years old. And when I had my baby he wanted to know all the details, if I liked it; even my mother told him not to ask me these things.

Margarita searched for the cause of her condition throughout the time I knew her. On different occasions she mentioned various possibilities. The attributions she gave reflected folk understandings, personal evaluations, and explanations offered her by different physicians which she incorporated into her own explanations. Sometimes she attributed her disorder to having eaten seafood, but then, she reasoned, other people ate the same foods and they did not get sick. At other times she thought her sickness was caused by an endocrinal imbalance, or a lack of vitamins.

Then she concluded that "When I make an anger I get sick because of my husband's behavior and his jealousies." She considered the possibility that witchcraft may have been performed on her: "Since all the doctors told me there was nothing wrong with me, and I am sick, I must be bewitched." She assigned culpability to her present husband's ex-wife and possibly her first husband's grandmother. And sometimes she attributed her sickness to a state of nerves because she experienced many frights and had an "aggressive character."

On close reflection, however, Margarita associated her disorder with her life. She volunteered:

I am sick because of my situation as a woman, my mental norms and moral rules. My situation is not the way I wanted it. I could not do anything. If I wanted to work to earn money I would have had to leave the bosom of my family, and where would I go with my child, who would support me? They had me up against the wall. To improve myself I would have had to abandon my family. That was too much pressure on me. And physically I was weak. I was very badly nourished, I was very skinny. Now I am the weight I should be and my family situation is stable, nevertheless I am still sick.

When I asked Margarita what she had wanted to do in life, she replied,

I would have liked to be a journalist, a ballet dancer. When I was in high school I received a scholarship to ballet school but my father would not let me go. I had other abilities, too: I told him I wanted to be a journalist and he told me that he didn't want a very liberated woman. I told him I wanted to study to be a bilingual secretary and he didn't want me to do that, either. He wanted that all my life I would be in his store [pharmacy]. He said he didn't want me to be a secretary because all the secretaries became the bosses' lovers. He wanted me in his store and all these things together provoked my physical and mental decline.

Finally, she attributed her condition to the fact that her husband had lied to her all the years they had been married by telling her that he had no money, whereas he earned twice the amount he had told Margarita. She usually paid for all the household expenses, including entertainment. "He used me because he gave me nothing." Since she had found out about it eight months earlier, she decided not to spend her money for the household, and she required her husband to pay rent, while she was saving her earnings. She said, "When I have saved up several million pesos, I will feel safe."

Subsequent to her first hospital visit, Margarita returned to the hospital at least five times at two-week intervals, on follow-up appointments. During this time, she felt variously better and worse. She was closely attuned to her bodily states and she reported every minute change. "Sometimes I have pain as if I were menstruating, as if I were having a baby, I get into knots, and when I get this pain I cannot breathe and I wish to cry."

Margarita usually followed the indication a physician gave her. Her records showed that she had taken 492 medications prescribed for her in the last several years. None, however, had helped her. She had numerous tests done, including a glucose test the hospital physician had ordered, the results of which showed her glucose levels to be normal. She drank the sodas and juices recommended by the hospital physician but these remedies failed to alleviate her condition.

Yet during the years I met with Margarita, she changed from a sick person to a self-confident woman who was no longer experiencing any symptoms. The process was lengthy, and over the course of the years she attributed her improvements to a series of factors leading to her recovery and well-being. Among the reasons Margarita gave for the alleviation of her disorder was that the attending physician at the hospital assured her that she would not die, that she could die more easily being hit by a car, and because he told her that her glucose curve was high, predisposing her to diabetes. This diagnosis absolved her from considering herself a neurotic.

Margarita also received a cleansing in a Spiritualist temple,[11] where, she disclosed,

> They told me to think of myself, as a free person, that I was put on this earth like a bird, to live freely, to do what I want. When I left there I felt a weight came off me that I had carried. They told me that a lot of people were envious of me but that I should not worry about other people and do what I thought best. Because they deal with the unknowable, the sense of awe it gave me contributed to my improvement.

She also attributed her improvement to the psychiatrist, because he "talked to me about my childhood, my conflicts," and gave her advice. She did, in fact, follow the psychiatrist's recommendation: she took a lover. This change seemed to have helped her for a while. She recounted:

> When I was sixteen I knew a man who had worked in the neighborhood in which I now live. I sought him out and we started having an affair. I can call him at any time but I am afraid of my son. He [her lover] loved me in a disinterested way. We have a friendship. All my life I had tried to make people love me by buying them off and they always had some ulterior motive, but this person was totally disinterested. My lover was the only man who respected me.

As her affair progressed she became nonchalant about her husband. "I am just totally indifferent to him. I agree to make love on occasion because I feel sorry for him, but I hide my eyes so that I don't have to look at him or see his face." Margarita raised her arm to her face to demonstrate how she hid her face from him and said, "I felt a bit bad at the beginning about having taken a lover. But I no longer feel that my house is going to fall when there is a wind or when it rains. I like to leave the house now, and if he [her husband] gets angry, let him get angry." Significantly, Margarita feared her son but not her husband, who was present during one visit when she spoke about her lover. She indicated that she had remained with her husband only because of her little girl.

At the time Margarita spoke about her lover she also talked about Mexican husbands in general and how they treated their wives. As she spoke, she acted out the role of each person. She spoke about how husbands do not care about their wives, how they go to their offices and watch the secretaries shaking their butts, and while they are having a good time with the women in the offices the poor wives sit at home. She observed, "My problem has been that I was born a Mexican woman rather than a European woman. I did not want support from my husband, I wanted his love, and no more."

On other occasions Margarita returned to a recurrent theme in her discourse—her sense of being out of place.

> I should have been born in Europe or North America, so that I could be a normal woman. For me, women here in Mexico are not normal. They are conditioned, first to be mothers. Men do not allow mothers to go out of the house. Once you are married you cannot go out to see the sun, or for coffee, or to dance, as men do. The woman must be loyal. The Mexican man thinks that a woman cannot do the same as he. He is a man and since he runs around with

other women and he is satisfied, he does not need to hug his wife anymore, or say nice things to her. He thinks the woman is his property. She has to be there if he wants to lay down with her. He just grabs her, he does not care whether she is all right.

When he leaves the house he tries to make other women feel good, and I know this by having seen how people conduct themselves. When they step outside the house, they are free, single, they can see anybody they want. When they are about to go home they remember their wives; but they go home out of obligation, and when they are in bed if they have desires they say OK but if not they go to sleep and snore while the woman endures [*aguantando*].

Well, now I am going to go and do what I want. I began thinking this way only recently. I always knew that I was different from the others, although my parents accustomed me to be like the others, to be like people here in Mexico, but I realized that nobody can make you be this way. My parents, my father, required me to think that a woman needed to be humble, censured, deprived of liberty as a person and as a human being, and that she could not have her individual likes, individual ways of thinking, and in this way women become depersonalized. That is what I realized—that no human being has the right to deprive one of one's own way of being as an individual. Since I have been eleven years old people have manipulated me.

Margarita, like most Mexicans, believed that one's character is determined at birth. She was born, as she described,

with a sensitive spirit, noble, delicate, and when somebody does something to me I am very pained. When one sees that one makes others suffer one feels terrible, but I am learning not to let it affect me. When I see a person feeling sad I feel sad, but I am losing these feelings. There are many people like me—people who feel bad for others, who feel sad, most all women are like that. Men are not like that, men are more practical, men are not sentimental or romantic like I am. I need to be loved and have the man show his love. When they [men] leave the house they forget their wives, whom they say they love, they forget their children, and when they leave the house they feel free. They say, "I am going to work," and when they see a woman they follow her at work. They don't remember the wife; they look at the secretaries, they imagine them naked and think of going to bed with them.

Margarita's observations on male behavior bring into bold relief my earlier discussion of Mexican male-female relations;[12] they also reveal the extent to which the nineteenth-century notion of the feminization of love is entrenched in Mexican women's ideology. However, when I asked Margarita why Mexican women accept their situation, she responded: "The Mexican woman acquiesces because her mother did the same. Even though they are sad and they cry, they acquiesce because the woman's husband is the father of her children, even though she knows he runs after other women. But I am not like one of the old ladies, worn out."

Margarita was disillusioned by her relations with her family, but with this disillusionment she was also freeing herself from them.

> I have done many things to gain the love of my family, my father, my siblings, my friends, and then I saw that I didn't get it even when I was a good friend, a good daughter. I realized that I got love when I gave money, buying things, for example, and working hard. I remember when I gave my father all the money that was earned in his business he was happy. Even when I was small my father would tell me that I was hard working and better than my brothers, that I brought in more money in the pharmacy than my brothers. So I tried to bring in more and more money and he hugged me and he said to me "my child" (I didn't like when he said "my child"). When I got married and my husband saw I earned more money than he, he did not say anything. I thought that if I worked hard and earned a lot of money—and I would have a bank account—everybody would love me. I always worked for my father, for my mother, for my siblings who wanted money from me, so that they would love me. I have worked since I was eleven years old and I will continue to work all my life because I like to have my money and give my children things. That is very important for a person and that is why I feel well. I no longer care what they think.

Margarita attributed the changes in her social interactions to the psychiatrist she had seen in the hospital, who "let me know that love cannot be bought with money. And now what I am going to do is work for myself and for my children. Nobody else, not for my parents, not for my siblings, or my husband. The only ones that I care about are my children, that is all."

In effect, the psychiatrist's advice enabled Margarita to remove herself from the family unit in which she was embedded and to anchor herself in the individual she wished to become. She accomplished this not only by taking a lover, whom she subsequently left, or by having Spiritualist cleansings to remove any evil hovering around her, but also by becoming a karate expert. In fact, Margarita attributed her complete recovery to karate.

Margarita became fully absorbed in karate on her own initiative, gradually transforming her life and her health state. Her immersion in karate was apparent by her mirrored walls, where she plastered pictures of Bruce Lee, a karate master. Karate had changed her life in several ways, including her relationships with people. She declared, "When I see other people [men] get angry, and they want to hit me, they cannot because I have very good reflexes. I have been with men who were larger than I and they could not throw me over. Before I felt old. Now I feel young. Now the

people who wished to harm me and who have affected me are made angry."
Margarita laughed. "I wish to show them that I don't care what they think."

Margarita's absorption with karate also brought about changes in the
customary reciprocal social relationships with family and others in her
circle. In the process of individuation and separation from her family, she
became less concerned about other people's responses to her. "Before, I was
a bit like my mother. I gave flowers, gifts, money. Now I think more of
myself, and I don't give gifts anymore. My sisters are angry because I don't
give them anything anymore." To achieve the newfound freedom, Margarita in effect removed herself from the people who made her angry.

> Now when I see that something can affect me and make me angry, I avoid it. I
> don't speak to these people. Before I just suffered, felt nervous and depressed
> when people humiliated me and didn't appreciate me. Now I feel much surer
> of myself. Before I felt useless, because nobody said I was doing well. Now the
> karate teacher tells me that I am doing well. I received medals and diplomas
> and this made me feel good. Karate teaches you physical and mental involve-
> ment, justice, courtesy, tolerance, and respect for God and for colleagues; its
> not just exercise. It's not that the mind can control the body. It requires total
> concentration and it gives tranquility.

Margarita's sickness led her to the realization that she needed to
refashion her life and herself, and she consciously decided to do so.

> I decided that I would change and I did, I will not allow that they harm me.
> One must have a strong mind, and I achieved it through karate. The pills did
> not help me. I realized I had to learn to control my nervous system, and my
> character. Karate and exercise allowed me to do it. And now when something
> emotional happens, I say I will not allow it to affect me. I control it.

The karate altered her existence as well as her appearance. Margarita
substituted her glamorous look for one of assertiveness. She was thinner,
looked smaller, and changed her hair from jet black to a honey color.
Wearing her karate costume, she looked tough. Her twenty-seven-year-old
karate master usually practiced with her in her house.

Margarita spoke of karate in much the same way a religious convert speaks about his or her new religion—in ecstatic terms. She proudly
demonstrated her karate prowess for us (my assistant and I) and testified
that by becoming a karate master she gained self-confidence, allowing her
to express her "angers, but now these are good angers." In a relatively
short period of time, she gained extreme proficiency and acquired the

highest possible karate belts. Her schoolmates named a new karate move "Margarita."

As Margarita advanced in her karate, she lost interest in her husband and shed all her symptomatologies.

> By exercising my mind I became totally distracted and I stopped paying attention to my husband. Now I don't feel that he is manipulating me and it really is not important even if he is, it does not affect me. I think all men try to manipulate one mentally, sexually, economically. I think one person ought not humiliate another, and one humiliates oneself when one loves. He is a computer engineer, he works on machines, and he manipulates me mentally in the way he manipulates his machines. I think he is envious. He humiliated me and forced me to "make angers." His daughters want to humiliate me; they didn't like me. They wanted him to go back to their mother, and these things have harmed me [because they could have performed witchcraft]. He is envious that I make more money than he. But now, when he makes angers, I don't care that he is envious or angry. I used to "make angers" but now I tell my husband, "If you make me angry you can leave, because you don't pay for my medicines." He wants me to be as I was before, and he doesn't even give me money. My husband does not wish to leave me now because he knows it's better here than elsewhere. He would have to pay for another house, to have his laundry washed and meals made.

Karate provided Margarita a powerful defense against her husband—one she would not hesitate to use. In fact, she noted, smilingly, when her husband attempted to hit her because she separated from him, she used a karate technique on him and he was terrified by it. Margarita's husband has appealed to her sense of motherhood.

> He tells me that I only think of myself, that I don't think about my child, and that I am an egoist. I love my little girl, and I will not have him blackmail [*chantajear*] me in this way. He manipulates my daughter. She told me I must love her father because he was her father. He said he would not divorce me. I want to be free. If I want to swim I will swim, if I want to do karate I will do karate, and I will go out the hour I want.

On my last visit with Margarita, three years after I first met her, she was a new person and I hardly recognized her. My visit was especially rewarding, and somewhat discomforting, because she openly expressed gratitude for the influence we had on her: "You and your visits have taught me that women can be friends."[13]

Margarita was feeling perfectly well without having taken any medications in the intervening years. She recounted how she had amazingly recovered. She and her husband had gone their separate ways, though he continued to reside in the house. Margarita's karate teacher became her lover, although, she said, "He was twenty-seven years old and he exhausted me." She delighted in describing how muscular and strong he was, and using her finger, she laughingly and with great astonishment demonstrated how long his penis became when they made love. The liaison made Margarita happy, but it soon became too taxing on her and she was relieved when her lover left for Japan. Despite his expensive presents, she refused to accompany him there because she had found a new life when she became friends with four women. Margarita had not experienced friendships with women before and said, "I was happier than ever before to have women friends." They went out to dance halls, and Margarita admitted, in a mischievous way, that she enjoyed taunting men and then leaving. Significantly, whereas before her point of reference had been her husband, during our last meeting she only mentioned her husband once to say that they were estranged. Her concerns were her friends and her son, whose studies in England she financed.

Analysis

The details of Margarita's life are instructive. They demonstrate how life's lesions are produced and how they may become alleviated. Of the numerous women I got to know in Mexico during my studies—and many I know extremely well and also admire—Margarita stands out in my mind. Most of all, I was impressed by her stunning intelligence and her coherent, logically articulated narrations, which she delivered in a monotone voice sometimes for eight hours, about herself and her perceptions of the world around her.

Margarita's story is the story of many women in Mexico, and yet the confluence of the forces at work render her life unique. Her story points to personal predilections and judgments and to ideological crevices and contradictions in Mexican society that brought Margarita into a struggle with entrenched cultural understandings that other women tacitly accepted. In contemporary times, Margarita's experience is certainly not unique to Mexican culture. Sexual abuse and its devastating effects resonate the world over in people's lives, but many of Margarita's conflicts arose out of the socio-cultural setting of which she is part.

To account for Margarita's life's lesions we must examine her life from several dimensions. The hospital physician diagnosed Margarita as an "obsessive compulsive, and extremely unstable." He medicalized her condition by converting her distress into a "prediabetic" impairment. He rightly berated the father for stimulating the girl by "awakening her instincts" and the acquiescing mother for failing to report it to the authorities.

We could objectify her condition and label it as a depressive disorder, attributable to her childhood fixated relationship with her father. The little girl who idealized her father became exploited by him as the mother looked away. We could explain Margarita's fear of leaving her house as a symbolic expression of her forceful confinement to her home, first by her father and then by her husband. Her father locked her in, her husband locked her in, and then she locked herself in with her fear of leaving the house.

These reifications may account for Margarita's pains, but the fact that Margarita's affliction was alleviated by a change in her circumstances suggests, more compellingly, that we must look for the roots of her disorder in the circumstance of her life and in the contradictions that she herself recognized related to her being a woman and to her having moved against cultural norms in her desire for individuation. As we can see from her narrative, central to Margarita's life's lesions is her having been caught between living up to the ideology of motherhood and wifehood, and her sexuality, which was awakened and whetted by her father's abuses; between the cultural emphasis on the mother-child bond that Margarita attempted to live up to in her quest to retain her son, and the woman-child she herself was; and between the independent individual she wished to become and the kinship obligations she had as a member of her natal family.

These conflicts were not experienced by all the women I met. Margarita was one of the few who openly expressed her sexuality and her desire for individuation. Undoubtedly, Margarita's conflicts came into focus in her life precisely because she was comfortably situated economically and she had few children to concern herself with. Generally speaking, poor women's sexual desires become attenuated and submerged by their obligations to their families and children and by their day-to-day search for a livelihood.

Margarita's dependence on her husband for love and affection, in addition to sexual satisfaction, was no doubt fostered by her alienation from her mother and her siblings. As we have seen, Mexican women are generally close to their natal family, toward which they look for affective ties. Margarita's aloofness from her own family produced a greater dependence on her male companions for friendship, which she sought out even more than sexual gratification and which her husbands were incapable of giving her.

A major theme in Margarita's life was, of course, her humiliation at being in the position of a woman—the one who must beg, the one who is "less." Although her husband earned less money and had fewer desires than she, she had to live with the notion that she was a woman and therefore was "less," and this humiliated her. She tacitly accepted that she must not refuse her husband sexual favors, but she questioned why he refused her, which aggravated the conflict between the docile woman and the sexual woman, "the aggressive woman," the whore. This was a contradiction she could not reconcile for herself until she became physically as powerful as a man when she became a karate master.

Margarita railed against the double standard and women's lack of freedom. Not coincidentally, she identified herself with the birds Spiritualists spoke to her about. She clearly sought to free herself from cultural constraints, and when she accomplished this, facilitated by her economic independence, it promoted her recovery.

Margarita was able to resolve successfully the contradictions and to alter the circumstances of her existence as a result of a number of converging factors. Undoubtedly the psychiatrist, who gave Margarita "permission" to take a lover, opened the way to the individuation that she so desperately sought. He allowed her not only to satisfy her sexual desires but to act on her own, to take the initiative by seeking out a lover. Previously any initiative she took was usually rebuffed by her husband. The psychiatrist also redirected Margarita's reference from her family and mother to herself. She was able to accomplish this transition owing to her economic independence from them and from her husband.[14]

Margarita's desire for individuation and her lack of independence and dignity were at the core of her life's lesions and expressed in her various symptomatologies. She achieved these qualities by immersing herself in karate. Margarita's choice of karate echoes the advice Simone de Beauvoir gave when asked, "Are you in favor of violence in women's struggle?" She responded,

> In the present situation, yes, up to a point, because men use violence toward women, both in language and in action. They attack women, they rape them, they insult them. Women should defend themselves with violence. Some are learning karate and other ways of fighting. I am in favor of that. They will feel much more at ease in their own skins and in the world when they don't feel helpless in the face of aggression. (1980: 148)

Margarita was freed of her husband, and her newly gained power, coupled with her friendships with women, allowed her to retaliate as a woman by goading men and to continue to be the rebel.

The nuances of Margarita's life I present here provide an understanding of women's concepts of themselves and are also instructive about the gradual character of the healing process. Biomedicine fails to perceive and aid in resolving the contradictions that wear on Margarita. Her narrative sheds light on the forces instrumental in the alleviation of her symptoms and her resolution of contradictions in which she was engaged. The psychiatrist's advice allowed her to act; the cleansings she received in a Spiritualist temple absolved her from evil. But her "conversion" to karate imbued Margarita with the autonomy, independence, and self-confidence she had sought, transforming her into a new being. Life became coherent.

Not all Mexican women seek individuation and autonomy. Nor is individuation an option for all women in contemporary Mexico, especially those who are deeply entrenched in the society, as Margarita was not. As she herself recognized, she was an outsider born in the wrong place. Alicia, the subject of the next chapter, does not search for independence; she is caught in the contradiction between motherhood and sexuality, as the "other woman."

Notes

1. This refers to the Shrine of Guadalupe, which is revered by Mexicans of all classes; it is located in a working class neighborhood.

2. Margarita is referring to Nembutal (sodium pentobarbital), a barbiturate.

3. She used the word *envidia*, which suggests jealousy but also implies the potential for witchcraft. Her husband gave all his earnings to his adult children, but Margarita was not distressed by this.

4. Margarita, like many others, lapses into the third-person singular when speaking about herself. In Mexico, it is not uncommon for people of both sexes to avoid the usage of the first person singular when speaking about themselves.

5. Such as Inderal for arrhythmia and hypertension (chlorhydrate of propranolol).

6. Her pressure was at all times 120/80.

7. The doctor prescribed an antidepressant (Tofranil, a tricyclic antidepressant) and a tranquilizer (Stelazine, trifluoroperazine in the form of a chlorhydrate).

8. When people speak of high and low blood pressure, they are referring to the vicissitudes of their existence, when one is dejected one's pressure is low, and when one is agitated and angry one's pressure is high. For a full discussion of typical Mexican symptoms, see Finkler 1991 and glossary.

9. Margarita weighed 104.5 pounds and was 5'1" tall.

10. In Mexico it is not uncommon to regard "mental problems" as neurological problems (see Finkler 1991), and general practitioners usually refer patients with what they assess as mental disturbances to a neurologist.

11. See Finkler (1985b) for the detailed significance of this: cleansings usually remove any evil that lingers around the individual.

12. Out of curiosity, I asked Margarita on several occasions whether she had been in touch with feminist groups. She claimed she had not been in contact with any group, attesting to her acute powers of observation and analysis.

13. In fact, as it is often customary among Mexicans, she gave me for a souvenir a picture of herself taken in Cancun, on the back of which she wrote a lengthy note of appreciation for our having taught her that "women can be friends and you gave me your friendship." All along she had stated that my assistant and I had contributed to her recovery, and now she repeated it. While the anthropologist's role is not to intervene, one of course does inadvertently and unintentionally, in much the same way as all human beings leave a mark on one another even after a casual meeting. The photo was also emblematic of Margarita's having left the house to take a lengthy plane trip.

14. As I discuss in Finkler 1991, psychiatry has not taken a foothold in Mexico for several reasons, one of which is its focus on the autonomous individual rather than family. Margarita, as an outsider to her culture, grasped the concept of autonomy quickly and acted on it.

8. Alicia: A Mother and a Mistress

Alicia was an attractive, short, chubby woman with sharp eyes, short hair, and a mischievous smile. Despite being only thirty-two, Alicia wore dentures, which, during a conversation, might sometimes fall out of place. As I got to know her, I found her to be an intelligent, fun person—upbeat, with a wry sense of humor. She liked to say that she was just happy with herself and her life.

Alicia lived in a Mexico City working class neighborhood in a tenement (*vecindad*) comprised of 106 small apartments off a long hallway, reminiscent of jail cells. Alicia's apartment, next to her sister's and cousin's, was visibly a cozy little nest, pleasant by comparison with the majority of the housing accommodations I had visited. Alicia lived in the apartment, which was fully furnished with standard kitchen appliances, with her two children and her lover. The family had moved there two years earlier, and she was pleased because, she said, she had separated herself from her mother: "I always lived with my mother, and by separating myself I live my own life, and she does not interfere. I used to go with her to the market, I ate breakfast with her—now I am more tranquil, as if I were freed."

Alicia came to seek treatment at the hospital for pain in her ovaries. Her abdomen felt distended, and she had had a recurrent mild pain for six months. She did not know what was wrong with her, but she came to the hospital because she was confident that the hospital "had many machines" and because she was fearful of uterine and breast cancer. She said wistfully, "I fear the pain and the suffering my family will have if something happens to me."

Alicia also reported to the doctor that she forgot things and was very fearful that she was suffering from brain cancer, especially because one of her nephews recently died of a brain tumor. She had been forgetting things for the past four to five years. "I am not nervous, I don't have any problems. But I forget everything, it's like being a child in kindergarten. I was always forgetful, but recently (about two or three years ago) it got worse and I began to have problems." In fact, one day she even forgot to pick up her six-year-old son from kindergarten, and she became frightened:

It's illogical that I should be forgetting things and I'm afraid I will get old and I will get lost. I want to be treated now before something worse happens. Even when I was in high school I loved to study, but I could never remember dates and numbers. I was never good in mathematics, so I said I cannot study and I cannot ever have a career. It [forgetting] makes me nervous. It's illogical.

Alicia saw a private physician who informed her that there was nothing wrong with her ovaries. "The tests he took showed I was well. But I told him I have pain when I carry things." Since her ovaries were normal, she believed she had a hernia. This possibility frightened her, "because I carry so many heavy things. I carry heavy boxes with soft drinks, and they are as heavy as the devil. Then when I have to go to the main market and carry heavy gunny sacks, I am afraid I will not be able to do it, that is why I am afraid of a hernia." Alicia was only mildly reassured by the physician that the results of the ultrasound he ordered were normal and that she didn't have any cysts, or "a *fibroma* as they call it."

Alicia was prescribed two analgesic-antipyretic[1] medications for when her pain became very severe. She declared: "I have gone from one hospital to another to see what was wrong since the pain began." Her mother, with whom she continued to be very close, told her to bathe herself with herbs usually used after the birth of a child. But these baths had not alleviated her problem. "Originally, the pain was mild but it increased, especially when I have sexual intercourse." Alicia's pain was particularly problematic for her because she could not have sexual intercourse with her lover. She hastened to add that:

> He was not bothered by it but I am because of our happy relationship; we have pleasure, especially since we don't go to the movies. We are not rich, and for me this is my pleasure. I like my man and we have good physical relations. It pains me that I cannot be with him. Logically it [our relationship] will have to end, and I don't want it to end. I don't know, but one day it will, maybe not that soon. I am thirty-two years old and at fifty, if I get to be that age—and I don't believe I will—he could leave me, so I want my problem treated. I am afraid that it is cancer of the ovaries.

When the doctors failed to treat Alicia, she sought help from a folk healer who specialized in "fallen ovaries and fallen testicles," but the healer could not remedy her pains, so she went to the hospital.

The hospital physician ordered a series of analyses and an ultrasound to rule out ovarian cysts, because Alicia reported that she menstruated irregularly. She even had had a false pregnancy. "One day I stopped menstruating for nine months and then I bled, but there was no baby." The results of the tests ordered by the hospital physician were all negative and the diagnosis Alicia was given was "hormonal problems [gonadal ovarian glands] and obesity,[2] mental disturbances of a vascular type, confusion, emotional problems and possible colitis."[3] The doctor referred Alicia to the neurology department for a computerized tomographic magnetic resonance scanning analysis or an electroencephalogram (EEG) to determine the cause of her forgetfulness. Neither test was done because the machines were out of order, but Alicia was given the diagnosis of "presenile dementia." The neurologist suggested that she take vitamins to alleviate her forgetfulness.

Alicia had been healthy all her life. "I don't have any pain in my head, and in the lower back" (*cintura*). And to emphasize this point, she repeated:

> I have no aches there—nothing. I am very calm. Only my menstruation has been irregular. I would like to have children every year but I cannot; I don't even have enough money for children. I like having babies. I don't like them when they get to be big, but I like being pregnant. I feel perfectly well when I am pregnant and I feel tranquil then. I like to show that I am pregnant because it is normal to be pregnant.

In fact, Alicia even suspected for a second time that she might have been pregnant at the time she came to the hospital.

Alicia's parents had migrated to Mexico City, where they established their family and where her mother gave birth to twenty-one children, of whom eleven survived. Alicia was the youngest and her father's favorite. Alicia's sister recalled, "We were many, and some he loved and others he didn't; but he loved Alicia." Alicia and her sister reminisced about their unhappy childhood in Mexico City. Alicia's sister recollected, "My mother was always pregnant since I can remember. Only now that I am an adult I don't see her pregnant." Alicia added:

> My mother had two sets of twins and one set of triplets. We were eleven girls and ten boys; the girls lived and the boys died. I think boys die more than girls. My father and mother worked all the time to maintain us and we grew like weeds; nobody taught us anything, nobody helped us. My mother came home and she used to hit us because we did not do what we were supposed to and she was tired. My mother worked as a servant and she worked very hard. She went to work and left us in school.

The two sisters vividly described how their father beat their mother all her life, but not the children. If he tried to hit them they would not allow themselves to be hit. Alicia added with an embarrassed laugh, "My father beat my mother when he was drunk, and since he was drunk daily he beat her daily. He did not beat us, but I don't know what his problem was with my mother and why he beat her." Alicia's father had died nine years before I met her. Alicia added, "My mother is old—she is sixty—but she knows how to work. We were not rich, nor were we middle class but, of course, we never went hungry. We always struggled for the little we had."

Alicia had worked at different jobs since she was sixteen years old, noting, "inasmuch as I did not study." She worked in a factory, and then in the toy department of a department store. "Then, six years ago before the birth of my boy, my man obtained for me an ambulatory candy concession in an out-of-the-way section of Chapultepec Park [the major park in Mexico City] and I have been selling sweets there ever since. Don't think it's a permanent stand," she added, suggesting that an ambulatory stand is much less lucrative than a permanent stand. She sold fruits, ice cream, sweets, and sodas. Several members of her family, including her cousins, mother, and sisters, each had separate stands. Alicia remarked, "Sometimes we get run out by the authorities because they say it is not hygienic."

Alicia was an astute businesswoman. With the economic crisis of the time, she sold fewer items, but she compensated by charging more for each piece. Her economic situation improved when she increased the price of her merchandise and when Alicia's mother, upon leaving the city, bequeathed her stand to Alicia.

As the owner of two ambulatory candy concessions, Alicia had been politicized, unlike women who work in the house, such as Margarita. Alicia believed that she had no voice as an individual, but as a member of the union she could enter the local police delegation and protest if anyone from her family was removed from the park or fined. "If I go to the police delegation by myself, what can I do? Nothing, unless I know somebody in there; but if we have a union then they attend to us. I like those who can defend themselves like cats." Alicia regarded her vending enterprise as a "noble job," meaning that it was honest and dignified. "I worked in a factory when I was young, but it is much better to be selling—the prices are not fixed, and one can get more than a minimum wage. We used to earn about 100 percent profit on the sweets, but now it's about 20 percent only."

Alicia was fearful of the future. She believed that her small business would soon be a thing of the past. "One must prepare oneself intellectually by studying. I took a trip to the United States border, and when we crossed the border there were no taco stands, there were no ambulatory stands on the street, and this is the way we are going to be in the future. What are we going to do? How can we prepare ourselves for the future?" Alicia asked despairingly.

From the time she began experiencing her forgetfulness, Alicia had to make lists of the merchandise she lacked. Sometimes she even forgot the prices of some items; However, her twelve-year-old daughter worked along with her and her six-year-old son also helped. "My little girl really turned out well, and this is why I want to be treated now so that she will not have to help me all her life, so she can live her life. I told her that if she would do well in school, she wouldn't have to work, but since she wasn't doing well, she has to work. What would she do if she didn't work?"

Alicia could hardly recognize her daughter's father anymore. She recalled laughingly:

> One day I was walking on the street and a man approached me and asked whether I knew him, and I truly did not remember where I had seen him. He said, "OK, I am going," and then I remembered. My God—it was the father of my girl, and I thought, "Oh my God, he will want something from me." He disappeared as soon as I had gotten pregnant. You know how it is, typical, he was very happy, then he went out for cigarettes and he never came back.

Alicia gave birth to two other children after she established her household with the man she called her husband. She had had an IUD inserted but nine years ago she got pregnant and the child was born malformed:

> The baby had a large head and short limbs and he was very sick. He suffocated at birth. When they pulled him out, his head was completely damaged, and I was pretty sick. I was very sad because I thought I would have other children like that. I think it was hereditary, because at the same time two of my cousins had children with the same deformity but one of the children lived. I didn't want any more children if they would come out very bad.

The last child Alicia had, her six-year-old son, had a "big mole and it is very ugly. They operated on the child but it was still there."

> The doctors told me to have an operation [hysterectomy] but I didn't want to. I am not using contraceptives and maybe I will get pregnant. I was afraid that if I had an operation I would stop being a woman. The doctors say it's absurd, but I don't know.

Alicia's man did not want any more children. She was very concerned about her womanhood. She described herself as a "concubine," and this status placed her in an ambiguous position in society.

There was a time when my marriage had affected me very much because I was on the outside. I don't live with my man. He is married, and he has a wife and children. I tried to disengage myself several times from him but I couldn't. I simply couldn't. I love him. Frankly, I am very happy with him. He makes me happy. I adapted to the situation. It's been many years [ten], and we have a child and now it doesn't bother me anymore. But yes, it does. All my sisters are married, even though they say it is sad to be married, no? Most people think that the "other" [woman], that is how they refer to my situation, is beautiful and sexy. But I feel like any other woman. I feel bad, and I feel rejected living the life I do with this man, but in my house it is beautiful. He is very understanding and very loving. He is good to my daughter. But other people, most of all wives of other men, criticize me because I am not a wife, because I am not married and they are married, and because I am the lover of a married man. This does affect me.

Alicia was disturbed that she had not married. She continued,

But then I say if I have lived well I will have no reason to complain. I feel frustrated because everybody is married and I am not. I would like to marry him but he cannot marry me because he has another wife. He comes regularly and he is with me every day but he goes to sleep with her [his wife]. He never stays here at night. They won't let him. He leaves at nine at night for his house. I don't wash or iron for him. I just cook the main day meal for him.

The ambiguity of her situation was distressing for Alicia. She declared,

He could, as Mexicans do, leave his wife, but he is lazy [*bien conchudo*]. His wife is very clean. She has a nice house that is well taken care of where he can bring his friends and his boss. Why should he live here? He has me anyway, and he will support her and he will support me. I serve him as a woman and she washes and irons for him, and so tell me why should he leave her? She does not love him, she is one of these women who only cares about her children. She has eight children and they are everything to her. She does not care about her husband. She likes to have her house nicely done, and her children well fed, well dressed, and well bathed. We never fought, only because she is not interested.

Despite the fact that she wanted to be married, Alicia, like Margarita, looked down on the traditional wife-mother role. She faulted her sister for taking care of her children and bringing her husband his meals to his place of employment, as many Mexican women customarily do. "My sister does not earn money like I do, she thinks she should take care of her children exclusively, she washes for them, she irons for them, and they are pretty big. She does everything for them, and I don't think that's good."

But although she reproached her sister for fulfilling the wife-mother role, Alicia liked to be at home for her man and to prepare his main meal. She also usually asked for his permission to leave the house, "because he could arrive at an unexpected time. But I don't like to leave the house anyway." In fact, Alicia was perfectly happy with her man, who only drank occasionally and who took care of all her needs. As I watched the couple together, I was struck by how considerate the man was of Alicia; his demeanor was in no way reminiscent of Margarita's laments about how Mexican men act toward their wives. But then Alicia was not the man's wife—she was, as Alicia herself always realized, the concubine. They engaged in a lot of free bantering and there was an absence of tension between them, unlike the behavior in most households I visited. Alicia was aware of her special relationship with her man, and she noted that people could not believe that they kissed each other constantly. Her daughter resented Alicia's devotion to her man and reminded Alicia that she "ought to be a mother first and a wife second."

Alicia and her lover described how people have attempted to divide them. She said, "When people see a happy couple, they conspire to separate them. Nobody likes to see people happy—even one's own children want to disunite one, when they see one kissing. People are also envious [*envidia*] when one has a good job or a good friendship." Alicia and her lover regarded themselves as being in a very fortunate situation, yet as a pair they were fearful of people's envy.[4] She assuaged her fears of envy, however, by regarding herself as being too insignificant for anyone to be envious of her. She remarked, "People are envious of those who have something. I have nothing. I am not beautiful, and I don't have diligent children."

Alicia was a devout Catholic, but she had been expelled from the church because she cohabited with a married man. She used to attend church, but because she lived with a married man, no one would accept her:

> I don't have a social life, I don't see anybody, because my neighbors criticize me a lot. One cannot hide this, and it feels bad. When I go to church and I want to go to confession, no, I cannot do so, because I know that I am sinning. This makes me sad because I do love my religion, but I will not leave him for that. He does not want to leave his children because they are still at a difficult age. His children go to school, and he cannot abandon them. She is the only wife he has. Maybe he is right, I don't know.

Alicia's expulsion from the church was painful for her. "People must believe in something, people don't want all this violence." The violence in the streets distressed her deeply. She was frightened by police assaults.

We have remained without law. Here in Mexico, there is no law. Twice my sister was stopped by the police. She was paid twice a month and she received eighty thousand pesos [about three hundred dollars] as severance pay. On the day she collected the money, a policeman stopped her and said she was too young to have so much money. He hit her, pushed her down, and took the money from her. When I leave my house there is no guarantee anymore that I won't be robbed, and there is nobody to appeal to. So I go on a pilgrimage to the shrine [San Juan de Los Lagos] and there I ask the Virgin to save me from assaults by the police. I ask her to protect me from getting beaten by them. If we had a government the way it ought to be [*como debe de ser*], that respected those who behaved well and punished those who didn't, we would not have to go to church.

In fact, Alicia was frightened not only of the police, but of the government they represented. She declared:

A cultured people do not have a bad [corrupt] government, we do it to ourselves. They rob us and I am more frightened of the police than of a robber. The robbers steal decently, but the police kill people, or even worse they hit one and there is no one to complain to. They violate [rape] women and then they say "She let him into the house" or "She let him do it." But why would she let a man like that in [to the house]? Nothing is done to the police.

And Alicia laughed as she said:

If you denounce a rape, the judge says in disbelief, "Sure you didn't allow him in?" The family says, "Better be quiet," because it is a disgrace to us." The men say, "This is what women are for." No, we must be loved and respected. But we are not and this is why we [as a people] don't advance.

Despite the violence of the world outside, Alicia was content with her life. She stated:

I am happy with what I am. I would like to have been beautiful, but I don't envy those who are. I see tall women and I am very short but very happy. My father loved me, my sisters love me, my mother loves me a lot, everybody loves me and my husband loves me; what else can I ask for in this life? I am not rich. We went to Cancun and looked at the beaches that are for the very rich—all that luxury. It does not demoralize me because we laugh a lot.

Yet as satisfying as her liaison with the married man was, it created an inescapable and unresolvable contradiction of which Alicia was very much aware. She was acutely conscious of her dilemma of being a mother and a mistress.

Children demand a lot. Even when they are big, they ask you to go with them, and you forget the husband [referring to her lover]. For example, I am in a dilemma. I have to choose between my daughter and my husband. I don't know what to do, and that is why it is better if I went to a psychologist who would tell me what to do about the children. For example, when my husband comes, we talk, and watch TV, and the children are with us. We don't pay much attention to the boy, and then he goes out into the street, gets fresh with me, and I don't know how to control him. I just hit him. The kindergarten teacher told me to see a psychologist. I don't want my children to fail. I don't want them to be professionals, I just don't want them to have vices. I want them to let us live out our old age together.

Alicia, unlike Margarita and the other women we will meet, was unable to account for her disorder, although she recognized that she was in conflict about her role as mother and mistress. She failed, however, to see the relationship between the contradictions and her pains. To make sense of the pains in her ovaries, Alicia considered that perhaps the pains resulted from her having carried heavy things. Or, perhaps, they were due to the fact that she failed to take care of herself after she gave birth to her six-year-old son. She commented, "If a woman does not take care of herself well after she gives birth, she begins to decline, deteriorate." She had not bathed with customary herbs or massaged herself after she gave birth, and she worried that she would wither.

Alicia was baffled by her forgetfulness. She had sought many reasons. Perhaps it was a lack of vitamins, or, she thought, maybe because

We are not serious people. My siblings and I always tease one another, but I don't really think that's the reason. Why should I be forgetting things? I am not that old, and I don't have that many problems. My sister forgets things, but she failed in her marriage and she had a lot of problems. I don't have problems, my husband doesn't beat me or maltreat me. If I don't have problems, why do I forget things?

Analysis

Forgetfulness for Alicia was indeed a serious dysfunction and it is no wonder she was concerned about it. A well-functioning memory was crucial for keeping track of prices and inventory in her small business. Her fears of dependency on her daughter to conduct her business were particularly grave because of her ambivalence toward her mothering role.

Alicia, unlike Margarita, did not seek individuation or independence, even though she appreciated her independence from her mother. She continued to be embedded in her natal family and in her little house (*casa chica*), but she was caught in the contradictions of being the "other woman." On the one hand, life was as it ought to be with her man. She enjoyed a man's respect and had love of the kind that Margarita was unable to gain. The feminization of love in the private domain was advantageous to Alicia. She has even adjusted to societal ostracism, having her family to cushion its effects. But she was caught in the profound contradiction of having to reconcile the ideology of motherhood with her day-to-day satisfying experience of being the mistress. Her male counterpart who, she noted, was very healthy, was not confronted by this kind of contradiction.

It was not coincidental that Alicia experienced pains in her ovaries. Pain in the ovaries[4] is what I call a "typical symptom"[5] women present in reference to generalized issues related to sexuality or motherhood. In specific terms it may refer to having few children or having an "exhausted womb." In Alicia's case, her ovarian affliction was tied to the paradox of her sexuality, to her desire for children that she could not beget, and to her status of mistress rather than wife.

Fortunately for Alicia, her forgetfulness was selective. My talks with her flowed freely, and I never noticed any memory lapses as she recounted the past or spoke of the present. That Alicia once forgot to pick up her little boy from kindergarten may be associated with the unresolvable bind in which she found herself—being both mistress and mother.

For Alicia's lover, having a wife and a mistress reflected positively on his manhood, whereas for Alicia to be the mistress produced a profound contradiction. Her perceived dysfunctions cannot be comprehended independently of the dilemma facing her. Alicia, like Margarita, was enmeshed in contradictions that related to sexuality and motherhood, but she, unlike Margarita, could not extricate herself from them.

Alicia's pains will not be alleviated easily by medication or other modes of therapy. In fact, though Alicia's pain in her ovaries lessened, her forgetfulness continued, and it probably will persist as long as she is engaged in a profound dilemma for which she lacks a solution.

Alicia's case demonstrates the links between women's daily existence, cultural ideologies, and sickness, and the corrosive effects on health of contradictory gender ideologies that supersede even class position. Alicia is perfectly happy with her class status and even her gender, but she is faced with the paradox of being both mother and whore in the eyes of the society that nourishes her essence.

Notes

1. Neo-melubrina (dipyrone) and Prodolina (antiprinal + methylamine + methanol + magnesium sulfate), an antipyretic-analgesic.
2. Alicia weighed 132 pounds and measured 4′8″. Her blood pressure was 100/70.
3. For the physicians' clinical reasoning, see Finkler 1991.
4. This observation had been made to me by others; see Chapter 5, note 41 in this volume.
5. See Finkler 1991.

9. Julia: A Drunken Husband

When I first met Julia at the hospital, I was struck by her bleached blond hair, her capped teeth, her emaciated,[1] short body, and her shy demeanor. As I listened to her speak, I noted that her soft-spoken, childlike voice was housed in the body of a thirty-three-year-old woman.

Julia lived in Chimalhuacan, a developing shantytown at the eastern extension of Nezahuacóyotl, about three hours from the hospital by train and minibus. The new settlement, one of the most impoverished in greater Mexico City, lacked most urban amenities, including a drainage system. The minibus made its way through vast stretches of flat land dotted by small cardboard and tin shacks and some cinder block constructions, all placed symmetrically and parallel to the main road. These habitations were connected by thick webs of crisscrossing electrical wires, pulling electricity to individual dwellings from a few centrally situated electric posts.

On my first visit to Julia's dwelling, which occurred during the rainy season, the unpaved roads were flooded and few vehicles could make their way through protruding rocks and creviced roads. In the dry season, dust storms arose from the unpaved roads, momentarily blinding my eyes and leaving my throat dry. Julia's house was situated one block away from the major road at the end of the private minibus line that serviced the colony.

Julia's four-room house stood on a corner lot. This was an auspicious location for the general store that Julia established shortly after she had moved there three years before. In one room she sold soft drinks, eggs, vegetables, and corn; she used the other rooms for living quarters and storing her merchandise. The rooms, separated by bed sheets, were cluttered with things, including a television set and console, a washing machine, a bed, and a stove. Turkeys, pigs, and chickens roamed around the small garbage heaps distributed in the inner courtyard, which was enclosed by a cinder block wall. In one corner of the courtyard there was a well from which Julia drew all of her water.

Julia had moved to this dwelling from the heart of Mexico City, where she had lived close to her in-laws. Her husband's father had helped the family purchase a piece of land in the new colony. It was cheaper to buy a small plot than to rent a room in Mexico City. Julia hated living in the new house because, she contended,

> It is very ugly here, at night the drug addicts come out. In the middle of the night one can hear shots, and in the morning, when I get up, I am very frightened. I see young sixteen- to eighteen-year-old people dead and it is very ugly. I think last Saturday somebody was shot. On the weekends it's worse, and since I am alone then, I am very fearful. I cannot sleep. When I lived in the center of Mexico City, it was not like that. It is very dark here, and there is no electricity.

Julia arrived at the hospital to seek treatment for pains in her lower abdomen and back and for her headaches, which she felt especially around the lower part of her head (*cerebro*). About three weeks earlier she had had a bout of diarrhea, and she began losing weight. She felt her abdomen was distended, and she experienced pain during sexual intercourse. Normally she had experienced these symptoms intermittently, but during the past weeks the symptoms were unrelenting. When I met with her a few weeks later she reported that she suffered from "pressure" (meaning high and low blood pressure) and, she disclosed,

> I feel very hot and choking; I think that is why I have pains. When I am in the subway I sweat, and my pressure goes down. I feel weak. I don't know when my pressure goes up or when it goes down. I have pain in my heart for a minute or two and then the pain ceases. I have pain in my ovaries. When I stop washing laundry the headaches stop. I always had pain in the back of my head [*cerebro*] and in the lower back [*cintura*] and I don't know why. Everything I eat makes me sick. And it's been this way for about nine years, since I got married—before then I was never sick.

At the urging of her husband, Julia arrived at the hospital after she had been unsuccessfully treated in a private clinic and after she had sought treatment from a *señora* (a term that usually refers to a folk curer of an unspecified kind). The *señora* had informed her that she suffered from a "fallen womb."[2] The folk healer promised to help her conceive a child on the condition that Julia follow her instructions for two months. The curer's indications included bed rest and cessation of her usual activities, including laundering, ironing, and sweeping the floor. But, Julia lamented, "since I must do these things I just go on like this." For a time Julia continued to carry out her daily chores and her business activities despite having been in excruciating pain, because, in her words, "I just don't have any time for that. I just go on doing everything; it goes away. I just wait for it to go away."

Julia recounted to me (as she had to the doctor, using the same words) that her symptoms had intensified three years earlier when, she reported, "I had an operation and I lost the baby I was carrying." The operation was a watershed event in her life. At that time, she was taken to the emergency clinic but she was uncertain why the operation was performed. "Somebody said perhaps it was because the baby was out of place, or perhaps I had a tumor." Julia believed that during that operation they removed a fallopian tube and an ovary, or "something like that." Maybe it was an ectopic pregnancy, she was not really sure. She had been pregnant several months. Julia bemoaned, "I don't know, my husband spoke, and I have no idea what it was, it was very serious. I have never gotten pregnant again, I cannot get pregnant again."

Following the operation, Julia couldn't walk for half a year because the scar on her abdomen opened up twice.

> Since that time I have been feeling faint, and I have not menstruated regularly. Before I was operated on I was much fatter. Since the operation I lost weight and everything started hurting me. At first I had pain intermittently, and I had to lie down, I couldn't even sit. But now I get pains more often, especially when I have to get on a bus.

Julia repeatedly articulated two recurring themes in the same breath when she mentioned her symptoms and her pains: she spoke of the operation when her ovary was removed and of her husband's perpetual drunkenness. Again and again, she reiterated how she was transported in a comatose state to one clinic and then transferred to a big hospital, how she was fed intravenously, how the doctors came to ask about her condition, and how she unceasingly fainted. She recalled, "I did not have enough blood and I was interned in the hospital for about a month and a half. I weighed sixty-six pounds, and I have not gained weight since. And now people remark censoriously on how skinny I am."

After taking Julia's medical history, the doctor noted in her medical records that she had had an "extrauterine pregnancy and intestinal obstruction." He diagnosed her abdominal pains as a "malabsorption syndrome," because a piece of her intestine may have been cut accidentally during the ceasarian. Julia was referred to a gastroenterologist, who prescribed an antiparasitic medication[3] and a medicine for ulcerative colitis.[4] The medication alleviated Julia's diarrhea, but the ovarian pains persisted for several months; she ceased seeking treatment after her hospital visit.

Julia spoke about her life in a matter-of-fact way.

> My mother died when I was one year old, and I was raised by my [paternal] grandmother, who died two years ago. I came to live in Mexico City with an aunt who also had her own children, and I had to work. My father had a second wife, and I have nine half-brothers and -sisters, but I do not feel close to them because I have been here [Mexico City] since I was small. My father and half-siblings live in Chihuahua [in northern Mexico], where I was born.

Julia lived with her husband, who worked as a mechanic, and her sixteen-year-old son, whom she originally introduced as her nephew.

> I had this child when I was young. We did not live together [with the boy's father]. I saw him from time to time, and when he heard I was pregnant he came to see me. He was a [bus] driver and one day he left and never returned. Then I moved and he did not have my address. The boy helps me a lot, he has turned out well.

Julia had lived in Mexico City for over twenty-five years, since she was eight years old, and had been working from the time she arrived. For many years she was a store cashier. She had married nine years ago.

> I worked all the time. I started working when I was eight years old so that I could buy my own clothes. I worked two blocks away from the shop where my husband worked for fifteen years, and that is where we met. I worked for a year after I married, but then I stopped and we came to live here. I did not get pregnant until about six years after we married, and then I got sick.

To listen to Julia speak about her interaction with her husband was to see the shaping of life's lesions on her body.

> My husband comes home sometimes, and sometimes he does not, and he does not bring any money with him. He swore off drinking for four months and then he started again. No matter, nothing can be done. We didn't speak for two months because, instead of helping us with the store, he got drunk. He started drinking when he was fourteen years old, and his brothers drank, too. Only two of his brothers who have big stores don't drink. My husband does not help me, he just drinks.
>
> At one time he used to beat me a lot and I have been sick since then. Since my operation he has stopped beating me. He was drunk at the time. I think that is why I was operated on, because he beat me, and since that time I have

been sick. When I was operated on, I did not know what was wrong with me. My husband was told that my ovary and my fallopian tube were removed, and from that time on I have been unable to get pregnant.

Because of the beating episode, Julia had lost her child and had the operation in the hospital. She has had pains in her ovaries since then. "I am not supposed to carry heavy things and I am supposed to rest, but I have to do the washing, and buy my supplies for the store."

For the first three years of their marriage, Julia's husband did not drink heavily, or not heavily enough to beat her into a stupor. Typically Julia absolved her husband from the responsibility of drinking, when she pointed out that he drank because "he goes out with his friends in the mechanic shop, and they start drinking. When he drinks, he gets up in the middle of the night, turns the hi-fi up and I cannot sleep. He goes out into the street and it frightens me, he may get hurt." When I asked Julia about the fact that she could not bear any children, her response focused on her husband's wishes, rather than her own feelings.

Sometimes he says, "We need a baby and maybe something can be done so you could have a baby," but he does not get angry that I do not have children because it was his fault when I lost our child. He says nothing. The doctors were angry with him. They called him in for two hours because I had these bruises on my back, and also in the area where they operated [around the abdomen]. They told me to tell the truth, whether or not my husband had beaten me. I said, "No, I fell," and they said, "No, he beat you, because you have many bruises." He beat me a lot and he kicked me. When he beat me, I did not say anything because when I scolded him he got worse, but he does not beat me anymore.

After the operation I left him. My father came for me and he said I should go home. I sold the furniture—everything—and I left. I went to my father's house in Chihuahua. Eight days later, my husband came for me and I went back with him. He promised he would never beat me again. After that he beat me only occasionally. He is not bad now, before he was terrible. Well, he is from Oaxaca [a state in southern Mexico], a bit aggressive, and when he drinks he must have what he wants—his bottle, or his beer. If not, he gets angry, and then I don't always have the money.

At the time I met Julia, she could not conceive of leaving her husband. She regarded her husband's drinking as an uncontrollable vice, intrinsic to his character and, in her stereotypic view, to men from the south of Mexico. I sensed wistfulness rather than rancor in Julia's voice when she spoke of her husband and the tragic beatings, especially the beating that resulted in the death of her unborn child.

Although Julia had no illusions about romantic love, she was grateful that her husband got along well with her son. She and the boy worked closely together in building up her business.

> The boy was not with me when we married, he was with my uncle, but then I brought him with us because I missed him. My husband never scolded him, nor did he ever beat him. Well, if he did something bad, he hit him. My son helps me with the store, but my husband does not. My son never leaves the house, except when he accompanies me, such as when we go to buy merchandise for the store. My son goes because my husband cannot go, since he drinks from Saturday till Monday. I don't ask him any more to help me.

Julia spoke with affection of her mother-in-law. "She is very nice, she comes to see me and she tells my husband to stop drinking." Significantly, when Julia and her husband moved to their present dwelling, her husband became abusive and he drank more than when they had resided with his parents. Julia, in fact, received the brutal beating immediately after she and her husband had moved to their present dwelling, away from his parents.

Julia got up twice a week at three o'clock in the morning and traveled for two hours with her son to the central market of Mexico City to purchase supplies for her store. They returned with heavy gunny sacks filled with corn, beans, animal fodder, sweets, and vegetables, carrying these on their backs in the subway and the minibuses.

> I set up this store when we moved here. It is doing very well. Everything sells in this neighborhood. There are not many stores here because it is so far away. We are open from early morning until nine in the evening. When my husband arrives I close. Thank God we have customers daily. Sometimes my husband wants me to go out, but I don't want to because people can come to the store, and then one can lose [a sale].

As an afterthought Julia added, "I have enough money." She decided to launch the store because, she said, "my husband didn't bring in any money; he didn't give us any, what could I do? Sometimes we had no food to eat and no money for clothing and shoes, and so I started buying things little by little."

I wondered where Julia learned how to run a store. She said she had started out selling sweets. Then, "I added vegetables and I didn't know it [the business] very well. I asked people, and then I bought things that didn't pay off well, such as tomatoes; but as one works, one learns. Things have been going very well." Indeed, during the time that I knew Julia her store prospered. It grew from a little grocery store to a relatively large general store. Each time I visited her she had more employees, more merchandise for sale, and more customers streaming into the store than before. Julia was able to expand her store by raising and selling pigs in her courtyard. She used the money she earned from the sale of the animals to expand her inventory. She reinvested all her earnings into the store, enabling her to purchase a commercial refrigerator; being able to sell cold soft drinks greatly increased her business.

According to Julia, as her store expanded other store owners in the neighborhood stopped speaking to her. "People are envious [*envidia*], especially because I sell grains—animal fodder is a lucrative item—and because one needs to have a pleasant personality to attend to people," suggesting that people might be envious of her character. Indeed, when Julia served her customers, she revealed a powerful personality lodged in her fragile body; her childlike disposition gave way to that of a tough merchant, succinctly and firmly attending to her customers.

As the store grew, Julia's health improved. Each time I visited her, she told me she felt better and that she had stopped taking all her medications. Julia also looked better. She had gained some weight, and she smiled often. She was visibly proud of her store even though she found it harder and harder to get up in the middle of the night to travel to the city to do her marketing for the store. Julia added, "But then I got used to having money," so she continued her thrice weekly trips to make her purchases. When I saw Julia on one of my last follow-up visits, she looked and felt relaxed, despite the fact that her maternal grandmother had died. She had spent three weeks in the country and had enjoyed her visit.

The recurrent theme in Julia's discourse was her husband's drinking. Every time we met, she repeatedly talked about it. But as I watched her store grow, I saw her distancing herself more and more from her husband. Although his drinking habits intensified to four days a week, Julia's pains gradually disappeared and her husband receded into the background. As her health improved, she even stood up to her husband, which she had never done before. For example, when I asked her how her husband felt about the store, she responded that he was angry because he insisted she give him the profits rather than reinvest them in the store. But Julia said, "No. Now he does not help us at all, he doesn't even go with me to the city to buy merchandise. He wants me to give him the money but I don't. We scream, but now everybody is for himself; he earns his money, and I earn mine."

During my initial visit to Julia's house, I asked her (as I did all the women), "What would you do if you could change your circumstance?" Like most of the women, Julia could hardly conceive of the possibility that her life could be altered in any way. Finally, she said she would like to live alone, but then she added that "it is not possible to leave. I am already used to my husband, and he to me. If I leave he will come and look for me again, and that would be even worse. He drinks so much, and we get angry but then what would I do? Better to continue this way." In Julia's words, "It is a question of luck. I married this man and he turned out to be a drunk."

Julia's financial success enabled her to free herself from her husband's grip. Her perception of her marriage also changed—from the view of inevitability, or as she put it, "a question of luck" to the view that, in her words, "for all that I suffered, and the money we had to pay for this house on installments, for me to leave, and leave everything, no, I could not do it now." In fact, she noted that "when I get angry I tell him to leave." Julia ceased regarding her marriage to her husband as inevitable, a victim of bad luck, and she began seeing herself as a person of property who had invested too much to walk away from it. When I saw Julia for the last time, her store had grown considerably, and she was flourishing. With the exception of a brief bout with the flu, all her pains had disappeared. Concurrently, she had became oblivious to her husband. Or as she said, "I ignore him." She was no longer bothered by the fact that they did not speak to one another.

Julia's business accomplishments had taken a toll but not in ways that affected her health. She remarked that she was feeling isolated where she lived, away from her aunts. She avoided any association with the people in her neighborhood. "The people here are different from the ones in the center of town. I keep a distance from everybody." Internal class dissensions are marked in this neighborhood, and they require Julia's vigilance. She noted that

> Here, people are very poor, there are some who don't even have any money for food, and then if I talk to them they ask me to lend them money, or they want something else, and then there are problems. My husband does not like to have anything to do with them. The only people I trust [*tengo confianza*] are my aunts, or my father. But here I have nobody to talk to. There are people in this neighborhood who have a lot of money and they think they are more important [*se sienten más*] and one should feel bad about this.

Remarkably, too, some of Julia's neighbors blame her for her husband's drinking. She stated, "There are some who say I shouldn't work in the store because that is why my husband drinks. They say I get him used to earning money and then he does not have to do anything and he can just drink." Significantly, but not surprisingly, the people who tell her this are her competitors.

Analysis

Julia's sickness undoubtedly was associated with the appalling public health conditions existing in her neighborhood, which fostered parasitosis, but her sickness was not only associated with parasitosis. The intestinal problems coupled with life's lesions grated on her body and were expressed in ovarian pains: pains that were anchored in her husband's drinking and his physical abuse, which also resulted in the lost possibility of Julia bearing another child. From this perspective Julia's life's lesions were rooted in gender relations. It cannot be said, however, that Julia was entwined in any specific contradictions between norms or between norms and actuality. She presumed that she was just "unlucky" to have married a drunkard and that was a woman's lot. Not having been enmeshed in any glaring contradictions facilitated her recovery with changes in her actual circumstances.

Her gradual recovery began not only when the parasites in her body were eliminated by the medication she was prescribed, but when her life's lesions slowly receded into the background as her store enlarged. As Julia's store thrived, so did she, and her relative prosperity, achieved by her own efforts, enabled her to extricate herself from her husband's authority in the household. Although Julia did not seek individuation, the circumstances of her unexpected economic achievement fostered it for her and nurtured a newly found self-esteem.

Julia's relationship with her husband transcended cultural dimensions; it was not unique to Mexican women. Her marital situation is replicated in numerous women's lives the world over. But individual circumstance enabled Julia to grasp an unexpected opportunity to establish a small business. Ironically, Julia's tragedy of having only one child turned into an advantage. With only one child, she could dedicate herself to a business with the assistance of her son; she also launched her store in a newly developing neighborhood. Given this setting, Julia was able to transform herself from a battered woman into a successful businesswoman. Julia sought economic independence for survival if not individuation, and with excruciatingly painful, hard work she succeeded. Or, as she said, "It just happened," concurrently submerging her life's lesions.

Julia and Margarita were two women whose life's lesions, along with their symptomatic expressions, were healed owing to the changes in their situation rather than to ministrations of any kind. But for many women their life's lesions grind away at their bodies, as was the case for Rebecca, the subject of the next chapter.

Notes

1. Julia weighed 70 pounds and measured 5′0″; her blood pressure was 110/70.
2. "Fallen womb" usually refers to the same condition as pain in the ovaries (see Chapter 8).
3. Metodine (diiodohydroxyquinoline + metronidazole).
4. Azulfidine (sulfasalazine).

10. Rebecca: A Woman on the Verge of Disintegration

When I first met Rebecca, a thirty-seven-year-old, petite, thin, woman with stylishly cut short graying hair, wearing torn shoes and an expensive-looking coat, I immediately noticed a fear in her gaze that also conveyed a sense of desperation and isolation.

Rebecca resided in a pleasant lower class neighborhood of Mexico City, where the cleanly paved streets are lined with trees, adding a sense of calmness to the surroundings. Her rented apartment, one of four apartments in a house built around a patio, was dark but comfortably furnished with worn furniture, indoor plumbing, and running water. She had lived in this house for three years and since that time her rent had doubled to thirty dollars a month. Before moving here, Rebecca and her family had lived in a tin-roofed shack in the same neighborhood.

Rebecca reported that her major symptoms and also her central concern were pains and a burning sensation in her *pulmon* (lungs, meaning upper back).[1] The burning in her back led her to think that she might have cancer. She also suffered from pains in her shoulders that were accompanied by numbness in her arms. The back pains were especially unbearable when she did her laundry. Her appendix and ovaries ached, and she suffered from low blood pressure, nerves, tiredness, and headaches. Rebecca also feared that she was going crazy, by which she meant "confused in one's ideas, wanting to run away, not knowing what one wanted."

After her physical examination, the hospital physician concluded that she was suffering from "parasitic colitis,[2] lumbar scoliosis [unstable spinal column], and flat feet." For these reasons she was experiencing headaches. While taking the routine medical history, the physician elicited from Rebecca that she was experiencing amenorrhea and his diagnosis included "secondary amenorrhea." All else was normal, including her blood pressure. Rebecca's amenorrhea had a lengthy history. She reported that from age thirteen until she married at age twenty, she menstruated normally.

After she gave birth to her first child fifteen years ago, however, she menstruated only intermittently. Subsequently, she had two other children now ages twelve and six. Ten years ago Rebecca gave birth to a little girl who died a week later. Rebecca failed to recover from this tragedy. In fact, shortly after the death of the infant, she experienced a "nerves crisis."

On the basis of his diagnosis, the doctor prescribed for Rebecca two antiparasitic medications[3] and for her husband yet another medication.[4] The physician indicated that she needed to abstain from sexual relations for at least five days, if not ten. The doctor also instructed Rebecca that her husband had to abstain from drinking while he took the medication[5] indicated for him. The doctor prescribed aspirin[6] and a muscle relaxant[7] for the aches in Rebecca's back, and a vitamin. He told Rebecca to take the medication for three months and referred her to the orthopedic department. Rebecca was pleased with the referral to a specialist particularly because, more than anything else, she wished to have an X ray done to reveal the reason for the excruciating pains in her back. Indeed, the orthopedist ordered an X ray, and later he prescribed for Rebecca a special brace that would "bring together my cervical vertebrae and reposition my spinal cord." The specialist noted that Rebecca may have been suffering from rheumatism, although she thought that the distress she felt in her back was due to nervous tension. The orthopedist prescribed two other medications for her pains.[8]

Before she arrived in the hospital, Rebecca had sought treatment from several health practitioners. She saw one physician, whom she had told that she could not stand being in the house. But, Rebecca recalled, "he didn't give me any medicine for this. I analyzed the situation myself and I concluded that it was very difficult for anybody to heal me." She didn't think there was anything anyone could do for her. She tried home remedies. Her mother, who worried about her, massaged her back with *savila* (aloe), but these treatments were to no avail.

A month before she came to the hospital, Rebecca had gone to a naturalist, "because he was the only one available on the weekend," when her pain had greatly intensified. She could not afford to buy the medicine the naturalist prescribed, but he gave her a massage with olive oil which made her feel better for a while.

One time when Rebecca felt sad, she went to a hospital, but there they wanted to treat her for amenorrhea by administering hormones and fertility pills. She refused that treatment because she was afraid the hormone injections would produce cancer. Besides, she felt better when she did not menstruate, because she didn't want more than the three children she already had, even though her husband wanted more children. She added, "I did not have the courage to tell him that we didn't have any money to buy shoes for the children we have."

Three years earlier, at the same time her husband's business failed, she suffered from an episode of crying and inexplicable fear. At that time she went to a Spiritualist temple but the ministrations there had no effect on her. She then turned to the church, where she went twice a week to beg the saints to alleviate her condition.

Rebecca also consulted a specialist who was both a "doctor and sorcerer." This practitioner told her that she suffered from low blood pressure, and that her husband had another woman who was bewitching Rebecca. Rebecca avowed she did not believe in witchcraft, but it frightened her. She did, however, follow the sorcerer's instructions and she sewed a red ribbon in her husband's socks to ward off evil. This "doctor sorcerer" informed her that her condition was incurable. The practitioner prescribed vitamins, gave her a special cleansing, and ordered her to place a special platter under her bed to protect her against evil. This practitioner cleansed Rebecca with a special stone which she then burned. Rebecca's condition improved with these ministrations. Despite Rebecca's protestations that she did not believe in witchcraft, she retained her husband's untied socks the way the sorcerer instructed, kept red flowers on her table to catch "evil things," and placed basil around the house for the same purpose.

As with most all the other patients, the pains Rebecca experienced in her back and her feelings of sadness were timeless. Occasionally she would say that she had experienced these pains for a month; at other times, she indicated that she had been sick for eight years, or ten. Sometimes she dated the beginning of her sickness to when she got married, sixteen years earlier, when her husband beat her on their wedding night.

When she felt sick about a year ago, she had asked her husband to take her out to the movies. She didn't want to be in the house, but he did not pay attention to her. She recounted,

> And when he did take me out I felt worse; when I got to the movies I left in the middle and he got mad. He did not understand me. He said I will never get better. I didn't know what I wanted or what I liked. Two years ago, I was so sick that my mother and my husband had to hold me back. I was so bad that my mother didn't even pay attention to me because I was feeling sick every minute, and she told me to stop complaining. Then the earthquake made me scream. I was deeply affected by it.

Rebecca was born in Mexico City to a very stern father. A well-established weaver, he used to beat his nine children, including Rebecca. He even hit his twenty-eight-year-old son in the head. He never beat his wife. Rebecca was the oldest of the nine children, and she had to care for her younger siblings. After she finished high school she worked for five years as a typist until she married a boy from her neighborhood in a civil and religious ceremony. Her husband, a car mechanic, did not permit her to continue working after they married, and she remained in the house by herself, separated from her family.

When she was about to deliver the child who subsequently died, she was deathly ill at home. She attributed her illness at the time to the fact that, in her words, "I had not eaten, and I did not have any food for my children." She thought at the time, "How is it possible to be married and not have food for one's children?" When her husband came home, she told him she was deathly ill, but he left the house. When he returned, she was bleeding and she fainted; only then did he finally take her to the hospital. When the baby was born, it had blood coming out of its ears and the doctors could not do much for it. Rebecca blamed the nurse who, according to Rebecca, mistakenly bathed the baby and caused the infant to have an attack of pneumonia.

Since the child's death, strange things happened to Rebecca. Immediately after the child died, she became very fearful because Death had pursued her. A woman with long hair in a white dress stood at her feet, next to her bed, holding a sword. "I don't believe that I am subject to suggestion, but I know that I have seen Death and I was very sick then. Now I feel only nervous tension."

The pervading theme in Rebecca's discourse was her relationship with her husband, and she was very concerned about her sexual relations with him. Every conversation turned to her lament about the way her husband had treated her from her wedding night on to the present. On the one hand, as a good wife, Rebecca believed she ought to have sex with her husband, and she accepted the fact that "a man must have sex and therefore I must not deprive him of it." On the other hand, she could not bear having sexual relations. She stated:

> From our first night together I was strongly disturbed because he had no preparation for sexual intercourse. He didn't know how to do things, he was clumsy, and I would not allow him to do what he wanted. I didn't know anything and we fought. He treated me brutally. He beat me because I wouldn't let him do things, and I imagine this has affected me terribly the rest of my life. This was the worst thing that had ever happened to me.

We have relations every month or twice a month and that is bad. The truth is I don't feel any desire even when we have relations twice a month. I feel uncomfortable, but I have heard that a man cannot be without sexual relations for a month. The fact that he does not seek me out and he does not feel any desire for me is not normal. This depresses me because some people tell me that their sexual relations are very nice, and so I get depressed because I would like to be like them.

Rebecca recounted, "My husband beat me when I was seven months pregnant with my last child." During the course of their marriage, however, Rebecca's brothers have warned him not to beat her and he has not laid a hand on her for the past five years.

When he used to beat me I didn't even protest, or tell him that he was bad, that I was feeling bad. I felt that things had to happen in a marriage. I felt that it was normal. Since childhood I had many stresses and I thought it was supposed to be like this with my husband. All my life I had been scolded and told not to do this, not to do that, to get up, to sit down, sometimes it wasn't even words, it was just with their [her parents'] eyes. When I was a child I was very shy and I was even afraid to speak. Now I cannot stand up to my husband.

Rebecca believed that a good wife was expected not to say anything to her husband. Her husband's drinking added to the difficulties.

Rebecca "made many angers" and found herself screaming at her husband. When she did, he told her she was crazy. In fact, they had had a fight about three days before she came to seek treatment at the hospital. She had not had sexual intercourse with her husband for three months, and they had become totally indifferent to each other. Rebecca repeatedly made reference to the fact that her husband failed to have sexual intercourse with her. She reasoned that it was not necessary to have sexual relations. Crying, she said, "It's even painful, but it's the indifference that makes me sick." Rebecca, however, blamed herself. "I have made many mistakes." She had considered looking for another man, but concluded that "it would be the same, it makes no sense even to try to change things."

Rebecca had separated from her husband three-and-a-half years earlier, and after the separation she felt very good. But her husband took one of the children away from her, and she refused to give up the child, so she returned to him. Rebecca echoed a common theme in Mexico for why women remain with an abusive spouse when she said, "Children need their father, especially the eldest." She accepted this belief even in light of the fact that the father mistreated the elder boy.

Rebecca was troubled by her relationship with her children. Her

husband beat the two boys, especially the oldest one. She too had hit the
oldest child since the time he was small, but she could not explain to herself
the reason for doing so. She blamed it on her nervousness. She worried
about the boy because he was not doing well in school. She observed
wistfully:

> My husband gives them things, but he beats the eldest boy with great rage.
> The other day he kicked him in his testicles, and he told me that I should never
> interfere when he beats him. He does not do it often but when he does it
> frightens me. He hits them in the head. He hit the boy with a stick. I gave my
> husband a belt instead, because I prefer that he hit him with a belt rather than a
> stick; it is less dangerous. If he had been drunk when he beat him I would have
> excused him, because alcohol does not know what it does, but he was sober
> when he beat him.

Rebecca's eldest son was angry with her because she sided with her husband, and she commented, "I am between a rock and a hard place. I want to
embrace my boy and tell him not to cry, but I restrain myself because my
husband accuses me of spoiling him. I don't know what attitude to take
with my husband. He never touches the youngest child, the girl."

When Rebecca saw the priest of her church about her problems, he
told her to have patience with her husband. In fact, during the past years,
she had turned to the church and to the priest, who gave her advice and
even helped her economically; she was able to confide in him. More recently, she had had a falling out with the priest and lost him as her friend.

Rebecca's close relationship with her natal family sometimes alleviated
her pain. She felt closest to one of her unmarried brothers who also had
helped her financially. She visited her parents regularly, even though her
mother lost patience with her condition. Rebecca's husband had searched
for work in another state, but she refused to leave Mexico City because she
did not want to be away from her parents.

Rebecca's feelings of ambiguity toward her husband surfaced in every
conversation. For example, she said, "When he left at the time to look for
work, I felt relieved, but I also missed him, and when he gets sick I even feel
sorry for him." Not unlike other women whose husbands remind their
wives of their stupidity, Rebecca felt she was going crazy because, she said,
"my husband always tells me that I am stupid, that I am not good for
anything." She thought maybe he was right. "I confuse ideas, I don't even
know what I want, and what I am doing, if I want to go out, or want to
work, or not work."

The broader ideology advances the notion that women more than men are affected by poor marital relationships, and Rebecca's statement reflected this belief when she noted, "These problems affect us women more than men." Undoubtedly, this ideology contributes to Rebecca's acquiescence to the brutal situation in which she found herself, but in actuality the ideology mirrors the reality. The woman is indeed more affected than the man by the marital relationship. Whereas the man usually builds his life with another woman, as Rebecca's husband had done, the woman, if she replaced her husband with another man, would not be assured that her situation would be ameliorated, as Rebecca recognized.

Rebecca's pains were perhaps the saddest for me, even though of all the women I had known, her apartment and living situation were more comfortable than most I had visited. Afraid of saying anything to her husband, Rebecca remarked that "many times it is not the economic problems even though there are many, it's the problems of not getting along, of love."

When I entered Rebecca's apartment, I felt engulfed by a deep sadness as I watched her move in the apartment like a caged animal. Although Rebecca had worked in an office, she was unable to get a job at this time in her life. She recounted that about three years earlier, when she realized that her husband's treatment of her was not normal, she began looking for work. She responded to several calls for office workers, but she was told that at her age (thirty-four at that time) she was too old to work as a typist or secretary, relatively prestigious work for women from the working class, as she had done before. The only work available to her was as a seamstress, but she could not do this work because of the pain in her back. And she could not work as a cleaning woman, especially since she had worked once as a secretary, because it would have lowered her status. Besides, to get a secretarial position, she would need good recommendations, but she had lost contact with her previous employers. Nor did she have the proper clothes in which to present herself at a job interview. Rebecca lamented, "At thirty-seven a man is at his height and a woman is no longer anything at that age. And worst of all, to have gray hair, even my son remarked on that."

Since she was unable to find office work, Rebecca turned to the informal economy; she sold brushes and apparel door to door with money she obtained by participating in a rotating credit society. With the hardships of Mexico's economic situation at the time, she was unable to get even her family members to buy anything from her; her husband reminded her that she was not good at selling things anyway. The unsuccessful venture left her in debt.

Rebecca had no idea about her husband's earnings. She knew that he drank a great deal and that he also contributed to his father's maintenance. He usually gave her ten thousand pesos (three dollars) twice a week for her household expenses; but he did not even give her this amount on a regular basis. Rebecca's brother's financial assistance enabled her to maintain her household, otherwise she would have had no money for food. On the day of her sixteenth wedding anniversary, she did not have any money to pay the police when they brought her drunk husband in during the middle of the night and charged him with breaking into his own car. That day she had waited for him and hoped he would take her to the movies. Rebecca insisted that it was not that she did not want to "buy out" her husband from the police, but she just did not have any money in the house to bribe the police to release him.

Rebecca's sickness impeded her from carrying out her daily chores. She neglected the house and she could not do any washing; her house was in disarray. Her children took care of these chores for her. She spoke about feeling exhausted and her weariness was clearly observable. I saw Rebecca at two-month intervals, and each time she looked more worn. She was usually by herself in the entire compound, and she had less and less to do because her husband stopped coming home for meals. Rebecca's aspirations were minimal; all she wanted was to live with her husband happily and to be able to get the necessary items her children needed for school.

Analysis

Rebecca failed to understand why she was sick. She was, in fact, in conflict about the causes of her illness. She acknowledged that many people suffered as she did, and she could only conclude that she was experiencing a "crisis of nerves" that produced the excruciating pain in her back and her lack of desire to do anything. She sought other reasons as well.[9] On one occasion, Rebecca considered the possibility that she was nervous because of the economic problems she was having and the fact that she was dependent on others to survive. Ultimately she rejected the "crisis of nerves" explanation. She believed that the pain in her back could not be only nerves, and so she embraced the physician's diagnosis of a deviated spine as the cause of the pain in her back. At one point, she associated her disorder with her lack of sexual activity on the basis of the not uncommon belief in Mexico that sexual intercourse is curative for women.[10]

The hospital doctor treated Rebecca for parasites, although she had never complained of abdominal pains, and the orthopedist recommended a brace. She took the medications prescribed for her (antiparasitic medication, Naxodol, and aspirin) but she had no money to purchase the brace. In Rebecca's case, her visit to the doctor may have even aggravated her situation rather than alleviated it, owing to the physician's instructions for her to cease having sexual intercourse for several days. This order created a terrible problem for Rebecca because she was fearful that in the event her husband would want her at the time she was taking the medication she would have to refuse him, and, in her words, "he would get angry"; she was certainly afraid to ask him to take the medication as the doctor had ordered.

Rebecca could not comprehend that her husband was not meeting his obligations to support his family. She repeatedly observed, "How is it possible to have a husband and not have food in the house?" Her narrative focused almost exclusively on her longing for a loving husband, the way a marriage ought to be. He ought to support her—after all they were married by civil and religious ceremony—whereas in actuality, he treated her poorly by abusing her physically and perpetually reminding her that she was incompetent and mad.

Predictably, Rebecca did not improve during the time I knew her. On my last visit she felt worse than before; her back pains had intensified. She was home by herself because her husband no longer ate meals at home. She looked frightened and dejected, and there was a visible deterioration in her demeanor. Nothing in her life circumstance changed.

Rebecca continuously denied that her husband may have had another woman. She claimed it was impossible because he had no money to support another household. Yet despite her denials of this fact, she considered that the "other woman" was bewitching her. And, as we saw earlier, she had followed the doctor sorcerer's instructions.

We could attribute Rebecca's life's lesions to her own deficiencies and her failed development in childhood. Rebecca's affliction and anguish are more than the sum of her childhood experiences lingering on in the adult woman, however. Her harsh past did undoubtedly contribute to her present pains, and true, any dignity she may have had was beaten out of her by her father and later by her husband. To the extent that Rebecca had accepted her husband's vision of herself as incompetent and stupid, and blamed herself for her husband's brutal actions, we can hold Rebecca culpable for her condition. But if we accept, as I believe we must, that notions about ourselves are framed by others and by broader societal ideologies, then Rebecca's pains emerged out of life's lesions rooted in the disorders of her domestic relationship and lodged in societal ideologies.

Besides the poverty in which she lived and the death of her child, which aggravated her anguish, Rebecca was enmeshed in contradictions that immobilized her and registered as severe depression and excruciating pain in her upper back. The prevailing ideologies framed Rebecca's moral judgments. Her husband, unlike herself, had failed to fulfill his obligations to provide her what was rightfully due her as a wife—to be fed and protected. Pitted against this conviction were the harsh realities of her marital relationship, which from its inception festered at her life's lesions and sickness.

There were no medical treatments for Rebecca's disorders. She had few options, and certainly none was available until her children were grown. In light of present Mexican demographics and cultural comprehensions, women past their twenties lack any opportunity for gainful employment to help them become financially independent of their spouses. In the absence of such transformations in her life, it was unlikely that Rebecca would recover in the near future.

Notes

1. Pain in the lungs usually refers to upper back pain.
2. Her physician, like most hospital physicians I studied, usually diagnosed patients as having parasites; see Finkler 1991.
3. Mebendazol, an antiparasitic, and Farmeban (diiodohydroxyquinoline + dimethicone + methylbromuro of hematropine), an antiamebiasis.
4. Flagyl (metronidazole), an antiamebiasis.
5. The doctor's rationale for prohibiting sexual intercourse for the duration of the medication period was, he told Rebecca, "When you have relations, his penis will again get dirty, but don't divorce him if he does not want to take the medication, because it is his problem if you infect him. Let him wash his penis after intercourse with soap and water." If her husband had the same problem he could also infect her.
6. Buscapina, a popular brand of acetylsalicylic acid (aspirin).
7. Robaxisal (methocarbomol + acetylsalicylic acid), a muscle relaxant and analgesic.
8. Naxodol (naproxen + carisoprodol), a muscle relaxant with analgesic and anti-inflammatory action.
9. During one of our meetings, Rebecca reflected that she must have been suffering from a crisis of nerves because "I felt better after I talked to you [referring to me and my assistant]; our talk helped me a lot. I felt it brought me good luck to speak with you." It also made her feel better that I was present during the medical consultation, she said.
10. See Finkler 1991.

II. Juana: In Search of Dignity Amid a Garbage Dump

Of all the people I studied, Juana was undoubtedly the poorest. Twenty-six years old, with three years of primary school, Juana came to the hospital with her five-year-old boy, whom she was unable to control. Juana had crossed eyes, short hair, and an elongated, freckled face marked with brown patches and bruises, which could have been inflicted on her by a fall or a beating.

Juana lived in a two-room shack constructed mainly from stone and wood but with cardboard walls, an earthen floor, and a tin roof shot through with holes. A white sheet served as a door, separating her shack from the four neighboring shacks and from the garbage heaps scattered on an otherwise empty lot. Before the 1985 earthquake the lot had been a soccer field, but after the earthquake it was covered with debris and converted to a garbage dump. Juana's shack was cluttered with broken beds, a broken table, and a two-burner stove. The outhouse and water faucet were located about ten feet away from the shack. Juana paid 5,000 pesos ($2.50 at that time) a month rent for these accommodations, but she refused to continue paying any rent after her daughter was violated.

Juana had shared the shack with her mother-in-law and her family for six years. "Then there were problems because of the children," she said, and her husband's parents moved back to their natal village, leaving Juana's unmarried brother, who made no contribution to the maintenance of the household, in the shack. Juana fed him anyway because his mother minded Juana's children in her house.

On our first meeting, Juana's three children lived with her mother-in-law because Juana could not feed them and because they were being beaten up by the neighbor's children. Juana explained that one of her boys had "failed in school because he was hungry." The neighbors would tell the child that he was dark, but Juana noted, "My husband is dark, and I don't like when my child is insulted. He is dark [*negro*], so is my husband. The neighbor's children are light. What can I do with the child, kill it?" Juana was unable to visit her children because she lacked money for the bus fare to the village where they lived. Eventually, her children returned to live with her.

A recurrent refrain in Juana's narrative centered around her concerns about her health because, she said, "My children will be left without a mother. Their father is not concerned about them, and if I got sick what would they do?" Juana presented a series of symptoms, including pain in her back, heart palpitations, "pressure," headaches, faintness, shortness of breath, and feelings of desperation. She reported to me, but not to the physician, that her menstrual period was irregular. She also commented:

> I feel as if I were pregnant because I don't use contraceptives. When I don't menstruate I get frightened because I may be pregnant, and when I menstruate too soon I bleed very little and I am colicky. My heart goes "pum pum." I have pain all the time and I cannot breathe. It's been like this for at least a half a year, but recently it has gotten worse, especially at night. I get up in the morning with pain. When I was pregnant with my last child I fainted and I was told I had a heart murmur. I have not been sick like this before.

During a second doctor's visit, two weeks later, Juana reported that she had stomach pains:

> I have pain in the abdomen all day but it is worse when I get angry. I cannot breathe when I make an anger or when I want something and I cannot buy it; but then I sigh, and I feel better.

Juana, who described herself as "a very angry person," observed:

> I make frequent angers and then I feel my heart murmur. I make an anger when I go out to sell and I don't sell anything. I make angers because I haven't sold anything and he [her husband] asks me, "How much did you sell?" I tell him nothing and I start getting angry. I make angers when I don't sell and I feel that I stop breathing. I make angers when he comes back from work and then leaves the house. He tells me he is leaving for an hour and he doesn't return. He, of course, has the right to leave the house but I don't. When I make angers my pains in my abdomen are terrible, and when I feel sick I lack any desire to do anything.

Juana's pains lack a fixed time of origin:

> I have pain in my upper back because I worked a lot. I have done a lot of washing since I was a child. I began having this pain a half-year ago when I went to wash clothing for this woman, and her clothing was very dirty. I

worked from 8 A.M. till 6 P.M., and she gave me 2,000 pesos [75 cents]. The clothing was filthy. It was very difficult. Washing clothes is very hard. The jeans they gave me to wash were very dirty. Before that, I was well.

Later Juana reported that she began feeling sick when her now ten-year-old girl was violated by a neighbor's boy three years ago. Shortly after this unbearably traumatic event for Juana, she dispatched her three oldest children to live with her mother-in-law in another town.

Before she came to the hospital, Juana treated her back pains with a mustard plaster, aspirin, and an analgesic-antipyretic,[1] types of patent medicines that have become folk remedies. But these alleviated her ailments only temporarily. She sought treatment from a neighborhood doctor for back and heart pains and for "pressure." The doctor told her there was nothing wrong with her. "What can the doctor tell me? I don't have enough food and he gives me a prescription which I cannot buy. When I have an Alka-Seltzer, I take it and it partially relieves my aches."

Juana visited another doctor for her ailments. He suggested she exercise. She asked, "What kind of exercise can I do? I run around all day, and I am the thinnest person in the neighborhood. A neighbor named me 'The Board.' Running is for weight loss, what kind of exercise can I do?"[2]

On Juana's first visit to the hospital, the doctor concluded that there was nothing wrong with her; he prescribed aspirin.[3] On the second visit, when she reported abdominal pains, he prescribed antiparasitic medication. Juana, however, was most distressed by the brown blots on her face and she had wanted some medication to eliminate them, but the doctor ignored this concern.

The aspirin Juana was prescribed by the hospital physician had diminished her pain, but she continued to feel sick. She blamed herself for not getting well because, she said, she lacked money to refill her prescription. Juana added, however, "My headache disappears when I take Alka-Seltzer, but I observed that when I eat well, I don't have headaches or pain in the back of my head [cerebro]."

Juana, the youngest of three children, came as a child to live in Mexico City to help her sister when the sister got married. She said:

> I tell my children I did not have a good childhood because of our economic problems. When I bought something for myself, there were fights with my father. He used to beat my mother, and I tell them [the children], "You are living in glory when you are with me," if they ask me for something and I have the money I give it to them. I go to work and share my money with them.

Juana began working as a maid when she was ten years old. When she spoke of her symptoms, Juana remembered how "I used to wash forty-four-pound buckets of wash daily. When I left school I came home and I washed laundry. I always liked working and earning money but now it is different. Now I have my children, I cannot spend money the way I did before."

At the age of fifteen, she ran off with her husband, after having known the boy for a month. They went to live with his family. Now she deeply regrets having eloped with a man who did not care about her. She asked rhetorically, "But what can I do now?"

Juana's father had died four years before I met her, and her mother lived in another state (Puebla) with her sister. "My mother cannot read, and she is old. She cannot leave her home to come to Mexico City to help me." The sister who lived with Juana's mother was bewitched and she went mad. She broke people's windows. Her father had done everything to try to cure Juana's sister; he even sold his land to help cure her madness, but all the medicines made her worse, until she received a cleansing from a folk healer.

Juana lamented that she could only visit her mother on rare occasions, for the same reason she could not visit her children: she lacked money for the bus fare. She received some financial assistance from her only sister for whom she also worked. But this sister had very limited resources, especially because she was left with debts after their father's burial expenses were paid.

Juana was miserable living with her husband. In fact, soon after she had married twelve years ago, she had separated from him for two years because he beat her:

> He beat me because I didn't have children right away. He said to me that he married a man, that I didn't know how to have children. It took me a year to get pregnant and for this reason he beat me. He came home from work and he started to beat me. Then I had a child; now he does not beat me but I also don't let him beat me anymore. I live with my husband but it is a sad life. Many women leave their husbands and they go with this and that person but I have not considered looking for somebody else. I told my husband one day I will meet a man, but in truth, I wouldn't like to have another man's children, it is better to have children from one father. I will have children with another man and it will be worse. For this reason I just put up with it, endure.

Juana's husband was inattentive to her. She described his attitude by saying, "What ever I say, one ear in and out the other. He is out all day. When he comes home—late at night—he goes to sleep." Juana complained bitterly that in addition to not paying attention to her, more important was that he failed to assume any responsibilities for their four children, ages twelve, ten, six, and five:

> He doesn't even like to hit them [meaning to discipline them]. I hit them more than he does, but I don't like to do it. I do it when they don't obey me. The children don't listen to me, and it makes me very angry. I am the mother and father and he does not even care when my boy gets beaten up. My neighbor's son hits my son as if he were a dog and this is when I make angers.

Juana's husband worked as a day laborer—a painter's helper—and he earned about 39,000 pesos (about $18.00) a week. He gave Juana between 15,000 and 20,000 pesos a week (about $7 to $10). Juana declared, "And that does not suffice for anything, soap, oil, clothing, shoes." Her husband ate out at street stands and so she did not need to feed him with that money.

Juana said, "I did not want to have my last child. I did many things." She injected herself with various herbs, including rue, oregano, and also chocolate. Her husband's sister helped her with the injections but they were to no avail.[4] She continued, "Then, I was afraid my son would be born crazy because I did so many things. I cannot use birth control pills because they make me sick, they give me headaches. I had an IUD once but it fell out and the other one I took out myself. My husband wanted more children but I didn't because I don't want them to suffer any more." Juana was afraid to have a tubal ligation or a hysterectomy, but she warned her husband she would have one. She added, "Now my husband watches me," and for the past five years "he finishes outside me" (coitus interruptus).

Despite her unhappy life with her husband and her wretched poverty, Juana was most distressed by her conflict with her neighbor and her neighbor's children. Her neighbor had moved into the shack next to Juana's three years earlier, about the same time Juana developed all of her symptoms. In fact, before that time, Juana felt very well. Every time I met Juana she complained bitterly about the neighbor with whom she had to share water and an outhouse. She repeatedly told of how the neighbor's boy violated her little girl when the girl was seven years old. Juana recounted with great anguish how the girl remained traumatized:

> I can see it [the trauma] because she doesn't listen, she does not study, she failed in school. She doesn't have any friends and I am very worried about this because as she gets older she will go out with a boy and instead of behaving well, then what? When she sees a pair embracing or kissing, she remains watching them. I imagine that she gets anxious doing the same things and this

is why she cannot stop watching. That is the way I see it. I tell her never to allow boys to do anything to her.

Juana agonized about her daughter and whether she was still a virgin, even though a doctor who examined the girl assured her that the child was fine. Juana believed that something terrible had happened to the girl, especially since she saw blood in her anus at the time the child was violated. Since that time the child liked to play only with men. Juana said, "She even went into my father-in-law's bed and the grandmother didn't even want to keep her. She will get pregnant."

The child never told Juana outright what had happened because, Juana believed, she was afraid. The boy threatened her daughter that he would kill her if she had said anything to her mother. Juana went to the police and had the boy arrested but they released him three days later. Juana angrily stated, "He should have been punished. He wasn't because I didn't give them any money. I didn't have any money to give them. I think it's the obligation of the law to take care of it [such outrageous conduct]. My father-in-law told me I should have given them money." She took the girl to the police station for an examination and they said nothing had happened to her.

To Juana, her sense of dignity was central to her understanding of herself as a human being.

> I tell my children, "Although you are poor, you must be respectful, honorable." Wherever I worked I could have stolen money any time, but I never did. There are many things in the houses of the wealthy, but I never took anything. I say this with pride, I was appreciated by them. There were some people who didn't feed me and they paid me poorly. In those instances, I left after a month; but in two houses where I worked, the people were very good. I was never fired because of any bad conduct or bad work—to the contrary, they came to look for me in my sister's house. What is most important is one's honor [*Lo que vale es la honra*].

Juana, confronted by her neighbor day in and day out, experienced a sense of outrage because her neighbor's children failed to give her that "sense of honor," the respect she believed they ought to have given her. The neighbor's twelve-year-old boy made Juana furious and her rage became visible as she spoke. She declared, "He leaves me trembling because he sees himself equal to me and tells me that I am crazy. I am older than he and his mother does nothing about it. My neighbor is terrible. She talks and I cannot listen to her. I go out to the bus station and I collect things there just not to listen to my neighbor."

Juana tried unsuccessfully to protect herself from her neighbor. She sought a cleansing from a folk healer, and she asked the healer to intervene spiritually so that she would not be harassed by the neighbor. She asked the Spiritual healer to tell her what had happened to her daughter. Juana was skeptical about folk healers, however, and normally she did not seek them out. "They tell you things, they invent things, and I don't want to know these things. They suggest that somebody is 'working' [performing witch-craft] on you and I don't want to know that. I wanted to know about my daughter and they told me I have problems with my husband. I don't want to hear this. When I asked about my daughter they told me other things." Juana even went to the Shrine of the Virgin Guadalupe. For 1500 pesos (.60 cents) they gave her a red pillow to protect her from her neighbor, but even this talisman failed to ameliorate the neighbor's behavior.

Juana was unable to take a regular job because she had to attend to her youngest child, who was troublesome. She earned about a dollar a day helping her sister and selling candy in school:

> I go to my sister in the afternoons. I help her iron and wash, and she gives me food. I feel faint a lot, and I noticed that this happened when I didn't eat well. I eat in the morning and then I have no more money for food. [Her little boy gets breakfast from a special government program.] On Sundays, I go to my sister in-law and I wash for her. Everything I earn goes for food.

Juana could not return permanently to her natal village, as her mother-in-law advised her to do, because her husband would not permit her to take her children with her. She could not tell her family about her afflictions because she did not wish to burden them:

> I don't tell my mother about my disorder because she is exhausted and it makes her feel worse, and I don't tell my sister because she too has many problems. I tell my husband but he ignores me; he says, "Go to the doctor," but I tell him it's useless for me to go to the doctor if you don't give me money for the medicines. All he says is, "Go to the doctor."

Analysis

Juana's life's lesions with their attendant symptomatologies were anchored in her experience of hunger, her husband's debauchery, and her dilemmas relating to her neighbor, who, she felt, had stripped her of her dignity. Above all else in Juana's life, it was Juana's neighbor and the neighbor's boy who made her "cry from anger" and caused her pains. Her poverty numbed her and impeded her from exercising her role as mother the way she ought and she sent her children away. But Juana was most profoundly affected by her demeaning social interaction with her neighbor, from whom she demanded respect and dignity as her equal. Her moral indignation at her neighbor and the violation of her child were compounded by her moral outrage at her husband's behavior. Juana refused to accept her mother-in-law's complicity with the son. The mother-in-law reminded Juana that Juana had known her son was poor when she married, and said she ought to have looked for a wealthy man. Juana's response to her mother-in-law was: "I met him as a poor man, but it is one thing to be poor, and another to be irresponsible. If they told me that Miguel [her husband] was poor, I knew that, but irresponsible is something else. People call me stupid [*cabróna*] because I demand of my husband responsibility, and they tell me to look for a millionaire."

To make sense of Juana's life's lesions, we must attend to her poverty and her disabling physical deprivations. Had Juana existed in better circumstances, she could have avoided living in such close proximity to her neighbor and undoubtedly she could have more easily avoided the charged social interactions. We must equally consider, however, her moral comprehensions. Having been surrounded by poverty all her life, Juana accepted the actuality of her situation, but she stubbornly refused to tolerate her husband's irresponsibility and indifference: she despaired as a moral being over her social interactions intrinsic to living in human society, and when those relations were embedded in a garbage heap, the self-respect Juana longed for became buried within it.

At the time of my last visit to Juana's shack, about a year after I had met her, she reported that her pains had been alleviated. The circumstances in her life had turned around; they were as they ought to be: her children returned to live with her, her husband stopped drinking, and hence she had more money for food. She continued to wash clothing for her sister and sister-in-law. Most important, her neighbor had moved away.

Notes

1. Neo-melubrina (dipyrone).
2. Juana weighed 112 pounds and measured 5′2″. Her pressure was 100/70.
3. ASA500 (acetylsalicylic acid).
4. Abortions are illegal in Mexico.

12. Carlota: From Proletarian to Housewife

Thirty-year-old Carlota—short, chubby, freckle-faced, with long curly hair—had a pleasant smile and a twinkle in her eyes. She was, like Margarita, exceptionally articulate. Her extensive vocabulary was especially surprising in light of the fact that she was semiliterate and had only three years of primary school education.

Carlota, her husband, and her six-year-old child lived with her married sister and her two children in a rented cinder block house located in Nezahuacóyotl, one of the biggest poor residential areas surrounding Mexico City. The house contained two little apartments, with one room having been designated for a kitchen, and faced an inner courtyard where chicks and roosters roamed freely and where the cistern was laden with debris.[1] This dwelling, for which they paid 60,000 pesos (about $35) a month, was an improvement over their previous habitation, which had been constructed of stone, cardboard, and tin. Carlota, who regarded herself as being in a poor state of health, reported a series of symptoms, including low blood pressure, jabs in her chest, shortness of breath, dizziness, pain in her left arm, upper back pain, and pain in the back of her head (*cerebro*). She also felt that sometimes animals crawled in her head. Carlota reported to the physician that she felt "oppressed in my chest and tired, as if I had received a blow on my arm." The symptoms were aggravated when she left the house, and tended to subside when she fell asleep. Then she woke up feeling very tired, dizzy, and in even greater pain. At one point Carlota diagnosed herself as suffering from "dejection, what I mean is pressure."

After having given her a thorough physical examination, the hospital doctor ruled out heart disease because, according to his diagnosis, "there were no murmurs, and there were no pathological manifestations in the chest cavity." At first he concluded that Carlota suffered "from arterial hypotension, and intercostal neuralgia on the left side, originating from anxiety and nervousness due to economic problems in her private life." He attributed her nervousness to "her lack of money for rent and food to feed her children." Later, in keeping with this doctor's understanding of sickness as rooted in poor economic conditions, the doctor concluded that Carlota's problem was not of organic origin at all but "a problem of hunger."

The doctor assured Carlota that there was nothing wrong with her heart. He prescribed for her an antidepressant,[2] several anti-inflammatory medications, and a muscle relaxant.[3] He also ordered an electrocardiogram, and he instructed her to continue taking a medication prescribed by a private physician for low blood pressure. Carlota resisted taking any medications on the ground that a previous prescription from a private physician had, in her words, "made my breast explode."[4]

On all subsequent recall visits, Carlota reported that she had taken the medications but continued to experience the same symptoms. In addition, she developed pain in her spine. The physician revised his diagnosis on each visit. On a second recall visit the doctor diagnosed her condition as obesity[5] and "arterial hypotension," for which she had been treated before with a vasopressor.[6] On her last visit to the hospital, in the doctor's clinical judgment Carlota suffered from osteochondritis, because her husband was cheating on her and because she was afflicted with a "conversion neurosis." He arrived at the latter conclusion on the grounds that "the Evadyne [antidepressant] improved her condition" (Carlota had not stated that her condition had actually improved).

Carlota resorted to various home remedies and alternative healers to alleviate her symptoms. Her sister prepared cinnamon tea for her and gave her Coca-Cola, which she believed to be good for blood pressure because, she said, "It has cocaine." She had already seen numerous private physicians, including one at the Social Security hospital.[7] Each physician she saw gave her a different diagnosis, advice, and treatment. These many diagnoses only added to her confusion and distress. She had been treated with medications that, she claimed, had made her head "explode." At an emergency clinic X rays and electrocardiograms were taken, but these failed to show any disease. She was prescribed nitroglycerine tablets because she felt she was suffocating, and in the Social Security clinic she was injected with penicillin because, Carlota concluded, "I had amoebas and my pressure went down even more. I wasn't told anything else. You know how these doctors are, they never explain anything. To the contrary, when you speak they say, 'Yes, be quiet, I am the doctor and you are the patient.' They stop you and they don't let you say anything."

Some physicians told her she suffered from low blood pressure, another said she had cardiac insufficiency, and yet another diagnosed the problem as asthma. The hospital physician told her there was nothing wrong with her and that "the principal motor in the body," her heart, functioned normally. One private physician instructed her to stop washing laundry. It was impossible for her not to wash laundry, however, because she needed to assist her husband in gaining a livelihood, albeit without his knowing, because he had forbidden her to work.

Before Carlota sought treatment at the hospital, she saw an herbalist and a Spiritualist healer. The herbalist prescribed special teas for the nervous system and for rheumatism, but these remedies had no effect on her. Carlota declared, "People go to the Sonora market[8] and buy all these things and it is all cheating. They just take your money." The Spiritualist healer's ministrations had no effect on her condition because, she observed, "I don't believe in their ministrations, nor do I believe in homeopathic medicine."[9] Confused about all the medical diagnoses and having exhausted her economic resources, Carlota arrived at the hospital in the hope that there she would be told the nature of her sickness and that a cure would be found for her.

The onset of Carlota's sickness was not fixed in chronological time. Sometimes she said she had begun feeling sick immediately after the birth of her six-year-old girl when she had a curettage. At that time she was also told by neighbors that she was bewitched, but she did not believe in witchcraft. At other times, she claimed that she had started feeling these pains a year after the birth of her baby when the infant became deathly sick. Most often, however, Carlota pinpointed the onset of her pain to the moment when she had been fired from her job. At that time, she had also received "blows" in her heart, chest, and arms during a union conflict in the factory; she forfeited her Social Security health care benefits and had not worked since. "When I left the factory, that is when I really felt sick, and when I began suffering from pressure."

Before she fell ill, she would do all her chores and go to work even when she had a grippe. Nothing tired her. Now, her sister cooked the meals, bought tortillas, and even fetched her child from school for her. Her husband was not angry with her for being sick. She observed, "He knew how I was before I fell ill, how I liked everything to be clean. Recently I have neglected my house but he does not say anything."

During the time I knew Carlota her condition fluctuated. On occasion she would report she felt better, but later she would disclose that she continued to experience chest pains. The antidepressant (Evadyne) she was prescribed made her feel sleepy, although she noted that her "pressure went up," meaning she felt more spirited and more able to do her daily chores without her sister's assistance. Then the pains in the lower back of her head (*cerebro*) became even more acute than before and her arms continued to feel numb. Subsequently she revealed that her pressure went down, she felt dizzy, and her feet felt cold. She also felt sleepy and lazy. She ceased taking the antidepressant medication because she was experiencing digestive problems, for which she was treated with an antiparasitic. When the hospital doctor changed his diagnosis to osteochondritis, he eliminated the antidepressant and he prescribed aspirin. The results from the electrocardiogram confirmed that her heart was normal. This finding made Carlota feel worse, however, because, she reasoned, "If my heart is not impaired, then what is wrong with me?"

Carlota could not herself explain the reason why she was feeling sick. Her sister was convinced that Carlota was sick because she remained in the house all the time. But Carlota believed it was because of a poor diet in childhood, when meat was eaten only once a week. At other times Carlota wondered whether she was ill because, in her words, "I had amoebas when I bought food from street vendors when I worked in the factory." But when she remembered that she had been successfully treated for these parasites, she eliminated the possibility that her sickness was due to a parasitic infection. Carlota then considered that "perhaps it was hereditary. My sister had high and low blood pressure, but then I suffer only from low blood pressure, therefore, it could not be hereditary. Or maybe because I got tired from all the work."

Carlota, the youngest of twelve children, was brought to Mexico City by her childless sister with whom she shared the house. Even though she was only eight years old when she left her parents' home, she had not missed them. She recalled, "My mother had a lot of children, and she did not spoil me. She had no preference for any of the children, maybe because she had so many. All the children were the same to her. My father loved me very much but I don't miss him, I got used to it. He even asked for me when he got sick." Carlota stayed with her father for several weeks when he fell ill, but she refused to remain in the village as her father had wished. She liked living with her sister better than in her village in Puebla.

Carlota had a long work history. "I got tired of being a child and I started working." She began working when she was sixteen years old at a candy stand, and from there moved on to cleaning stores, working in a beer factory, and lastly working at the candy factory where she had worked since she was nineteen years old. Three years ago she and thirty other people were fired from the factory. The events that led up to the loss of the job and the actual firing were a watershed in Carlota's life, and she returned to these events on every occasion we spoke.

Carlota worked in the factory for eight years sealing candy bags by machine, and she met her husband there. She liked working and she liked her job. But she and her husband were fired as the result of a conflict between the majority of workers, who wanted to form a new union, and the shop union that represented the employer. She and her husband had not taken a stand but the owner had not believed them. Carlota recounted, "The opposing union sent strikebreakers to beat us, and it got violent. We demonstrated and we held meetings and we did not eat normally. One day fellow workers beat us up. The owner sent them because the owner did not want the union. I escaped but they even hit women."

Carlota and her husband were pressured from all sides. One day she was called in by the owner and asked to which union she belonged. When she said, "The same as always," he told her she was lying. When she heard from one of the employers that he did not care if somebody died in the conflict, she became terrified. "It gave me an empty feeling in my heart because it was even more serious than I thought. And I felt a great deal the loss of my work and I got sick." She repeated, "I felt a lot the loss of my work because I was accustomed to being an active person." Since the time she was fired, she said, "I became very frightened. I also got very sick, and I have been in the hands of doctors since then. I have not felt well." Carlota "made angers" at the time and she reported that "my mouth even turned crooked. I almost died of nerves, until one day my face and arms, tongue and mouth became numb because of all this tension, because they wanted to get rid of us. I started feeling dizzy, sleepy, and lazy and my pressure fell." She was warned not to make angers any more. "But what could I do? The loss of my work was very important in my life. I was used to having my money, and I was free to give something to my mother. At present, the economic situation is very difficult and my husband and I are left without work. We need to buy milk for my little girl." Carlota had not searched for other work because now high school certificates were required to obtain work in factories and she had not even finished elementary school.

When the couple left the factory they were given the obligatory severance pay, the equivalent of about one thousand dollars at that time. They invested the money in a small business selling clothing. That venture did not succeed because their child fell ill and Carlota became sick. In fact, they used much of their severance money first for the child and then for Carlota's treatments. As a result, they went into great debt.

After the strike, Carlota experienced another fright (*susto*) when her little girl almost died from a severe sickness. The illness of this child was particularly terrifying in light of Carlota's reproductive history. She recounted the great difficulties she had had bearing a child, and she was fearful that she could lose her only daughter. Carlota had had a stillbirth about seven years earlier and she was greatly saddened by the event. When she had a miscarriage, she was terrified by the heavy bleeding. She declared, "I had carried heavy things in the factory, that was why I lost the child." Subsequently she had difficulty conceiving, and when she finally gave birth to her one child, it was born with a urinary tract infection. Carlota reported, "She bled from the vagina and she was like a skeleton. I have never seen a child bleed like that. I got frightened." Carlota attributed her child's ill health to injections (she said progesterone) she had received during pregnancy to retain the child, because according to one doctor the medication had affected the child. Happily the baby's condition improved, and Carlota was even able to return to work after forty days.[10] Her sister cared for the child when Carlota went to work. For two years the child was fine, but then the girl became deathly ill, causing Carlota to experience the *susto*.

During the baby's second illness, Evangelicals came to pray over the child. They helped Carlota find a children's hospital where her little girl was successfully treated. Carlota attributed the child's recovery to the Evangelicals' prayers. She declared, "They don't believe in cleansings, in witchcraft, all they did was pray." When the child's condition improved, Carlota converted to the Evangelical creed and later convinced her husband, sister, and mother to convert as well. Her father would not join, however.

Conversion to the Evangelic church was yet another important benchmark in Carlota's life. Carlota provided several reasons for her conversion, including the fact that her husband was a heavy drinker. Before her conversion, her husband smoked and drank a lot and they fought:

> He hit me because of the alcohol, even though I was sick, and my sister had to protect me from him. My parents fought, and I did not want my daughter to experience the same thing. He disappeared for four or five days. He used to swear on the Virgin of Guadalupe that he would stop drinking for a week and he did. But then, after the time elapsed and he had fulfilled the promise, he began drinking again.

She wanted to leave him but she reconsidered. "What could I do, I cannot read, I have a child." After some debate he agreed to enter the church and then he was content. She remarked:

> When my husband entered the Evangelical church, he stopped drinking and he even started working. Our church teaches us to show respect to the man. The man ought not disrespect the woman because we are all human beings and we should not treat each other like animals. We were never practicing Catholics, but we changed a lot when we became Evangelicals. Before, we were always fighting with other people. I used foul language, even with my daughter. Since I converted, I stopped using vulgar language. I learned to respect people, and even when someone tells me something I don't like, I don't answer. I keep quiet. I learned to behave in a very different way.

Carlota pointed out that her church was "a church of order, not like the Catholic church that is of disorder. There are no drunks and drug addicts in our church. In the Catholic church they criticize others. We don't do that in our church."[11] When they joined the church, they entered a special literacy program, and both she and her sister were relieved when they learned to read and write. They remembered how embarrassed they had been by their illiteracy.

Both Carlota and her husband regretted not having more children. But she was told, she said, that "One cannot have children when one's pressure is low. Besides, I had a cesarean the last time and therefore I could not have any children in the normal way." After the birth of her girl, she had an IUD inserted but, she said, "My womb became swollen, and it [the IUD] was removed. Then I refused to use anything because it made me nervous. My husband watches me" (meaning they practice coitus interruptus).

Carlota and her husband have lived a peaceful life since their conversion to the Evangelical church. Her husband was concerned about her health and the treatment she received. He even accompanied her on office visits at the hospital, although he was getting impatient because he wanted to know what was wrong with her. Carlota had lived with her husband in a common-law marriage for seven years. Prior to giving birth to her daughter, she refused to marry him because she was afraid she would regret it. She did not care that she would not be married in "white" (as a virgin). But then when she had her child, they married in a civil ceremony and she said, "Now we get along well. He is not jealous. I did see him with a girl once and I got angry, but it wasn't serious and that is his character. Now, in our church, people can only have one mate so he cannot be unfaithful, and when they are they are criticized."

After Carlota's husband lost his job, he worked in a bar. It was dangerous work because he came home after midnight and at that time of night people could be robbed and killed. He was also not paid overtime. He could not find another job until he started working as his father's helper, cleaning floors and doing other menial tasks for 45,000 pesos a week ($20.00). Carlota's husband gave her 15,000 pesos (about $7.00) a week. To make ends meet further, Carlota, unbeknownst to her husband, helped her sister wash laundry. They charged 1,000 pesos (about 40 cents) for a dozen articles. Carlota also crocheted miniature baskets and flowers that were distributed to guests at weddings and at other family celebrations, for which she received about 4000 pesos (about $2.00) per thousand. Carlota observed, "I don't like to feel useless." She could only knit about 500 a week, earning 2,500 pesos (approximately $1.35). She could not crochet any more because she needed to take care of her other daily chores, which included daily attendance at church services at 5 A.M., preparing her child for school, cooking the main meal for her husband, and as was customary, taking it to his place of employment. Carlota reported, "I get up with a pain in my head, and when I wake up I feel like a drunkard. But I must fulfill my obligations. I have to prepare his meal and send my girl to school."

Carlota rarely left the house other than to attend church, and she occasionally went out to people's homes to proselytize. Carlota had minimal aspirations. She would like to be more active and improve her economic situation a little. She added, "I would not mind being poor, if only I were not sick and I could do my daily tasks with ease."

Analysis

On first glance, we can easily objectify Carlota's disorder by labeling it as classical depression, with its accompanying symptoms of sleeplessness, tiredness, and the typical symptomatology of Mexico, "low blood pressure." We could attribute her dysphoria to intrapsychic dynamics associated with early childhood experiences. True, to the degree that depression is associated with loss. Carlota's suffering may coincide with a psychoanalytic explanation of her condition. Carlota's suffering cannot be designated simply as depression, however. Throughout Carlota's narratives, the single most important themes of her narrative were loss of her work, conflicts at the factory, being fired from her job, and the blows she received during the strike. After all the years she had worked in this factory, her dismissal was contrary to her sense of justice and her moral sense. Her vitality as a worker was sapped and turned into inactivity, especially because she was unable to find new employment under contemporary economic conditions in Mexico. In addition to her moral indignations, Carlota also experienced inordinate fright when her child became deathly ill, grating further on her life's lesions and inscribing on her body the various symptomatologies she reported to the physician.

Carlota had not recuperated from these events even after her conversion to the Evangelical church. She claimed that the prayers she recited in church gave her a sense of tranquility but did not alleviate her pains. Neither the doctors, nor her newly acquired religion, nor her caring sister and brother-in-law, nor her husband could restore Carlota's balance. None of them could transform her back to the independent woman she once was from the dependent wife she had become.

Carlota's life's lesions were moored in Mexico's economic conditions and the lack of access women had to gainful employment. Within the confines of the economic currents, uneducated women's options are even more limited than those of men, as is reflected in Carlota's life. Although both Carlota and her husband lost their jobs, Carlota (unlike her husband who had been well throughout their marriage) had lost the economic independence to which she had become accustomed, along with her dignity as a person. She became newly dependent on her husband for her subsistence, eroding her self-respect and festering her life's lesions. Moreover, as the mother of an only child, a large family to care for was not available to offset the injury to her self-respect that accompanied her loss of employment. Carlota's sickness prevented her from having more children, which added to her anguish and aggravated her life's lesions in turn.

It is also highly likely that Carlota was engaged in the contradiction of both believing and disbelieving that she had been bewitched during the strike, particularly since she had become an Evangelical Christian. As an Evangelical she was precluded from seeking cleansings to remove her disorder. Carlota's inability to resolve the contradictions fueled by conflicting ideologies no doubt contributed to the persistence of her symptoms.

Given the conditions under which Carlota exists, there is no alleviation for her life's lesions. It is probable that as long as she continues to be confined to her home, her symptomatologies will persist intermittently.

Notes

1. Carlota and her family were the only people I saw who filtered the water from the cistern through a cheesecloth to eliminate the earthworms, tapeworms, and other debris before they used it for drinking and cooking.

2. Evadyne, a tricyclic antidepressant.

3. Naxodol (naproxen + carisoprodol), prescribed as a muscle relaxant; Naprosyn (naproxen), an anti-inflammatory; Robaxisal (methocarbomol + acetyl-salicylic acid), a muscle relaxant; Dolo-Neurobion (vitamins B1, B6, B12 + di-pyrone), an analgesic.

4. She had been prescribed a vasodilator for the heart.

5. Carlota weighed 146.3 pounds and stood five feet tall.

6. A.S.Cor (hydrochloride of d1-m-oxyphenyl (1) + ethanol (1) amino (2) (norfenefrine)), for arterial hypotension.

7. In Mexico two kinds of medical care are available—private and institutional. The latter includes government hospitals available to all Mexicans and hospitals administered by the Social Security system that are only open to employed individuals. For a full discussion see Finkler 1991.

8. This is a market devoted entirely to herbal medicines.

9. In Mexico homeopathic medicine is widely practiced and a legitimate alternative to biomedicine. See Finkler 1991.

10. "Forty days" refers to the *cuarentena,* or the customary time women usually are confined to rest after giving birth.

11. See Finkler 1983 for an analysis of the reasons why people in the rural sector join dissident religious movements such as Spiritualism. I identify the same reasons for people becoming Spiritualists as Carlota narrated to me here in reference to her conversion to the Evangelical church.

13. Josefina: "All My Life I Worked Very Hard"

In contrast to Carlota, who had wanted to work, Josefina had spent all her life working and she was tired. A forty-six-year-old mother of five children, Josefina was a big, chubby[1] woman with graying hair gathered tightly away from her face in a bun. When I looked at her high cheekbones and the high bridge of her nose, I saw the classical features of engraved Mayan codices. Josefina was an incessant talker and an enthralling storyteller. She needed no prodding to recount her pains and unfold her life. Yet, despite her intense absorption with her afflictions, the smile on her face conveyed a generosity and kindness of spirit.

Josefina lived in a neighborhood located on the slopes of a mountain at the northern extension of Mexico City, about half an hour from the last metro station in the city. The self-contained neighborhood was comprised of little houses and unpaved streets littered with garbage. Josefina did not have a permanent home. Sometimes she stayed with her son, sometimes with her daughter, and at the time we met, she resided with her parents and brothers in a compound. This compound was comprised of three small apartments surrounded by a wall and housed Josefina's three brothers, their families, and her parents. The families shared a cistern for drinking water. Josefina used to live with her daughter and son-in-law in a dwelling located on top of the mountain, which was difficult for Josefina to reach by foot. Her son-in-law had built an additional room for her, but during a recent rainstorm the tin roof collapsed on Josefina during the night while she slept. This event frightened Josefina and she returned to live with her parents.

Josefina experienced a multitude of symptoms, including pain in her lungs (referring to her upper back), dizziness, blurry vision, jabs in her chest, burning sensations in her hands and feet, and, as she put it, "pain in the mouth of her stomach." She repeatedly referred, however, to her relentless pain in the lungs. She cried, "I have done many things for the pain in my back, but it never stops." There were times when Josefina's "pressure" went up and sometimes down. At such times her symptoms intensified; her heart pounded and the pains in her chest became unbearable. "I feel fear [I am afraid]. I don't want to be left alone. I feel I will fall and I will die when I feel my pressure going up." Josefina reported to the physician that she felt very nervous because of her dizziness, dry mouth, and her desire to cry. "I cry because of the terrible pain in my lungs."

Josefina confided to me, but not to the physicians, that she was afraid she had AIDS and that she could transmit it to her children and her parents. She believed she had AIDS because her sister's husband was in the military and, she said smilingly, military men were afflicted by it. Josefina worried that her sister may have transmitted it to her. She was told it was incurable, and she had been sick for so long.

The hospital doctor diagnosed Josefina's problem as muscular dysfunction—resulting from a deviated spinal column that affected her musculature and nerves—potential hypertension and obesity, and aging. He urged her to lose 44 pounds, and he assured her that with the weight loss her pains would recede little by little. He warned her that if she failed to lose weight, she would develop "high blood pressure, throbbing in her ears, sparks in her eyes, dizziness, palpitations, arrhythmic heartbeat, muscular pains, and an unstable spinal column." The doctor observed, "If you didn't have that rubber [spare] tire you would not have any pain in your back." Later he also noted that she had gastritis.

Josefina disagreed with the physician about being overweight. Besides, the doctor had instructed her to follow an expensive diet which she could only keep for a month.[2] He prescribed a muscle relaxant[3] and ordered a series of blood and stool analyses, urine tests, and X rays of her lungs. He also referred her to an orthopedist. The results of the tests and X rays showed no pathology, her glucose was normal, she was not anemic, and she had no uric acid problems.

The orthopedist diagnosed Josefina's condition as a "deviated spinal column and a sprain" and told her that her muscles "were stretched out." She was advised to exercise and to place plastic bags with tepid water on her back three times a day. On subsequent visits to the hospital, the doctor prescribed exercise and medication for hypertension,[4] which Josefina could not afford to purchase. She was referred to the ophthalmology clinic because she reported, "I cannot see when I don't eat well." The ophthalmologist diagnosed her condition as myopia and he prescribed glasses. But Josefina could not afford to pay fifty dollars for glasses.

Josefina had seen numerous physicians and various folk practitioners for her pains prior to seeking treatment at the hospital. At home, Josefina massaged her back with alcohol and tomatoes when her pains were especially severe, and she drank herbal teas.[5]

Most doctors she had seen prior to the general practitioner and the orthopedist at the hospital had assured her that there was nothing wrong with her or her lungs. According to the physicians, she suffered from nerves and muscle pain. She was told that she was old and that her pains were also due to the onset of menopause. Josefina, however, claimed she menstruated regularly. A private cardiologist informed her that her heart was healthy and he concluded that she was feeling the pains because she must have had family problems. Josefina was decidedly dissatisfied with these diagnoses. Josefina wanted to know why she could not breathe, and why, as she said, "I couldn't even make angers [get angry] or experience fright." One physician prescribed a painkiller,[6] but Josefina informed the doctor she would not take any palliatives—she wanted a cure for her pains. She did take the medicine, but it had no effect on her.

Since these various physicians had not produced a cure, Josefina sought out a folk healer, who gave her an injection that made her feel even worse. The folk healer provided her some pills with a juice, but Josefina feared she could be poisoned and she vomited the pills out. After her encounter with the folk healer, Josefina returned to a doctor and he, too, told her that it was nerves. Dissatisfied with this diagnosis, Josefina sought the advice of a naturalist after having heard his commercial on the radio. The naturalist declared that Josefina was lethargic, but that it was nothing bad, she had just worked very hard and that was why she was so sick. He treated her with herbs, administered "little capsules," and explained that her blurred vision was due to a lack of calcium. He gave her injections to regain her energies and, she said, "to make me feel strong." This practitioner instructed Josefina to drink milk with lemon and garlic and to massage her back for thirty minutes with a cool iron wrapped in a towel. All these treatments and the injections were to no avail. In fact, they made her feel even worse.

Because the doctors could not cure her, Josefina sought out a sorcerer. The sorcerer advised her that she had been bewitched. "I was buried somewhere" (meaning in effigy). "The sorcerer told me I had the 'bad sickness,' two neighbors wanted to harm me, so they took my robes and made a doll from it and buried it." The sorcerer cautioned Josefina that doctors' medicines would not cure her, and he treated her with cuppings[7] and massages. He also provided her with two out of three injections he had prescribed for her. Josefina refused the third one because, she said, "the sorcerer would kill me." The sorcerer claimed Josefina was very nervous and lacked confidence in him, but, nevertheless, he promised Josefina to remove all her pains and alleviate her distended stomach, for a charge of 3,500 pesos ($2.00). When Josefina arrived home after her visit with the sorcerer, she felt worse; she could not even lie down and she developed a colicky pain. She shivered. She recounted, "My entire body was in pain, my whole back was sore from the cupping."

Josefina regretted having gone to the sorcerer. She didn't believe in witchcraft but, according to her, "there are people who don't like me and can harm me." Significantly, Josefina struggled with the notion of whether or not she had been bewitched: "The sacred Bible says that people who believe in this [witchcraft] do not have the pardon of God, but I am in pain. My father got angry when I went to this sorcerer. I believe in the doctors, but I was disillusioned by them." Josefina, a religious woman who frequently went to church, feared she would be punished by the saints for believing in witchcraft. She vowed to go to confession for nine Fridays and she alerted the priest that she would instruct her son to respect his wife, all this to atone for having committed the evil act of going to a sorcerer, who failed to relieve her pain anyway. She observed that her belief in witchcraft "just made me fight with other people."

When she told her brothers the sorcerer's diagnosis of witchcraft, they told Josefina she was crazy and that the sorcerer had deceived her because witchcraft did not exist. Her brothers were convinced Josefina was suffering from nerves. She reminded them that she had gone to many doctors and they were unable to treat her successfully. What else could it be then, other than witchcraft? Yet the sorcerer's prescriptions and massages with special herb increased Josefina's distress.[8]

When her private physician heard that Josefina sought ministrations from a sorcerer, he became angry with her. He prescribed vitamins and concluded that her disturbances were due to her age and to her "pre-menopausal" state. After this medical encounter, Josefina again sought a folk curer who gave her a cleansing and warned her that if she did not believe she had been bewitched it was at her own peril. By now she began believing that her daughter-in-law was bewitching her, not her neighbors. She stated: "I don't believe in this, but then I began believing that it was true. My daughter-in-law behaved badly; one who is poor is always badly regarded by those who have money. I am very poor, and her parents have money. They are well dressed, they have a house, and I don't."

While struggling with the possibility that her daughter-in-law had bewitched her, Josefina finally uncovered incontrovertible evidence to substantiate her suspicions. About two weeks before she developed the excruciating chest pains and the desire to cry, she had had a serious dispute with her daughter-in-law, with whom she had been living when she moved to Mexico City. "Since that fight, I have been sick.[9] But the healer saw that I did not believe in witchcraft and she told me that I would not get well."[10] Immediately after the cleansing the healer gave her, Josefina's condition improved; the pain in the back of her head (*cerebro*) ceased: "The iron I carried in my head disappeared, and my head felt light." Soon after the cleansing, however, Josefina's pains returned. She prayed to the Virgin of Guadalupe but her disturbances persisted.

After all these quests for a cure, Josefina's parents and her five brothers urged her to seek treatment at the hospital. She had spent a great deal of money on private physicians and the folk curer, but her distress was not alleviated. Following her first visit to the hospital, when we first met, Josefina made thirty-four visits to the hospital physician, one visit to the emergency service, and five visits to the orthopedist during the course of one year.

Josefina's anguish was suspended in the timelessness of her experience. When she spoke of her symptoms, time was obliterated. Her narrative moved from when she had married her first husband to when she had moved to Mexico City only about six months ago. Every time Josefina spoke of her symptoms she remarked, "I feel these pains because I have worked so hard. The type of work I had was not easy." She continued:

> Yes, it's my work. I carried a lot, and I didn't have anybody to help me. I couldn't breathe because I carried cement bags. I took the children to school, and I had to have a cesarean with the last child. I collapsed from carrying heavy things, and I didn't have any money. I didn't have anything to eat. There were days when I didn't eat anything, and this made me sick. Now I have this problem. We never had enough money, and I am tired. There were days I didn't have any breakfast. I only had tea, and I laid down, and I feel this was what had made me sick. I washed and ironed a lot. I am gravely ill.

Later, Josefina claimed she was sick because, in her words, "I am tired of renting a place, and once I was thrown out with my small children. I don't want to continue suffering, and I should not have worked so hard."

To make sense of her pains, Josefina recalled many other experiences in her life, and every biographical fragment referred back to her condition. She linked the pains in her stomach to the fact that she had not cared for herself after she gave birth to her children. When she spoke of her chest pains and her inability to breathe, she spoke of her first husband who had always threatened her. She bemoaned, "He always turned a pistol on me when he was drunk. At such times he wanted to kill me. When he was not drunk, he was nice. I feared him, and because of the fright, I have the pain between my breasts. That was about nineteen years ago. I suffered a lot with my husband." In the same sentence, she turned to a recent explosion of an oil refinery (the San Juanico gas explosion) close to her dwelling that had frightened her in the same way her husband had. Josefina observed that during all these frights (*sustos*) her body shook and she was left sleepless.

Josefina also attributed her affliction to the 1985 earthquake in Mexico City. It frightened her terribly. And both the earthquake and the explosion left her fearful and made her sick, because during both of the disasters her children were not home. Then she reflected that her pains were due to her worries about her children, because when they were small she was compelled to leave them by themselves so that she could go to work.

Josefina's pains intensified when she came to live in Mexico City, about six months prior to her seeking treatment from the hospital physician. She sought reasons for her deteriorating condition. "I was very sad, and I cried, I didn't get used to living in the city because I am used to living in small towns that are beautiful."

Occasionally, Josefina doubted her experience of pain and faulted herself for her condition. "My brother says that a doctor told him that we make ourselves sick because we pay so much attention to it [our sickness]. Yet I am in pain. My brother read to me that sickness begins when one pays attention to it. If one does not pay attention to it, the sickness does not exist. My mother told me that my nerves overpower my existence, but I rejected these suggestions." She asked, "But why is it that I am in so much pain if I am not sick? I feel I am." Josefina laughed, "It is the pain that produces the nerves, angers, and fears. My mother tells me not to pay attention to it, but I feel the pain."

In the final analysis, Josefina concluded that it was her daughter-in-law's malfeasance that made her sick. She said, "My daughter-in-law offended me when she told me that I had children from more than one husband." Moreover, the daughter-in-law allegedly hit Josefina's son, and Josefina reminded her that she needed to be thankful that her son had not abandoned her in the same way Josefina was abandoned by the boy's father when the children were small.

Conflict over class position also emerged in Josefina's dispute with her daughter-in-law. Josefina reminded her son that his wife's parents had more money than he, and he should not have married the girl because she was from a higher class. Josefina also reminded the daughter-in-law that she had informed her that her son was very poor, that he was not going to provide her with a big residence or a car, and that she needed to adapt herself to her husband. She reprimanded her daughter-in-law by saying that it was shameful not to respect her, as the mother of her husband. Josefina had done everything she could, with her brothers' help, to provide her son with a church wedding five years earlier, and she even went on behalf of her son to ask the girl's parents for her hand.

As a result of the fight between Josefina and her daughter-in-law, Josefina moved out of her son's house and in with her daughter, because the daughter-in-law "did not want to live with poor people." About a week after this devastating conflict with her daughter-in-law, Josefina developed the excruciating pains for which she had been seeking treatment for more than a year.

In addition to these woes, Josefina had "made angers" on other occasions as well, and at such times her blood pressure rose and she felt sick. She made angers when her children failed to obey her, and when her son got drunk and acted like his father, she hit him. When she made the angers her vision became blurred, she lost her appetite, her heart pounded, she trembled, she felt nausea, and she believed she almost died. She said, "My husband always came home drunk and I suffered so much, I don't want any woman to suffer as I did. My father never drank."

Josefina began making angers when her first husband left her and threw her out of the house. She could not tell him anything or scream, because she was afraid of him. She could only cry. It was because of this anger that she was in such agony. Josefina also made angers when she was criticized about being a woman alone, and when other women complained that she was interested in their husbands. Such accusations were unjust and untrue and they made her very angry and sick.

In speaking about her life, Josefina recalled:

> I have worked for twenty-seven years as a washerwoman, and I ironed and sewed, but I didn't like it. So I worked with bricklayers and I carried cement and lime. It was hard work for a woman. I got the job when they were looking for men and women and I needed work, and a woman who was in charge of women workers placed me there. My children were small, and I left them by themselves from 7 A.M. until we finished at 6 P.M. I got home at 7 P.M. and my children suffered from hunger. I used to cook at night. One time one of the

girls was sick, she did not eat, she fell from a chair and she died. So I quit. Then I returned to work and I worked until two years ago when I got sick. My son came and brought me here because I was still sick. I have not gone back to work since. I have worked enough. I was left alone with the children. And I made angers from all I had to do in the house. One gets very tired—sewing and washing daily.

Josefina was the fifth of ten children and remarked, "My mother raised us on breast milk and I thank her for that to this day." She had two years of primary school, but most of her childhood she spent working with her father in the fields. She remembered those years with fondness. "My father planted peanuts, beans, and corn. It was so beautiful. In September we had corn, in November peanuts. And everybody said hello. They would even feed one; here [in Mexico City] people get angry." Josefina longed to have her animals and live in the village again.

We were born in a small village. When my brothers grew up they came to Mexico City to live: they found this lot. They worked and settled here. Later, they brought my parents. I got married in 1970, and I left the village. We went to live in Puebla because my husband was there, and I got used to it. Sometimes I returned to my mother's house with my children, but my husband came and brought me back. I wanted to live in a small town where I could breathe the fresh air.

Josefina married her first husband, a sergeant in the military, in a church wedding only, when she was about twenty-four years old. The husband left her for another woman after twelve years of marriage. Josefina was very saddened by it because she had loved him. In fact, when she found out, she lost consciousness and then also her sanity. "I lost my five senses [meaning sanity] and I cried a lot for three months. I followed him to his work. I would talk to him in my imagination. I imagined that he was there. My mother said I was crazy because I said I talked to him when he was not there." Her husband left her thoughts when Josefina moved to another state to stay with one of her brothers.

Because Josefina was not married in a civil ceremony she was not entitled to support or health care benefits from the military after her husband had left her, which made her very angry. According to Josefina's mother, at that time it was not common to marry in civil ceremony.[11]

Even before her husband had left her, he did not always come home. He would leave for days before returning. There was only one year when they stayed together like a couple. She related, "I had nine children with him [all but three survived], but he was almost like a lover, not a husband." She was frightened often during her marriage and was often angry.

> He used to arrive with his pistol, and he was always drunk. He wanted to kill me, and it was frightening. He used to throw dishes; he had a gun. Once he placed me against the wall and he beat me and he also threw me out of the house. I was left outside, and I had to sleep in my slip, barefoot. Of course I cried, and I was frightened. He never allowed me to raise my voice, and I had to hold in my anger. I couldn't tell him all that I wanted to say. One time he beat me when I was pregnant with my now eighteen-year-old son and I could not breathe. My husband never allowed me to explain how I felt, I could never tell him that I was in pain and frightened. He would not allow me to scream and I made so many angers [stayed angry all the time]. I suffered a lot with my husband, that is why I feel the pain in my chest.

At the time Josefina had the caesarean for her stillborn child, she requested to have a tubal ligation done without her husband's permission. When he found out, he got angry and later abandoned her, blaming Josefina for the child's death.[12] This was the first time Josefina had had a child in a hospital. Previously, she delivered all her infants "with Mexican valor," that is, with her mother's and midwife's assistance and without any medication, since she lacked money to go to the hospital. Her husband was never present when she gave birth. Three of her infants died when they were four months old, and three died at birth. Josefina declared unequivocally: "The infants died because my husband abandoned me." She was gravely pained by the death of all her children.

After her first husband left her, Josefina established a liaison with another man, who was the father of her two youngest children, now fifteen and eleven years old. She reported, "I worked when I lived with him for seven years, and he turned out to be the same." He took her to live in his parents' house, where she stayed for two years. The man's parents liked Josefina because they did not like his wife, but she felt deceived. When she found out that her second husband had a wife she wanted to kill him. "If he had told me the truth there would have not been any problem."

This man's parents wanted Josefina to stay with them so that she would take care of them in their old age, and they would have bequeathed their house to her. She, however, could not abide by her husband's deception and she left him. "I suffered greatly," she said. When she left, the man wanted the children but Josefina said emphatically, "The children are mine."

She had had three children, one of whom died at birth, with this man. She cried at the death of the infant, but she knew that she had lost her child

medication nor folk curers can erase the life's lesions inscribed on Josefina's body, forged by insupportable domestic relations and endless contradictions. None of the practitioners Josefina saw could undo her tormented life.

Her past marital relations and the angers her relationships had produced cannot be eradicated from Josefina's memory by any practitioner. The pains inscribed on her upper back, perpetuated by her memory, only affirm and give meaning to the past injustices, abuse, and hard work she had endured.

We must consider some of the recurrent contradictions in Josefina's story with which she continued to struggle and which heightened her life's lesions. Most important in Josefina's case is the possibility that she had been bewitched, despite her fierce disbelief in witchcraft. In fact, her pains temporarily disappeared when her daughter-in-law apologized to her and her son asked her to move back into their home. But the lingering doubts continued, as can be seen from her statement that "if my daughter-in-law has done me this wrong, she will pay for it." The contradictions entailed in the simultaneous belief and disbelief in witchcraft could tear a person apart, just as they harmed Josefina. A religious woman, Josefina feared God's punishment, and she did not wish to regard herself as an ignorant woman. Yet so many people had told her she was bewitched because the physicians had failed to cure her.

The conflict with her daughter-in-law was not only a clash of personalities. Josefina's account of the dispute with her daughter-in-law reveals how women reproduce male ideologies. By accusing her mother-in-law of having children with more than one man, the daughter-in-law reflected and reinforced the male ideology of the double standard that women must not have more than one man. Josefina, however, reinforced the ideology of male dominance, when she in turn reprimanded her daughter-in-law for not obeying her son, whom she was required to respect as her husband.

Josefina's discord with her daughter-in-law disclosed how regnant ideologies about male-female behaviors guide women's interactions. It also informs us how class relations become intertwined with male-female relations and are transformed into sickness. For as we saw, during the dispute, Josefina repeatedly reminded her daughter-in-law that her son was from a lower class and she ought not to have married him. The dispute also reverberated on moral issues relating to the obligation of married sons to their mothers and wives, because Josefina felt her son had failed to assist her.

Why did Josefina miss each man when he abandoned her, after all the pain she experienced in her marriages? To answer this question, we must keep in mind Josefina's distress at being criticized by the neighbors as well as her parents for being without a husband. The criticism reflects the powerful ideology that a woman must have a mate, overriding all painful experiences. In fact, this ideology drove many of the women we have met, including Rebecca, Margarita, and Julia. Only the latter two successfully shed these compelling forces in their lives concomitantly with their pains, whereas Josefina continued to exist with this illusion.

Notes

1. Josefina weighed 160.6 pounds and measured 5'1"; her pressure was 120/80.
2. The diet prescribed for Josefina included a glass of milk in the morning, a piece of toasted bread, vegetable soups without fat and salt, beefsteaks, and apples. This kind of diet was totally beyond Josefina's cultural or financial possibilities. Her usual diet consisted of beans, prickly pear cactus leaves, and epazote with tortillas. The doctor asked her why she ate these things, and she stated she had no money for other foods.
3. Robaxisal (methocarbamol + acetylsalicylic acid), a muscle relaxant and analgesic.
4. Aldomet (methyldopa, an antihypertensive).
5. She drank especially arnica flower tea (*Zexmenia Pringeli*).
6. Prodolina (antiprinil + methylamine + methanol + magnesium sulfate), an antipyretic-analgesic.
7. Cupping refers to using a glass vessel evacuated by heat to draw blood to the surface of the body; it is intended to relieve congestion.
8. The sorcerer prescribed massages with *hojas de naranjo* (leaves of an orange tree), usually prescribed for nerves and as a purgative; sour milk with lemon; and ground onions.
9. According to Josefina, her daughter-in-law took a piece of Josefina's clothing without her knowledge, when she and her son were out of the house, and she placed it under Josefina's bed. This is a sign of witchcraft.
10. Josefina provided the folk curer with all the necessary ingredients for the treatment, including branches *arbol de pirul* (California pepper tree, *Schinus molle* L.), twelve chicken and turkey eggs, pigeon eggs, and turkey feathers. The curer provided the candles and, after some bargaining, she charged Josefina the hefty sum of 20,000 pesos ($10.00) for the entire treatment.
11. My experience suggests that the man may have already been married in a civil ceremony to another woman (see Finkler 1991).
12. It is not uncommon for a man to blame the woman when a child dies (see Finkler 1985a).
13. During the time she sought treatment for her disorder she was prescribed approximately 25 different medications, including vitamins, antidepressants, tranquilizers, antihypertensives, anti-inflammatories, antibiotics, and medicines for ul-

cerative colitis. The medications she actually took were Cimetase (cimetidine) a gastric or duodenal ulcer medication; Aldomet (methyldopa), an antihypertensive; Alboral (diazepan + dicyclomine hydrochloride + magnesium hydroxide), an antacid and tranquilizer; Viterra Plus, multiple vitamin complex, and Diprospan (betamethasone), an anti-inflammatory. She had her back rubbed with herbs, muster plaster and Vicks Vaporub.

14. During a follow-up visit with Josefina's attending physician a year later, he told me that she had come to see him on various occasions.

14. Susana: A Woman Who Ventured into the Public Domain

By any standard, Susana appeared twenty years older than her forty-six years of age. Her high cheekbones, wide nostrils, missing front teeth, sad gaze, long braids, and short, slightly bent body suggested that she had not lived an idle life.[1] Susana had resided for the past five years in Neza-huacóyotl with seven of her nine children in a three-room house that belonged to her sister. The sister and her family returned to their native village and left the house to Susana. The house was furnished shabbily, and pictures of Christ hung on spotted, whitewashed walls. Baby chicks strolled around the rooms and the sound of pigs and piglets could be heard from the courtyard. The water and outhouse facilities located in the courtyard were shared by Susana's family and her dead husband's sister's household that was situated in the same compound. Because Susana's children ranged in age from ten to twenty-four, contemporary rock music blasted constantly from one of the rooms. Occasionally, Susana kept her two married sons' grandchildren who lived nearby.

Susana experienced pains in her upper abdomen (*boca del estómago*), kidneys and lower back (*cintura*), throat (*anginas*), head, and feet, and she had lost her appetite. She arrived at the hospital with several pressing concerns. She feared that she suffered from diabetes because she had a fright (*susto*), and that she was afflicted by cancer, which would cause her body to rot. Most important, she feared she was pregnant because, she said, "I stopped menstruating for a year and my stomach grew. Yet how could this be, in view of the fact that I am old." The latter preoccupation led Susana to seek treatment in the hospital.

After giving her a physical examination, the hospital doctor concluded that she was not pregnant. He nevertheless ordered a series of routine tests, including a pharyngeal exudate and a glucose analysis, all of which were negative. The physician diagnosed Susana's condition as parasitosis (despite the fact that the results of her stool examination were negative) and emotional disequilibrium, because in the doctor's words, she was going through "the famous period of menopause." His final diagnosis was that there was nothing wrong with Susana.

The physician prescribed for Susana the customary antiparasitic medication[2] and a vitamin tonic, and he ordered her not to eat spicy foods. According to the physician, Susana suffered from digestive problems which she mistook for pregnancy.

Susana has not had many illnesses in her life and she rarely sought treatment from any practitioner. The fifth of thirteen children, she had a serious illness many years before when her younger brother had died. He followed Susana in age, and she was very close to him. Her mother had urged her to compose herself at the time, but for a while she could not. Since then Susana had not fallen sick.

To alleviate routine musculoskeletal aches, Susana usually took aspirin and drank cinnamon tea. When she visited her mother in the village, she would seek out an herbalist or Spiritualist healer who would give her a cleansing. These ministrations diminished her muscle pains even more than the herbalist prescriptions.

At the time I met Susana, she had been sick for about six months. She attributed her illness to several causes. She fell ill after her twenty-four-year-old daughter, who had gone off with a neighbor's son, was returned to Susana by the boy, who then ran away from the city. The boy's parents had disapproved of the liaison, and when Susana's daughter became pregnant the boy's mother denied her son's paternity. When the baby was born, the daughter could not even help Susana with housework any more. Besides, Susana was deeply offended that her daughter was returned to her and was no longer a virgin. She mourned, "Now the neighbors laugh at me." Susana consoled herself with the thought that the boy's mother had daughters as well, and, Susana said, "She will see how she feels when this happens to her." Susana suspected the boy's mother of having performed witchcraft on her, and believed that that may have been another reason for her sickness.

In addition to the calamity resulting from the daughter's failed liaison, Susana's twenty-one-year-old son was arrested on charges of public drunkenness six months earlier, and Susana was unable to get in touch with him. Her inability to reach her son had made her sick as well. Moreover, Susana had been frightened by the earthquake. All these events, including her younger brother's death, had frightened her and that was why she fell ill. She trembled, she was nervous, and she wanted to cry. Susana added that for these reasons "I also have parasites." She described herself as an angry person, and her current affliction angered her greatly. The sickness also frightened her, and she noted that she was in a state of fright (*asustada*).

Susana was born in a small village in the state of Mexico. When she was eight years old she came to Mexico City to live with her sister, who worked there as a maid. She left because her parents were very poor, and she saw how they had suffered. They had had thirteen children, and only a small piece of land, and they lacked any income other than the meager yields from the land. Shortly after Susana arrived in Mexico City she started working as a maid and earned seventy pesos a month. She recalled, "At that time it was a lot of money and I would give my parents one month's pay and one month's pay I kept for myself. The most I earned was 200 pesos, never more than that."[3] Susana's father died when she was seventeen years old and she helped support her mother and siblings in their natal village.

Susana had three years of primary school and because of her lack of education she was very timid. All she could do was work as a domestic until she married when she was seventeen. Her husband, a mason, had not permitted her to work, and in order to maintain herself and her children she took in laundry at home in secret. Susana smilingly observed that she used to go out selling candy when she finished her daily chores and returned home before her husband so that he would not discover her activities outside the home. Four years before we met, Susana's husband had died from excessive drinking. After he died, she began openly selling chewing gum and other sweets next to her front door. She had then moved her stand to the local market; more recently, she placed it in front of a subway station. This location proved to be more lucrative, enabling her to earn about 2,000 pesos a day (about $1.00 at this time).

Susana despaired when she lacked money, and she wondered why some people had more wealth than others. She failed to comprehend why she had so little even though she worked so much and so hard in her life. In fact, these questions presented dilemmas for Susana, which, as a religious woman, she resolved for herself by accepting the fact that it was so ordained that she needed to work.

Susana spoke little about her dead husband. All she had said about him was that he drank a great deal, that he was a womanizer, and that she had lost a baby about eight years earlier because her husband's other woman had bewitched the child. The husband occasionally beat her, and he did not give her any money. But Susana now had a boyfriend, a widower. She said with a mischievous smile, "I see him secretly." In fact, Susana giggled like a young girl when she spoke of this man. She was compelled to hide the man's existence because she feared her sons' wrath, as is usually the case. Generally speaking, children—especially sons—vehemently object to their widowed mother having a liaison with a man.

When Susana was sick, the children behaved a little better and they avoided making her angry. Still, Susana's principal source of indignation were her children, who often failed to carry out their duties at home. While her two youngest children, aged ten and twelve, accompanied her daily to work and helped her sell sweets, the two oldest remained at home to take care of all the chores. Three of her children were in high school because, as she stated, schooling is the only "thing I can give my children."

Susana felt close to her sisters who lived nearby, her eldest daughters (aged twenty-four and nineteen), and her mother. She was suspicious of everybody else, however, because she believed that she had a weak character, making her especially vulnerable to becoming bewitched.

Susana left her house every day at noon to set up her stand, which was located about two hours away from her house. She usually returned home at midnight because her stand was situated close to a dance hall, and at nights and weekends there were a lot of people around to buy her merchandise. She liked selling sweets and chewing gum, particularly because she lacked an education that would have permitted her to do something else. She, like Alicia, regarded her vending activities as an honorable profession. She always liked small commerce: "My mother used to sell rice and fruits, and she used to take me along to help her sell from the time I was small."

During the time I knew her, Susana and other street vendors were being hassled by representatives of the dominant political party the *Institutional Revolutionary Party* (*Partido Revolucionario Institutional,* PRI), as well as by the marketeers from the nearby closed-in, permanent market. The merchants in this market claimed that the street vendors (all women) robbed them of their business, and therefore they wanted them removed. Some people were beaten up. Susana remarked, "The market merchants were envious. The more people have the more they want. They are fools— they don't have to be out in the sun, or in the cold. Why don't they let us be?"

As a result of the conflict with the market merchants, Susana had become active in the Socialist party about a year before. She insisted that the street vendors ought not be stopped from selling in the streets because, and she reiterated a point she had proudly made earlier, selling was a respectable profession. The Socialist party (*Partido Socialista Mexicano,* PSM) mobilized the ambulatory vendors located within the area of Susana's stand

and took on their cause to defend them against the dominant PRI representatives, who required the street merchants to pay a user fee for each spot. Susana attended the meetings of the PSM, but sometimes she felt like a traitor to the PRI. She had no choice, however, because the PRI representatives were extorting money from her and the other vendors. She was frightened by all the political activity because she thought they would take her and her merchandise away. This contributed to her state of fright. Nothing was taken from her, however, and Susana laughed nervously when she recalled how she bribed the overseer with a chocolate, as she said, "to quiet him down."

During the period of our association, Susana became increasingly involved in the PSM's activities and she also later became active in supporting a maverick candidate (Cuahtemoc Cárdenas) for president, although she knew that "the PRI always won."

Susana was forced to keep secrets all of her adult life. First she hid her selling activities from her husband. Then she hid the fact that she had a boyfriend from her children. She also kept her political activities a secret from her boyfriend and she did not tell him that she was a street vendor. Susana's various secrets required her to juggle her life, but she laughed about it. In fact, I was impressed with how much Susana enjoyed having kept secrets from the people close to her, including her husband, children, and boyfriend. Her situation was indicative of the stealthy strategies women needed to maintain with men in order to accomplish their goals and also maintain their dignity.

Analysis

On my last follow-up visit, Susana was feeling well. Her pains had disappeared with the prescriptions she had been given, and she was relieved to learn that she was not pregnant. She declared, "The doctor removed a weight that was on me."

Unlike those of the other women we have met, Susana's life's lesions were not deep, because her life was as it ought to have been. Only when her daughter was returned to her had her life gone in a direction contradictory to the path events ought to have taken. Once her daughter gave birth to a child, Susana was content with having another grandchild. Her children often did not obey her, but she was able to control them. Susana was acutely conscious of the paradox that although she worked very hard she possessed nothing to show for it. She reconciled this dilemma through her deep belief in God who so ordered it and through her active participation in the Socialist party.

Unlike Josefina, Susana was not troubled by the question of whether witchcraft existed. She knew that there was evil in the world, and she needed to protect herself against it. Because her pains subsided with the medications prescribed by the hospital physician, Susana had no grounds for believing that her neighbor (the mother of the boy who fathered her grandchild) had bewitched her.

Moreover, Susana was able to make the transition from the private domain to the public sphere successfully, having been thrust into it through her vending enterprise. She relished her participation in the Socialist party activities, which also had given her life new meaning and helped resolve her contradictions through the magnitude of the movement. Most important, the party she joined addressed the very contradictions of the economic injustices that had long nagged at her. And her well kept secrets added to her prowess and sense of accomplishment.

Susana's life's lesions had not penetrated her body deeply and her pains were quickly and completely alleviated. Susana's political activities, her secret lover, and her presiding over a large household provided her life with a sense of mastery and coherence, which was further restored when she learned that she was not pregnant.

Notes

1. Susana weighed 137.5 pounds and stood 5′1″ tall. Her pressure was 140/80.
2. Vermox (mebendazole), an antiparasitic.
3. At the time, about $17.50 a month.

15. Norma: "I Have Found God"

Norma, a short, heavy-set woman[1] with curly hair and a smile on her face, looked perpetually bewildered by life. She lived in a rented three-room apartment on the top floor of a three-storey house in Nezahuacóyotl for which she paid 30,000 pasos ($15.00) per month. To enter her apartment, which was full of broken furniture, I passed the owner's house and climbed a ramshackle staircase. The well and outhouse situated in the courtyard were shared by several tenants in the house. Norma lived in constant fear that she could be evicted from the apartment any time if her landlady required it for herself.

Norma had been experiencing abdominal pains for three years, but she suffered most from unceasing headaches that were not alleviated with any medication. The pain was so severe that she felt she was going mad. They happen, she said, when "I have a strong experience or when I don't eat." She worried that her pains could be cancer, because the pain was unbearable, especially during urination. Her feet were swollen due to the rheumatism she had developed from washing and ironing other people's laundry and from leaving the house in cold weather. She was unable to sleep or breathe easily and she felt as if she were choking.

Previously, Norma had attempted to treat herself at home. She took medication prescribed for a neighbor.[2] Neither these pills nor the various medicines prescribed by the pharmacist[3] diminished her pains. About a year earlier, she had sought treatment from a Social Security service hospital and from government health centers. There she was given X rays and blood tests, and all the physicians told her that there was nothing wrong with her.

But Norma could not understand how the physicians could contend that she was in good health when she felt so sick. "The doctors say there is nothing to be done, but they say this because the doctors experience no pains." During her examination, their poking felt as if she were being stabbed, and the medications they had prescribed, which she could not name, had made her even sicker than before. "Then they said that it was a psychological sickness, that it was my imagination." But Norma did not believe that she had imagined her pain. She declared, "The mind could not do that much harm to oneself." She failed to understand why people would not believe that she was sick.

When the physicians provided no relief, Norma sought a folk curer who treated her for a "fallen womb" and "open waist" by cupping her lower back (*cintura*). She described her visit: "The curer placed me upside down on my head to reposition my womb." The woman placed a band and a mustard plaster around Norma's waist and also gave her injections. Norma was prescribed herbal teas, but none of these treatments lessened her pain or helped improve her condition. In fact, the injection and the various procedures carried out by the folk healer made Norma feel worse. "All this hurt me, and didn't do me any good. I felt sicker than before," she said. Upon the urging of her neighbors, she went to another folk healer for a massage, but this woman's ministrations also failed to relieve Norma's pain.

After the various therapies failed to alleviate Norma's anguish, she sought treatment at the hospital. Normal disagreed, however, with the doctor's diagnosis when, after a thorough physical examination, he had told her that her problem was a deviation of her spinal column. "How could this be?" Norma asked. "All I have done is to kick a stone one time. This could not have distorted my spinal column." The doctor explained to Norma that her spine was deviated not because of any bending she may have done but because she was obese. She was also diagnosed as having an irritated colon and parasites, and she was prescribed antiparasitic and anti-inflammatory medications.[4] Norma agreed that she must have parasites, yet her concern was not the parasites but the headaches. Norma's Pap smear, given routinely to all women seeking treatment at the hospital, showed she had a mild vaginal inflammation, but the doctor did not give this finding any attention.

Norma took the prescribed antiparasitic medication, but it had no effect on her feelings of suffocation and experience of dizziness. She continued to feel pain in the left side of her abdomen, although it was less painful a month later than when I first met her at the hospital. Her headaches were partially alleviated because, in her words, "my son gave me money to pay the rent." She did not return to the hospital for her last recall appointment because, as she told me, "I had no money to pay for the X rays that were ordered by the doctor. I needed the money for uniforms and school supplies for my daughter."

Norma's pains had no precise beginning; perhaps they began twenty-five years ago, maybe eight years ago, or maybe only three years ago. Or they may have started six months ago when she came to stay with her married daughter. She was certain that she had been having headaches for twenty-five years. Norma recounted,

> At that time, twenty-five years ago, my husband gave me a blow to the head, and since then, I have had excruciating pains. Some people tell me it is because I don't eat well, or maybe it's because of my vision, or perhaps the work (maleficence) of a ritual relative [a *comadre*]. When I experienced these pains before, I didn't give them much importance. My children were small, and if I didn't work I wouldn't have anything to live on. The work exhausted me and here I am now.

Norma also attributed her symptoms to having worked hard in a factory where she had to lift very heavy things. "I felt as if something just twisted inside, but I didn't say anything and it subsided. Then I felt like I was being jabbed by an animal inside my body."

In addition, Norma associated her afflictions with an abortion she had had when she was thirty-two years old. She was content to have had six pregnancies and four children, so she went to a folk practitioner for an induced abortion. The practitioner administered a quarter of a bottle of tequila and two capsules of quinine. The concoction made her feel as if she would die. She bled a great deal and was convinced that "something may have remained inside me." She thought that perhaps that was the reason she was having stomach pains and headaches.

Norma, now forty-six, had come to live in Mexico City about twenty-five years earlier. She came from southern Mexico, where her parents still resided in a small village. The oldest of five children, she ran away with a young man at fourteen against her father's wishes. "At that time, women had to be very submissive. When your father said you will marry this person, you couldn't say no, even when you didn't love the man you had to marry." Her liaison with the man ended in disaster. She recollected, "For the first three months I felt well, but then he started hitting me. Since then I have not had a peaceful life." After about seven years she left the man because, in her words, "I could not stand the beatings he gave me. They say the time has passed when a man could beat a woman. Now, the women beat the men."

After the separation, Norma left her three children with her parents and came to stay with her brothers in Mexico City. Her brothers would not assist her because she had left her husband. Norma needed to fend for herself and to make her way in the big city. She moved from place to place.

About fifteen years ago she married a man who, as she put it metaphorically, "began like a horse but ended up like a donkey." She was happy with this man until she brought her children to Mexico City. Initially, she felt she was "living in glory" to have her children close to her. But shortly after the children arrived, her husband became disinterested in her and "worthless." He did not beat her but he was very lazy and he drank a lot.

The man, father of her thirteen-year-old daughter, left her about a year ago, shortly after she had joined an Evangelical church. It was not quite clear to me whether Norma initiated the separation or the man just left. She observed, however, that when she entered the church she was told that it was wrong to cohabit with a man in an unmarried state. Besides, Norma's oldest son, who supported her, threatened that if she reunited with the man he would leave the house and stop aiding her.

Norma wanted to have a husband and had hoped that she would live out her days with this man. Now she could not meet a man anymore because she was too "old and rickety." She said of herself, "I am like an old car that is out of service," particularly because she had stopped menstruating five years earlier. Cessation of her menses made Norma feel bad at first, like a "dry plant that will not give any more leaves." Her husband had even told her then that she was no longer a woman, and at the time she had felt sad. But she had few disturbances as a result of the cessation of her menses, and added, "They say it is like that [not being a woman], but now I see it is normal, everything that starts must also end."

Norma had always worked, even when she was married. For many years she had a job in a shirt factory. But thirteen years ago her youngest girl was born with a hernia. The child was operated on and she had to attend to her at the hospital. When she returned to the factory a few weeks later, she was fired, even though she had received permission to take the time off. She found work in several "underground" shops that provided no Social Security benefits, but they all went out of business. She could not find any work in a factory. She turned to washing and ironing laundry in people's homes, and she has been doing this work for the past two years, but on many days her aches and pains have impeded her from working.

A year and a half before we met, Norma had become a member of an Evangelical church. She said, "Since I was a small child, I looked for God. I liked visiting the church, the priests and the nuns. I thought they would give me love, but I did not find it there." She realized that, in her words, when "you open your heart to God, you don't need people." An important theme in Norma's narrative focused on changes in her social relationships occasioned by her conversion to the Evangelical church. Whereas before she was concerned with her interaction with other people, after her conversion she concentrated on her relationship with God. She oscillated between blaming others for her misfortunes by accusing them of witchcraft, and blaming herself. When she converted, she said, "I no longer minded that people criticized me because they no longer interested me. As a result I no longer felt nervous." Before Norma's conversion, when she was a Catholic, she liked going to parties, drinking, and smoking. She observed,

> I had my freedom. I was happy. I was well received and I had friends, and when I die, I will have many masses and God will forgive me. Now [after her conversion] I know I cannot blackmail God. It's one's conduct and how one behaves. God will forgive if we don't disobey him that much. I believed in all the saints, but I didn't think I believed very deeply. I no longer believe in saints, or images made by humans.

Initially, Norma joined the Jehovah's Witnesses. But she did not like to go to that church, because everybody was well dressed there, and she did not have any money for good clothes. Her sister-in-law took her to the Evangelical group, where people spoke in tongues (Pentecostals). Norma noted, "When I was baptized there I felt the presence of God." She had not reached the stage of being able to speak in tongues because, in her judgment, "I don't have the faith that I can speak in tongues. When they speak in tongues, they are receiving the Holy Ghost. I have not received it yet. Before I came to this church, I was an adulteress, but not any more." Her lack of faith may be related to the fact that she had not fully relinquished her deep belief in the Virgin Mary. "She [the Virgin Mary] is irreproachable. Jehovah chose her to be the mother of God, she who is like a precious pure glass, a pure woman." But, unlike the situation in Catholicism, "in my church she does not have the first place, as does Jesus."

As a result of her conversion, Norma felt much more tranquil and she ceased to feel desperate. "At one time, I used to think it was unjust that some people have a lot and I don't. And I was very angry. I scolded everybody, and I was always in a bad mood and badly disposed to everybody. Now I don't concern myself with injustice. Now God gives me money for food, and if I don't have a house, I haven't earned it." She knows God will supply her abundantly and will not permit her to die of hunger.

> When I was a Catholic, and I believed in all the saints, I believed that people were bewitching me. I used to go to a sorceress to give me things to protect me against other people. But with the faith in Christ, I don't need these things because He is the best doctor. With faith in God, I know one human being cannot harm another. When one is Catholic, one is always afraid of being

bewitched. I thought my *comadre* [ritual relative] bewitched me. Neighbors wanted to harm my daughter, they threw things into her house, spilled special waters in her courtyard. But nothing happened to my daughter. They were pressed to move and everything went bad for them. With the belief in God, everything bad that should have happened to us happened to them. Now I don't have these fears anymore, now no human being can harm me.

Norma was, however, frightened that if she disobeyed God she would be punished and that she would return to her old way of life. She had, in fact, removed herself from her friends with whom she used to party and who would tell her that they had some very nice men friends for her to meet. Her current friends were the people from the church who gave her support and even assisted her economically. She claimed, "They help people find rooms for rent and to find jobs." To Norma's lament, her sons would not participate in her church, but her daughters converted to Norma's new religion.

Norma was promised in the church that she would recover. "Because God, the father, protects his children, I believe I will get well." She reasoned that her condition failed to improve, however, because she still lacked complete faith. Sickness and death were due to sin, and Norma felt she had sinned a lot and that she had not merited healing. "I did things I shouldn't have. I disobeyed my father and I married a man I didn't love. This was my first sin, and from then on there were more."

The two youngest of Norma's four children were her thirteen-year-old daughter, who was in high school, and her nineteen-year-old son, who worked at a food stand. Norma supported her family by washing and ironing laundry in different households. This job was difficult for her because she needed to travel to these houses and she could not read the street names. Somebody needed to take her for the first time and then she memorized how to get to the house. The work paid her a living wage and, besides, she observed, "I am too old to find any other job."

Norma's nineteen-year-old son paid for her medical expenses, such as the X rays and medications. Her married daughter and her one grandchild visited her weekly, and her youngest daughter helped with her household chores. To Norma's chagrin her twenty-three-year-old son took off with a married woman who Norma described as having "had a past," and she did not want that kind of girl for her son.

Like most of the women I interviewed, Norma had modest aspirations. She wished she lived in a house where she did not have to pay rent or fear eviction; she wished she had been educated so that she could work in a place that was covered by Social Security and paid her health care expenses. She wished she did not have to work now because she had done so all her life.

Analysis

Norma's life's lesions were rooted in her harsh existence with her husbands, coupled with her total economic and ideological dependence on them. Norma endured a life of misery with both of her husbands, even though she had worked when she was married. As a middle-aged and illiterate woman, she was unable to find a job in a regular factory where she would benefit from having access to Social Security hospitals. Ideologically Norma, like Josefina, was wedded to the notion that she needed to be married to be taken care of; her brothers reinforced this notion when she attempted to venture out on her own by coming to Mexico City and they refused to help her. But Norma could not be simultaneously mother to her children and married and protected by a second husband. When she brought her children to live with her, her husband, as she had said, became "a donkey," obstinate. He refused to care for her or the children. Her husband's reaction was not uncommon: men in the poor social strata usually refuse to assume responsibility for another man's children.

In addition, Norma's sense of culpability for having disobeyed her father grated on her life's lesions, adding to her suffering. Although the single most important theme in Norma's life at the time I knew her was her conversion, unsurprisingly Norma's life's lesions were not alleviated by this event because she experienced a new feeling of blame. Her conversion brought her into a new relationship with people and with herself. It removed her from the intense relationships with friends and neighbors that generated her fears of being harmed through witchcraft, and the change resulted in Norma's feeling "less nervous." But it transferred the blame for her sickness from other people to herself. She could no longer accuse her neighbors or friends for her misfortunes. Instead she reproached herself and her past actions for her lack of resources and for being sick. She blamed herself for having been a disobedient daughter and for having lived a life of "sin" without having the benefit of Catholic confession. Norma was encompassed by an unresolvable dilemma; on the one hand, she absorbed the

Evangelical teachings and ideologies, while on the other hand, at the time of our association, her conversion was incomplete because she was not totally possessed by her new faith.

The symptomatologies inscribed on Norma's body by her life's lesions were not easily treated by medication or by her transformation to a new religion. In fact, the religion may have created new dilemmas for her, especially that of assuming culpability whereas before she had felt none. Norma left for her village to care for her mother who had become ill, so I was unable to follow her for more than our initial six months. I expect, however, that she will continue to experience her symptoms, unless her conversion becomes complete and she is able to immerse herself in her newly found religion, which will change her circumstances and also give her existence meaning.

Notes

1. Norma weighed 162.5 pounds and she stood five feet tall. Her blood pressure was 120/80.
2. Naproxen, an anti-inflammatory medication.
3. Aspirin, Neo-melubrina (dipyrone), an analgesic and antipyretic, Conmel (dipyrone), an analgesic and antipyretic, and two others she could not recall.
4. Metodine (diiodohydroxyquinoline + metronidazole), an antiamebiasis, and Profenid (Ketoprofen), an anti-rheumatic.

16. Maria: Out of the Frying Pan and into the Fire

Thirty-three years old and married with two children, Maria was a short woman with short hair, a round face, striking white teeth, and a warm smile. She resided in a newly developing neighborhood that lacked drainage, tap water, and paved streets. Water was brought in by truck twice a week and stored in a water tank. There were only a few electric lines that serviced the community. Maria and her family had moved to the neighborhood about a year earlier because land prices were still reasonable and because in their previous home—a one-room shack with a tin roof—Maria could not abide the noise at night when the rains came down. Their present one-room cinder block house with an asbestos roof was sturdily constructed, painted in bright colors, and furnished with the basic necessities of a bed, tables, and kitchen stove. On the whole the neighborhood was peaceful, except for some incidents of assassinations. According to Maria's husband, the assassins were people dispossessed by the earthquake who had relocated to their community.

When Maria came to the hospital she felt bloated as if she would explode inside. "I felt as if there were a child inside of me," she said. The pain extended to her kidneys (meaning lower back). She said, "In the afternoons my stomach just grows, and when I sit it gets worse. I am also constipated a lot." Maria experienced headaches (in both the back and front of her head) and at night she felt rheumatism-like pains in her legs, joints, and spine. She was bothered by varicose veins, and she usually had pains in one ear that had been perforated when she was hit by a truck at age eleven. Whenever she carried out strenuous activity, Maria was in pain. She felt very tired. She also had fungi on her feet and vaginal discharges, but these signs Maria regarded as normal and not sufficiently important to report to the hospital physician.

The hospital physician diagnosed Maria's condition as "spastic colon, parasitic colitis, and diverticulitis." He prescribed several medications.[1] On

subsequent recall visits, the doctor prescribed another antiparasitic medication,[2] and when she reported that she was having menstrual pains, he
prescribed a painkiller.[3] The doctor also reminded Maria that she must not
gain weight.[4] The physician ordered blood and stool tests,[5] but all turned
out negative.

Maria, like most of the women we have met, had seen many physicians
for the symptoms she was experiencing prior to seeking treatment at the
hospital. She had been treated with numerous medications,[6] but none
relieved her symptoms. Her various diagnoses included "ovarian problems" and "chronic nervous colitis," and some doctors had just told her that
she was plagued by "animals in her stomach."

Four years earlier Maria had seen doctors in the Social Security service
office, where they had performed numerous tests and analyses. She took all
the medications prescribed, but she failed to recover. She complained, "I
was not told what was wrong with me and I want to know what is wrong
with me." She even had her tonsils removed on the grounds that with this
operation her condition would improve, but she continued to feel sick.

The Social Security doctors referred Maria to a psychiatrist. Maria
explained that the referral was made "because I didn't want to have sexual
relations with my husband. We don't have relations because I always
remember what he did." The psychiatrist and Maria "just talked."

> He asked me questions about my sexual relations with my husband and how I
> treated my children. The psychiatrist told me that I should change, but if my
> husband who has made me so [sick] does not change, and he does not see the
> psychiatrist, then what difference will it make? It is just talk. What for, I will be
> the one who will change but my husband will not. I told the psychiatrist that I
> didn't like being with my husband and that he was seeing another women, and
> he told me that we [Maria and her husband] needed to talk; that we should be
> calm about it, and when he said, "Well, maybe it wasn't true" [that her
> husband had another woman], I didn't return. He gave me advice on how I
> should position myself during sexual intercourse, so that I would not be in
> pain. If I put myself in front of him I would have no pain. He talked only about
> sex and why I didn't want to have sexual relations. I am feeling sick and he told
> me I should not pay attention to it [being sick] and talk with my partner about
> it. He asked me if we did not get along, did I think a separation would be
> better. I did not return to see the psychiatrist. It made no sense to return to
> him. Better to seek a specialist.

The Social Security doctors became exasperated with Maria and told
her not to return. She then sought treatment from a homeopath; she took
the pills he provided, but these ministrations did not alleviate her symp-

toms either. "We spent a lot of money but the medicine did not help me at all. The medicines even made me feel worse," she said. Maria's godmother was a curer, and she treated her with home remedies,[7] but these remedies too produced no effect on her condition.

On my subsequent encounters with Maria, she continued to feel sick. The medications she was prescribed[8] had a positive effect on her condition initially, but later she continued to feel as if she were going to explode. Everybody told her it was nervous colitis. She commented,

> The doctors always asked me what is wrong and I always tell them, and they tell me that with the medications they prescribe I will get better, but I never get better. Then they tell me I am nervous. But I tell them that I am not nervous and I feel the same. When I go to the doctor I get nervous because I am being told that I am suffering from nerves. By saying this, they make me nervous and they make me tremble.

As was the case with the other women we have met, Maria's experience of her symptoms transcended chronological time. Maria reported that she had been sick all her life. She remarked, "Since I have had the use of reason for twenty-nine years, I have been feeling sick. My mother took me to a folk healer, and she unsuccessfully treated me for bolus (*empacho*) and headaches; then she took me to a doctor and he treated me for ameobas."

On another occasion she said she had felt fine until sixteen years ago: "Then, I started feeling sick again right after I got together with my husband." Much of this pain was related to Maria's discomfort with having sexual relations with her husband. "He told me, 'You don't ever want to do anything with me,' but I tell him it is because of the way I feel. I don't do it [have sexual intercourse] because I like it, I do it because I have to, and I feel bad, bad." After her husband had sexual relations with her, she would lie down in a fetal position and, she said,

> My intestines became swollen. Now we have relations every two weeks, every month, or every two months. Also my children are a bit wild. All this makes me nervous. My husband's angers make me sick, and every time he changed jobs, his behavior also changed. Three years ago, he took up with another woman and this harmed me a lot. At that time I began suffering from colitis.

Two years ago her husband's body got burned. As a result of this episode Maria experienced a fright (*susto*) that made her very nervous. She noted, "I have seen many doctors and everybody said it was nothing but colitis." Many doctors and other people told her that she suffered from nerves, and sometimes Maria agreed. "Since I moved in with my husband, I have been feeling very nervous. He has a very strong character [meaning he became angry often] and it makes me nervous."

Maria lost all confidence in the doctors she saw because "they tell me it's nerves." But she was afraid of cancer, "because when one has cancer one's body disintegrates." She was also afraid of AIDS, which she, like Josefina, heard about on television and radio. Maria saw how terrible these people looked, and one doctor even told her that she had AIDS. She wanted to know what was wrong with her, yet no one could tell her.

Maria, like Josefina, was distressed that people refused to believe she was sick. "Everybody says I look well, but if they would only see me in the afternoons. All morning when I must do my house chores I forget everything, but after I finish feeding my family and after I sit down for a moment, I begin to have pains below my chest. Then I wake up at three in the morning and I have insomnia."

The recurrent theme in Maria's narrative was the pain she had during sexual intercourse. She narrated, "And then he [her husband] kept sending me to doctors. I stopped going to them and I bought the medicines without their prescription. But they haven't done me any good." Maria observed that although her husband was generous enough to give her the money for the medicines and the doctors, he refused to believe that she was having stomach pains and that she was sick.

Added to the other reasons Maria gave for her sickness, she also related it to her reproductive history. She had difficulties conceiving her second child, and she went to a folk healer who had told her that her ovaries were out of place. The healer repositioned the ovaries, gave her a cupping,[9] and informed her she would become pregnant a month later. She did become pregnant. After she gave birth, instead of observing the forty-day seclusion period, she immediately returned to her household chores. Maria supposed that perhaps she got sick because as soon as she left the hospital she began cooking and did not take her forty days of rest. She explained she had had to do her chores because there was no one to help her, and for this reason she also avoided having more children.

Maria had two miscarriages, and one infant died shortly after birth. Her first pregnancy went well but thirteen years ago, four months after the birth of her first child, she became pregnant again. She feared the short spacing between the children because she could not care for two small children simultaneously. Besides, she said, "I didn't want to have another child. I had a lot of problems with my husband and I didn't want another baby to be born." Maria's aunt instructed her to take some pills to abort the child. She took an herbal remedy[10] and aspirin, but this treatment produced no effect. She then took, she said, "some black pills that had skulls painted on them." After she took these pills she experienced "a burning sensation." She remembered, "I hemorrhaged severely. I didn't know what was happening but my aunt said it was normal. The following month I didn't menstruate because I continued to retain the fetus. A nurse placed a probe inside me and she told me that if the baby were born it would have been sick." The child died and Maria's husband blamed her for its death. She stated, "He was very mean about it and I cried a lot." Maria's fourth pregnancy resulted in a premature birth because, according to Maria, she fell. A curettage was done and she almost died. After that pregnancy Maria's husband had a vasectomy.

Maria was born in a small village in the state of Puebla but she had spent twenty-nine years in Mexico City. Maria's mother had had a little store in the village and her father had been an itinerant merchant. When Maria was four, her mother became very sick, and the store went bankrupt. Soon after her mother recovered, the family moved to Mexico City.

Maria had been raised chiefly by her maternal grandmother, whom she considered her mother and whom she loved most in the world. She recalled, "My mother had the store and helped my father when he left the village to sell his merchandise. For this reason my grandmother took care of us." The grandmother, who suffered from the same stomach pains that Maria was experiencing, and who died five years ago, used to wash other people's laundry and take care of Maria's eleven siblings. In the village Maria's grandmother had a little bar and Maria remembered that when she was very small "my mother gave me five cents and with this money my grandmother gave me a little shot of anis (anise liqueur) and Ron Pope (eggnog) for my stomachaches. People told me I was a crybaby, but I felt that with this drink my stomach pains went away. My parents did not progress very much"—they had not improved their economic position in Mexico City. Four years earlier Maria's parents returned to their natal village.

Maria recounted that her mother and father married at the ages of fifteen and sixteen respectively. Her mother bore twenty children, of whom twelve lived. Maria was the second oldest child and she was required to assume great responsibilities for the household.

> My mother had a child every year. My grandmother cooked and we, as the oldest, had to wash diapers, clean the house, and sweep and wash floors. When

my mother came home, my grandmother used to wait for her with a bowl of beans, tortillas, and salsa and my mother would bring meat or whatever else there was. I always had children in my arms as if it were I who had been married.

Uncharacteristic of most Mexican women, Maria felt closest to her mother's sister rather than her mother. She recollected,

> This aunt took care of us a lot. Our mother never gave us the love of a mother. She was never with us, she was distant because she always took care of my father. We did not count, only my father, and we had to take care of the children. She did not worry when we were sick, or whether or not we went to school, but she did beat us a lot. Both my father and mother beat us because my father didn't want my mother to have to do anything; we had to take care of everything. My mother always went with my father. So we always went to our grandmother and our aunt. They defended us and took care of us. Now, I get angry with myself when I hit my children, but I don't hit them any more. I think it's bad, and besides they don't allow it. But I was beaten a lot, all the children were beaten, except my oldest sister. She was better treated and she even had better luck in marriage. Besides, I don't want my children to be angry with me. What hurts me most is when I remember how my family treated me and that is when I feel worst.

A recurring theme in Maria's narrative and her constant lament was that she had wanted an education. Reflecting on her life as we talked, Maria said, "My trauma was that I always wanted to go to school and they never sent me because they had so many children, and because I was so desperate I went with my husband." In fact, Maria, who had only one year of primary school, was resentful that all her siblings, except her, had finished primary school. She stated, "They did not send us to high school even when the school was very close. My mother would not let us out beyond the gate of the house. More than anything, I wanted to study and work to help with the household expenses." She attributed her misfortune of having to marry her present husband to the fact that she lacked schooling. Maria's highest aspiration was to be a secretary.

Maria repeatedly stated that her life in her natal home was insufferable and that because her parents did not enable her to get an education she had no recourse but to run away with her husband when she was only sixteen. "I didn't know him. I just went with the first person who came along because I was so sad. I didn't have any schooling. Only now I am beginning to know him."

Maria has had difficulties with her husband, particularly revolving around sexual intercourse, from the beginning of their common-law relationship. She said, "When he is home I get nervous, I want him to leave because he scolds me when he does not have his food immediately. When he is home all day it's unendurable, he gets angry and he always reminds me that if I don't like it I could go. When he screams I cannot ignore it."[11] Maria observed,

> I felt a big weight when I came to live with my husband and it makes me feel desperate. If I had returned to my natal home I would have been treated the same way. Even when I go back now to my mother's house, she screams. She wants to keep us locked up so that we do the cooking for her. Everybody had to work in the house and I was bothered that she hit me and screamed. Even my husband defended me from my mother once when my mother hit me. I thought it would be different with him but it was worse. He doesn't let me out of the house, he wants his food exactly on time. I could never tell my mother that my husband treated me badly. The family would say that I left them and now I want to leave my husband.

When she came to live with her husband, who was five years her senior, Maria forgot everything her mother taught her about cooking.

> I didn't even know how to prepare rice and how to prepare the condiments. He demanded so much and he got angry and he threw things. I wanted to please my husband, I wanted to be close to my husband. That is how I got sick, how I got nervous. He was never loving, he never hugged me, he was very critical, he gets irritated quickly, he curses.

Furthermore, Maria's husband disliked the children, and he beat them often when they were small. "My children cried a lot and they were very sickly, this made my husband angry and for this reason he beat them. Now that they are bigger [fourteen and twelve] he likes them."

Maria's husband was once a very heavy drinker, but he stopped about a year and a half ago. The last time he got very drunk he and Maria had a terrible fight and she returned to her mother's house after all. Maria's husband, who was present during part of one of my visits to their home, said, "My daughter was upset to see her father stretched out in the street and she had to bring me back home. I started to think about my son and how my father drank, and I did not want the same thing for my son."

When Maria left her husband and returned to her village, he made a promise in church. He signed a paper in a Catholic church that he would stop drinking. Maria returned a week after he had done so. Aware of the problems drinking had caused, Maria's husband said, "When I drink I lose myself and I have problems with Maria, and I told her that I have not drunk and that I will not return to drink."

There are, of course, many pressures on men to drink. The husband continued, "The priest gave me a receipt and when I meet with friends and they insist that we drink, I can tell them that I made the promise, and show them the receipt and then they cease to insist. One loses one's friends, and those who know I don't drink don't come near me, they don't invite me." Recently Maria's husband made friends with a person from Alcoholics Anonymous and this has helped him to remain sober. Maria feared however, that when the promise her husband made to the Virgin expired, he would revert to his weekly drinking habit. She noted that every time her husband changed jobs he would consume more alcohol. Her observation is explained by the fact that when men start a new job they need to establish a convivial relationship with their co-workers, and men usually do this by drinking together. But even when Maria's husband stopped drinking and came home regularly, he mistreated her. He repeatedly reminded her that if she disliked his behavior she could leave. His major concern was to have his meals prepared. "The day you don't want me I can find somebody else to prepare my meals," he told Maria. But then Maria reminded him that he would still have to give her money to support their children.

Maria was not in contact with her mother and because she had moved to the present community she had lost communication with her aunt. Maria had only her husband with whom she could share confidences. Her isolation from the rest of her family aggravated her life circumstances. Maria's relationship with her husband became exacerbated when he established a liaison with another woman, a nurse, three years ago. Maria had not known about it at first, even though everybody else did. Maria was adversely affected by her husband's infidelity. Maria cried, "I did not know how to act. My father was always very loving with my mother until late in life, when my father found another woman. When he did have another woman my mother would not sleep with my father and they became estranged. My mother even left him for five years."

At first, Maria did not believe the rumors. Although she knew that her husband and her sister's husband talked of such things a lot, her brother-in-law had not told Maria anything specific. Then she spied on her husband to confirm her suspicions, although her husband denied the allegation. Maria confronted the woman, and she asked her why she wanted her husband in view of the fact that the woman was already married—after all she had a home and a husband of her own.

Maria had no doubts that people could perform witchcraft. Her mother's convulsions were caused by witchcraft done on her, according to her mother. Maria remembered her mother had dropped to the floor and fainted, and used to bite her tongue.

> During such attacks my grandmother gave her alcohol, onions, and massaged her. Then she took her to many doctors and they could not cure her, and that was why my mother believed she had been bewitched by my grandfather's lover. When my mother was thirteen years old she went to my grandfather's lover and told her to leave my grandfather alone. They had a fight and that is how my mother was bewitched. After my grandmother died, my mother stopped fainting. My mother always took medications, she was always sick, and she always felt bloated like I do.

Maria believed that she, too, was being bewitched. She disclosed, "things have not been going right for us, we are not making any progress [economic headway]." Although Maria regarded herself as very shy and avoided her neighbors for this reason, she thought one of the neighbors was bewitching her. "There are many bad people. The neighbor used to rob my animals and also broke my water tank. The neighbor was envious of my daughter because my daughter liked to bathe and to look nice. Every time she saw my daughter the neighbor made an anger and that is why I don't let my daughter out of the house." When Maria and her neighbor quarreled, Maria's husband always took the neighbor's side. "My neighbor was a common person without any education. The neighbor moved away and maybe things will get better."

Maria, unlike most of the other women we have met, has never worked outside the home. Her husband was employed for nine years in a tortilla factory, until five years ago, when he was permanently laid off. When he lost the factory employment, he also forfeited Social Security health benefits, which produced a tremendous hardship on the family's resources. At that time Maria, her husband, and her sister and brother-in-law set up a butcher shop. Her husband worked with the brother-in-law for six months, when, according to Maria and her husband, they were cheated out of their initial investment and pushed out of the business. Maria and her husband were left without any funds and they moved in with Maria's mother, who had helped them out financially. When Maria's mother left Mexico City, Maria and her husband built their present one-room house, where they have lived for the past year. Maria resolved the conflict with her sister over the business by proclaiming that it was the brother-in-law's and not her sister's fault. To sustain the family, Maria's husband rented a taxicab, which he drove only within the neighborhood because he lacked a driver's license. He also worked as an apprentice to a mason. He was unable to find a factory job because he had not finished primary school, and Maria and her husband pointed out, as others have done, that these days there is no work for people without some schooling.

Maria's husband, unlike many other Mexican men, wanted his wife to find work, but Maria claimed she was unable to take a job and also meet her husband's demands. She made and sold tamales for a brief time, but, she stated,

> He wanted everything done exactly on time, and I couldn't manage both. Then he would say, "Look, you are working and you earn so little," and I had to tell him that I could not maintain the house and make tamales, too. That is why I want my children to study so that they can progress [economically] a little bit.

To Maria's grief, "Life is always the same: monotonous. I only go out of the house to go to the doctor, to buy food, and to school meetings." She could not stop being nervous and sick. She contended, "One cannot change, one cannot change how one was raised, and how one lives, because the rhythm of life is always the same and even though the doctors tell me that I ought not to be nervous, it's very difficult because first, my husband rushes me, and he wants everything his way and I have the obligation to give him everything." During recent years, Maria had changed in at least one respect that was worrisome to her. Previously she could recall and repeat every conversation verbatim, but since she had been sick, she claimed she was no longer able to remember conversations. She felt her mind was failing her.

Analysis

The recurring themes in Maria's narration were her lack of education and her unbearable life with her husband. She wanted at least a primary school education, but her parents failed to send her to school. Instead she had worked for her parents since she was eleven years old. The irony had not escaped Maria, however, that when she did the household chores in her natal home everybody depended on her and she knew how to do everything well, but when she married, she could not do anything right. Her husband constantly criticized her and all that interested him was to have his meals prepared on time. If she was not willing or able to do so, he said he could always substitute somebody else.

Given Maria's physical and social isolation, her relationship with her husband became the focal point of her existence, an existence that since her marriage had gnawed at her life's lesions which may have been produced by her moral indignation that she, unlike her siblings, was deprived of the education she desperately desired. When her husband found a mistress, Maria as a compliant wife was of no value, which assaulted her moral sensibilities. She had faithfully fulfilled her obligations, whereas her husband betrayed her. Unlike most women, Maria was unwilling to submit to the sexual demands of her husband in light of her dislike of him, undoubtedly aggravating their relationship even more.

The medical profession provided little assistance to Maria. The psychiatrist's advice failed to address her suffering. On the contrary, the psychiatrist incensed Maria because the counsel he gave her to submit to her husband's sexual demands was one of the causes of her pain. Moreover, the various physicians' denial of her symptomatology suffused her pain even more. They failed to see that her lesions were not just "nerves," but the expression of angers and moral indignations about her helpless and hapless existence.

Maria's temperament was probably more suited to carving out a life for herself professionally than to being a wife. But in fact, Maria, like many women in Mexico, have few choices other than marriage. Maria's plight was to escape out of the "frying pan into the fire," in the absence of any choices available to her. The consequences were the symptomatologies registered by her body and expressed in her anguish.

On my last visit with Maria she began feeling somewhat better and less nervous because she and her husband had not had any fights and the children were more obedient. She did not make many angers and she and her husband had started a small business selling fruit. With changes in her husband's comportment, Maria's life's lesions may heal in the future.

Notes

1. Hemestal (1 (2,3-carboxy propionyloxy ethyl)-2-methyl-5-nitroimidazole), an antiparasitic, Oxibeldina (diiodohydroxyquinoline + Flalisulfathiazole + belladonna extract), an antiamebiasis and antidiarrheal, and Hidroxicina, an anti-anxiety compound.
2. Mebendazole.
3. Ponstan 500 (mefenamic acid), an analgesic.

4. Maria weighed 135 pounds and stood 4'9″ tall. Her pressure was 130/90.

5. He ordered standard blood tests and three stool analyses.

6. She had taken anti-inflammatory, antiparasitic, and antiflatulent medications, including Flagenase 500 (benzoylmetronidazole + diiodohydroxyquinoline), an antiamebiasis.

7. *Té de cancerina,* milkwood (*Asclepias*) tea.

8. Especially Oxibeldina.

9. See Chapter 13, note 7.

10. Goosefoot (*Chenopodium albam*).

11. The Spanish expression she used was *hacer concha,* literally "to surround oneself by a shell."

17. Conclusion

My aim in this book has been to deepen our comprehensions of women's lives and women's morbidity in a developing nation. I addressed the question of the disparity of sickness between the sexes. To begin to grasp this problem, I explored the meaning of sickness from an anthropological perspective. We saw that sickness is not exclusively a breakdown of the body's functioning, or the consequence of an assault on the body by noxious organisms. I proposed that, because humans have evolved as social and cultural beings, the society and culture in which they are embedded are extensions of the corporeal human body. For this reason, it is necessary to place under close scrutiny the individual's experience of his or her social and cultural worlds to discern an individual's life's lesions and penetrate the dynamics of his or her sickness, in the same way that we place physical organisms under a microscope to capture the characteristics of anatomical lesions.

I posited that life's lesions, viewed as the existential equivalents to noxious pathogens, become inscribed on a person's body as a result of a concatenation of factors, including perceived adversity, inimical social relations, moral evaluations, and unresolved contradictions between prevailing norms or between norms and lived experience. Life's lesions are shifting, changeable, and closely linked with a person's perceptions of his or her daily experience.

The concept of life's lesions eschews body-mind dualism; it rests on the assumption that to be human is to simultaneously perceive, evaluate, and embody the physical and social environments and to impose order on them. When the perceived order vanishes or recedes into the background, we experience disorder in our bodies; we become sick and cease to take our body for granted. Keeping these considerations in mind, I must emphasize that the ambiguities and complexities associated with life's lesions resist hierarchical classification and schematic representation.

Although this work is built on the efforts of many scholars, the notion of life's lesions emerged inductively out of the many life and illness histories I have collected, a few of which I presented here. With this immersion in people's experiences, I became convinced that life's lesions must be examined in tandem with physical insults to the body in order to gain an understanding of the person's sickness and its alleviation. In this endeavor, I have attempted to avoid ideological rhetoric and a priori fashioned conceptualizations of power and domination. Rather, I have scrutinized people's lives and the sense *they* make of their actualities within the parameters of the society and culture in which they exist.

My objective has been to present a snapshot of women's comprehensions of their experience, to illuminate women's health and show how women's sickness is intertwined with their lives. The aim is to pinpoint the subtleties of perceived existence associated with sickness. By so doing, we avoid reducing human pain and suffering to an amorphous and impersonal concept such as stress. Stress, of course, is inherent to human existence. From our early beginnings as hunters and gatherers we were faced with countless stresses. Similarly, the women we have met all live under stressful conditions. With the exception of Margarita, the women exist under various degrees of extreme poverty, and some, like Juana and Rebecca, even suffer hunger. The majority of the women arrived in Mexico City from rural communities at a relatively young age, and all ten women have worked continuously since their youth. Most of the women were abused by their mates. Foremost, however, is the resilience of these women and the ways in which they accommodate the miserable conditions of their existence. To regard them as victims of their environment is to do them a disservice. While we must never lose sight of the abominable conditions of these women's existence, we must also keep in mind that each of the women is, like all human beings, a thinking and moral being who is engaged in an ongoing process of judging the rightness and wrongness of other people's actions. Each woman knows the world as it is and also possesses convictions about the world as it ought to be. Each woman must struggle with ideologies laid down by the social history of Mexico. The overt similarities between the women that we note on first glance dissolve, however, into individual angers and anguish as we regard specific, subtle human experience that becomes inscribed on the body and expressed symptomatologically. There are disparities between Margarita's and Juana's torments, and the conflicts each woman faced explain in large measure their life's lesions.

Although both men and women experience life's lesions, my contention is that the actualities of women's lives as they unfold in the lived world—especially in domestic and marital relations and as reinforced by socially produced ideologies—submerge women more than men in situations engulfed by contradictions and in moral indignations that grind on their bodies and become expressed as non-lifethreatening subacute symptomatologies. On these grounds, differential morbidity between the sexes must not be reduced to artifactual causes, including that women more than men are able and willing to articulate their pains, that women may have more time than men to seek treatment, or that women seek to attain secondary gains by assuming a sick role. Barring women's conditions associated with their reproductive capacities and the fact that in contemporary society the woman's body has been brought under medical surveillance, women's experience of non-lifethreatening subacute symptomatologies must not be regarded as a pseudo-phenomenon.

I do not presume that men and women are inherently dissimilar due to anatomical and biological differences. I argue that women more than men are placed in day-to-day situations that offend their sensibilities, and women more than men are faced by inconsistencies that cannot be easily unraveled. The circumstances and paradoxes that shape women's lives ensue from historical processes and culturally produced gender ideologies. I presented various theories that attempt to elucidate the actualities and ideologies in which gender relations and gender differences are played out. As we have seen, there is no one theory that explains women's position vis-à-vis men in the past and present and in different societies. Women are not perpetually subordinate to men, nor are they in a position of powerlessness under all circumstances, Alicia being a case in point. Most theories, however, support the notion that gender differences emerge out of social-historical and not biological constructions.

We saw that women's subordination in the domestic sphere and the ideological underpinnings of romantic love in marriage became dominant themes in Mexico as elsewhere in the Western world during the nineteenth century. As a consequence of industrialization, complementarity of roles and economic interdependence were replaced as the mortar cementing marital relations by dependence and the notion of romantic love, which in turn led to the devaluation of women. Women in Mexico became increasingly removed from extended families, dependent on men for subsistence, and so vulnerable to the supremacy of the husband. The women we have met have each had to confront these prevailing ideological currents, which are also reinforced by the medical profession from whom they seek alleviation of their pains.

I submit that men and women are equally moral. Human beings in each society have imposed a moral order on the world and both women and men are engaged in making judgments about that order, about what is right and what is wrong. Each distinguishes between life as it ought to be and as it is. When this order disintegrates, the ensuing chaos on a social level is experienced as disorder on an individual level. The turmoil is recorded on the body and expressed symptomatologically. Certainly, the order comes apart for women more than for men within the domestic sphere. Men's privileges and prerogatives within the familial context promote abuse of women that provokes in women corporeal pain and moral indignations, angers, and sickness. The women we met were caught in a web of contradictory norms and discrepancies between what they knew ought to be and the actualities of their experience, which created disorder in their lives and in their bodies above and beyond their harsh conditions of existence.

There is a tendency in contemporary society to place the blame on the individual for the disorder he or she is experiencing. I propose that the circumstances as much as the actor are responsible for the disorder. To alleviate the disorder, order must be restored in the circumstances of the woman's life to the same degree that the individual must change. It could be argued, for example, that Rebecca's dysfunctions were rooted in her person and in her intrapsychic dynamics. While I do not wish to exclude these possibilities, I assert that the fundamental dilemma does not lie within Rebecca as much as it does with the circumstances of her life, especially her marital relationship.

A common Western therapeutic concept assumes that health—and especially mental health—requires a transformation of the self, reflecting contemporary assumptions about the nature of humans. Berger et al. (1974) have argued persuasively that the hallmark of the modern mind is its disposition to change. Modern humans are required constantly to remake themselves. They are never fully "baked" as human beings, they are always in a process of completion. Maria, like most Mexicans, recognizes, however, that her situation must change before order is reestablished in her life and her disorder alleviated. As we saw, Maria wisely told the psychiatrist that the transformation of herself will not relieve her condition unless her husband's actions change. Margarita and Julia provide us with excellent examples of the synergy between changes in the circumstances and in the person. These women were able to alter their circumstances, facilitated by the economic possibilities available to them, and gradually their ideologies and expectations of their marital relationships and their health were transformed as well.

A vibrant tension exists between the preponderant societal beliefs and an individual's subjective understandings of them. This strain manifests itself in my theoretical analysis as well as in the experience of the individuals studied. From a theoretical perspective, it cannot be said that human beings are mere sponges, passively absorbing dominant ideologies that they themselves create and by which they are encompassed. On the other hand, we have seen that human beings' understandings of themselves mirror extant societal beliefs and practices. A woman's appraisal of her being flows from the people surrounding her. The hegemonic view of women, the view in Western society, including Mexico and Latin America, was created by men. This view defines women as less than men and awards men the right to dominate women's existence.

In practical terms, the tensions we encounter on a theoretical plane reflect the tensions of the lived world. The tug between predominant ideologies and individual comprehensions foment life's lesions, as was the case for Margarita. She marched against accepted currents of the definition of womanhood, and the contradictions she encountered by doing so were at the core of her sickness. Thus although from a theoretical perspective the tugs between the individual life and society's definitions of it may never be actually resolved, in practical terms such tensions are the sources of life's lesions.

The lives of the people studied by anthropologists are usually bracketed by the people's memories and by a time period that corresponds to a research timetable. I presented the life of each woman as she remembered it and as she experienced it in the present. Needless to say, each life has no closure, it flows on, as does each woman's health state. Because we cannot predict what course a woman's life will take, we cannot predict the sickness she may experience. A woman's health status will vary with her life situation at a particular time in life[1] and with the actions of her mate and children. Attention to these nuances enables us to explain why some women experience more sickness than others. As I noted, in my previous work I found that women who experienced a sense of coherence, whose life was as it ought to be, including an absence of turmoil in their domestic and social relations, experienced fewer sickness episodes. We can also see from Margarita's and Julia's narrations that when women are enabled to alter their existence their health status improves as well.

The women we have met speak only for themselves. And yet, as I have shown, they also represent a large segment of society. We may then rightfully ask, To what extent can women's lives and health in this segment of society be altered?

The anthropological contribution is to illuminate the subtleties of people's lives and people's sickness. Anthropological analysis lends itself to identifying the issues more than to solving them. Like ancient biblical prophets, anthropologists supply incisive analyses of the quandaries but often lack solutions to them, perhaps because they recognize the complexities involved. In this as in all my previous fieldwork, I was confronted by ethical dilemmas, when several of the women who opened their lives to me asked for my advice about how to deal with their situation to alleviate their pains. The quagmires in which these women exist, however, lack facile resolution. Knowing their circumstances and their lack of options, I did not have any advice to give them.

For the majority of women I met, the socioeconomic and ideological constraints limit their possibilities and aspirations for transforming their situations and their sickness. When I asked women in what ways they would change their lives if they could do so, the question seemed puzzling to most. Their singular concern was dealing with their miserable poverty and feeding their children.

I could, of course, engage them in several sessions of "consciousness raising," on the commonly held assumption that to do so would benefit the women, for whom I had high regard. But as anthropologists we also recognize that the frequent attempts to raise women's consciousness in developing nations, to counsel them "to take control of their lives" and "to transform themselves," to regard themselves as autonomous individuals who act independently of a larger unit in which they are embedded, is Western presumptuousness.[2] We could instruct women to remove their "embeddedness" from family and transform themselves to individuated and separate selves. These, of course, are concepts derived from the Western contemporary mind.[3] Aside from the fact such advice reflects the anthropologist's conception of human aspirations and not that of the Mexican women, to promote these agendas but not provide avenues to carry out these newfound realizations is foolhardy. Such advice leads to frustration rather than to amelioration of the problem. What could we tell Juana, or Rebecca, or the other women we have met, unless we could also offer them choices on which they could act with impunity? Margarita and Julia altered their existence and their health because of the special circumstances in their lives that permitted them to accomplish the changes, whereas Susana was able to alleviate her pains by immersing herself in a movement that ideologically addressed the contradictions that grated on her life. As anthropologists we cannot remedy women's lives by altering societal ideologies, day-to-day relations, and extant contradictions. Nor can we single-handedly remove the women from their deplorable poverty. But it is at this elemental level that anthropologists, feminists, and others must address the issues rather than endeavor to deracinate them from their cultural being.

Not only anthropologists but also physicians lack remedies for these women's conditions. In some instances, the medical diagnosis may even aggravate rather than alleviate a woman's life's lesions, as for example a diagnosis of "obesity." Women seek biomedical treatments for their pain, but physicians lack medications to eliminate and heal the patients' disorders, because the biomedical paradigm fails to attend to the life's lesions that form part of the patient's sickness. It is not always medications that alleviate the suffering. What these women need is not medication but to change their existence to allow a restoration of dignity within the society at large and within the confines of their homes. In their cry for health they cry for dignity.

It is my hope that physicians would incorporate into the medical model the totality of human experience, and into medical history-taking questions that explore a patient's life's lesions, in the same way that physiological disorders are currently probed. Moreover, an important goal of this work is to help specialists engaged in implementing changes in developing nations become cognizant of the fine-tuned suffering that is not easily resolved with special programs. Too often professionals with the best intentions, and feminists wishing to alleviate women's anguish, furnish impractical solutions. Any alteration to women's lives in this social stratum must first come by laying the groundwork that paves the way for new possibilities and options. When more than one option becomes available, making it known to the women will be the real benefit.

When women are able to support themselves with dignity and able to assert themselves without fear, they will also be placed in fewer contradictory situations. At that time the disparity in health status between the sexes will disappear, and I anticipate that men and women will experience sickness on equal levels.

Notes

1. See Zavella 1991.
2. See Morsy 1991.
3. See Berger et al. 1974.

Bibliography

Abrahams, Roger D.
    1986   "Ordinary and Extraordinary Experience." In *The Anthropology of Experience,* ed. Victor W. Turner and Edward B. Bruner, pp. 45–72. Chicago: University of Chicago Press.

Abu-Lughod, Lila
    1991   "Writing Against Culture." In *Recapturing Anthropology: Working in the Present,* ed. Richard G. Fox, pp. 137–162. Santa Fe, NM: School of American Research Press.

Alcoff, Linda
    1989   "Cultural Feminism Versus Post-Structuralism: The Identity Crisis in Feminist Theory." In *Feminist Theory in Practice and Process,* ed. Micheline R. Malson, Jean F. O'Barr, Sarah Westphal-Whil, and Mary Wyer, pp. 295–326. Chicago: University of Chicago Press.

Amkraut, Alfred and George F. Solomon
    1975   "From the Symbolic Stimulus to the Pathophysiologic Response: Immune Mechanisms." *International Journal of Psychiatry in Medicine* 5:541–563.

Anderson, Joan M.
    1991   "Women's Perspectives on Chronic Illness: Ethnicity, Ideology and Restructuring of Life." *Social Science and Medicine* 33 (2):101–113.

Antonovsky, Aaron
    1979   *Health, Stress and Coping.* San Francisco: Jossey-Bass Publishers.

Apple, Rima D., ed.
    1990   *Women, Health, and Medicine in America: A Historical Handbook.* New York: Garland Publishers.

Armitage, Karen, Lawrence J. Schneiderman, and Robert A. Bass
    1979   "Response of Physicians to Medical Complaints in Men and Women." *Journal of the American Medical Association* 241:2185–2187.

Arrom, Sylvia Marina
    1985   *The Women of Mexico City, 1790–1857.* Stanford, CA: Stanford University Press.

Banerji, Bebabar
    1984   "The Political Economy of Western Medicine in Third World Countries." In *Issues in the Political Economy of Health Care,* ed. John B. McKinlay, pp. 257–282. New York: Tavistock Publications.

Barrios de Chungara, Domitila, with Moema Viezzer
    1978   *Let Me Speak: Testimony of Domitila, a Woman of the Bolivian Mines.* New York and London: Monthly Review Press.

Bebbington, Paul E.
   1978   "Epidemiology of Depressive Disorders." *Culture, Medicine and Psychiatry* 4:297–341.
Belenky, Mary Field et al.
   1986   *Women's Ways of Knowing: The Development of Self, Voice and Mind.* New York: Basic Books.
Bellah, Robert N., Richard Madsen, William M. Sullivan, Ann Swidler, and Steven M. Tipson
   1985   *Habits of the Heart: Individualism and Commitment in American Life* Berkeley: University of California Press.
Benería, Lourdes and Martha Roldán
   1987   *The Crossroads of Class and Gender: Industrial Homework, Subcontracting, and Household Dynamics in Mexico City.* Chicago: University of Chicago Press.
Berger, Peter L. and Thomas Luckmann
   1967   *The Social Construction of Reality: A Treatise in the Sociology of Knowledge* Garden City, NY: Anchor Books.
Berger, Peter, Brigitte Berger, and Hansfried Kellner
   1974   *The Homeless Mind: Modernization and Consciousness* New York: Vintage Books.
Berkman, Lisa F.
   1984   "Assessing the Physical Health Effects of Social Networks and Social Support." *Annual Review of Public Health* 5:413–432.
Berkman, Lisa F. and Lester Breslow
   1983   *Health and Ways of Living: The Alameda County Study* New York: Oxford University Press.
Bibeau, Gilles
   1990   "Being Affected by the Other." *Culture, Medicine and Psychiatry* 14 (2):299–310.
Birley, J. C. T. and J. Connolly
   1976   "Life Events and Physical Illness." In *Modern Trends in Psychosomatic Medicine,* ed. Oscar Hill. London: Butterworth.
Bossen, Laurel
   1975   "Women in Modernizing Societies." *American Ethnologist* 2(4):587–601.
Boyer, Richard
   1989   "Women, *La Mala Vida,* and the Politics of Marriage." In *Sexuality and Marriage in Colonial Latin America,* ed. Asunción Lavrin, pp. 252–286. Lincoln: University of Nebraska Press.
Brandes, Stanley
   1981   "Like Wounded Stags: Male Sexual Ideology in an Andalusian Town." In *Sexual Meanings: The Cultural Construction of Gender and Sexuality,* ed. Sherry B. Ortner and Harriet Whitehead, pp. 216–239. Cambridge: Cambridge University Press.
Briscoe, Monica E.
   1987   "Why Do People Go to the Doctor? Sex Differences in the Correlates of GP Consultation." *Social Science and Medicine* 25(5):507–513.

Brodman, Keeve et al.
    1952   "The Cornell Medical Index Health Questionnaire III: The Evaluation
            of Emotional Disturbances." *Journal of Clinical Psychiatry* 8:119–124.
Brody, Howard
    1987   *Stories of Sickness.* New Haven, CT: Yale University Press.
Brown, George William
    1974a   "Meaning, Measurement and Stress of Life Events." In *Stressful Life
            Events, Their Nature and Effects,* ed. Barbara Snell Dohrenwend and
            Bruce P. Dohrenwend, pp. 217–244. New York: John Wiley and Sons.
    1974b   "Life Events and the Onset of Depressive and Schizophrenic Condi-
            tions." In *Life Stress and Illness,* ed. E. K. Eric Gunderson and Rich-
            ard H. Rahe, pp. 163–188. Springfield, IL: Charles C. Thomas.
Brown, George William and Tirril O. Harris
    1978   *Social Origins of Depression: A Study of Psychiatric Disorder in Women*
            New York: Free Press.
Browner, Carole H.
    1989   "Women, Household and Health in Latin America." *Social Science and
            Medicine* 28(5):461–473.
Browner, Carole H. and Ellen Lewin
    1982   "Female Altruism Reconsidered: The Virgin Mary as Economic
            Woman." *American Ethnologist* 9(1):61–75.
Browner, Carole H. and Carolyn F. Sargent
    1990   *Anthropology and Studies of Human Reproduction.* New York: Green-
            wood Press.
Bryant, Christopher G. A. and David Jary
    1991   *Giddens' Theory of Structuration: A Critical Appreciation.* London and
            New York: Routledge.
Buckley, Thomas and Alma Gottlieb, eds.
    1988   *Blood Magic: The Anthropology of Menstruation.* Berkeley: University of
            California Press.
Cancian, Francesca M.
    1985   "Gender Politics: Love and Power in the Private and Public Spheres."
            In *Gender and the Life Course,* ed. Alice S. Rossi, pp. 253–264. New
            York: Aldine.
Cassell, Eric J.
    1976   "Disease as an 'It': Concepts of Disease Revealed by Patients' Presen-
            tation of Symptoms." *Social Science and Medicine* 10:143–146.
    1991   *The Nature of Suffering and the Goals of Medicine.* New York: Oxford
            University Press.
Cassell, John
    1974   "Psychosocial Processes and Stress: Theoretical Formulation." *Inter-
            national Journal of Health Services* 4:471–481.
    1976   "The Contribution of the Social Environment to Host Resistance."
            American Journal of Epidemiology 104(2):107–123.
Celentano, David D., Martha S. Linet, and Walter F. Stewart
    1990   "Gender Differences in the Experience of Headache." *Social Science
            and Medicine* 30(12): 1289–1295.

Chagnon, Napoleon A.

1983   *The Yanamamo: The Fierce People*. New York: Holt, Rinehart, and Winston.

Chaney, Elsa M. and Marianne Schmink

1980   "Women and Modernization: Access to Tools." In *Sex and Class in Latin America: Women's Perspectives on Politics, Economics, and the Family in the Third World,* ed. June Nash and Helen Icken Safa, pp. 160–182. South Hadley, MA: J. F. Bergin.

Chodorow, Nancy

1974   "Family Structure and Feminine Personality." In *Woman, Culture, and Society,* ed. Michelle Zimbalist Rosaldo and Louise Lamphere, pp. 43–66. Stanford, CA: Stanford University Press.

Cobb, Sidney

1974   "A Model for Life Events and Their Consequences." In *Stressful Life Events, Their Nature and Effects* ed. Barbara Snell Dohrenwend and Bruce P. Dohrenwend, pp. 151–156. New York: John Wiley.

Coles, Robert and Jane Hallowell Coles

1978   *Women of Crisis: Lives of Struggle and Hope*. New York: Seymour Lawrence, Delacorte Press.

Collier, Jane Fishburne and Sylvia Junko Yanagisako

1987   *Gender and Kinship: Essays Toward a Unified Analysis*. Stanford, CA: Stanford University Press.

Connell, Robert William

1987   *Gender and Power: Society, the Person, and Sexual Politics*. Cambridge: Polity Press.

Counts, Dorothy Ayers

1982   "'All Men Do It': Wife Beating in Kaliai, Papua New Guinea." In *Sanctions and Sanctuary: Cultural Perspectives on the Beating of Wives,* ed. Dorothy Ayers Counts, Judith K. Brown, and Jacquelyn C. Campbell, pp. 63–76. Boulder, CO: Westview Press.

Crawford, Robert

1984   "A Cultural Account of 'Health': Control, Release and the Social Body." In *Issues in the Political Economy of Health Care,* ed. John McKinlay, pp. 60–106. New York: Tavistock Publications.

Davis, Dona L. and Setha M. Low, eds.

1989   *Gender, Health, and Illness: The Case of Nerves*. New York: Hemisphere.

Day, R., J. A. Nielson, A. Korten, G. Ernberg, K. C. Dube, J. Gerhart, A. Jablensky, C. Leon, A. Marsella, M. Olatawura, N. Sartorius, E. Strömgren, R. Takahashi, N. Wig, and L. C. Wynne

1987   "Stressful Life Events Preceding the Acute Onset of Schizophrenia: A Cross-National Study from the World Health Organization." *Culture, Medicine and Psychiatry* 11(2):123–205.

Dean, Alfred and Nan Lin

1977   "The Stress-Buffering Role of Social Support." *Journal of Nervous and Mental Disease* 165:403–417.

de Beauvoir, Simone
  1980a "From an Interview." In *New French Feminisms: An Anthology,* ed.
         Elaine Marks and Isabelle de Courtivron, pp. 142–150. Amherst: Uni-
         versity of Massachusetts Press.
  1980b "Introduction to *The Second Sex.*" In *New French Feminisms: An An-
         thology,* ed. Elaine Marks and Isabelle de Courtivron, pp. 41–56. Am-
         herst: University of Massachusetts Press.
de Jesus, Carolina Maria
  1962   *Child of the Dark: The Diary of Carolina Maria de Jesus,* trans. David St.
         Clair. New York: E. P. Dutton.
de Lauretis, Teresa
  1984   *Alice Doesn't: Feminism, Semiotics, Cinema.* Bloomington: Indiana
         University Press.
De Leon, Friar Luis
  1943   *The Perfect Wife* [1584], trans. Alice Philena Hubbard. Denton, TX:
         College Press.
Deliege, Denise
  1982   "Classification of Social Problems Affecting Health: A New Concep-
         tual Framework." In *Psychosocial Factors Affecting Health,* ed. Mack Lip-
         kin, Jr. and Karel Kupka, pp. 219–240. New York: Praeger Publishers.
Devereaux, Leslie
  1987   "Gender Difference and the Relations of Inequality in Zinacantan." In
         *Dealing with Inequality: Analysing Gender Relations in Melanesia and
         Beyond,* ed. Marilyn Strathern, pp. 89–111. Cambridge: Cambridge
         University Press.
Dewey, John
  1929   *Experience and Nature.* New York: W. W. Norton & Company, Inc.
Diccionario
  1987   *Diccionario de Especialidades Farmaceuticas.* 33rd edition. Mexico City.
Dohrenwend, Bruce P. and Barbara Snell Dohrenwend
  1976   "Sex Difference and Psychiatric Disorders." *American Journal of Sociol-
         ogy* 81:447–454.
  1979   "The Conceptualization and Measurement of Stressful Life Events:
         An Overview of the Issues." In *The Psychology of the Depressive Disorders,*
         ed. Richard A. Depue, pp. 105–124. New York: Academic Press.
Douglas, Mary
  1966   *Purity and Danger: An Analysis of Concepts of Pollution and Taboo.*
         London: Routledge and Kegan Paul.
Doyal, Lesley
  1979   *The Political Economy of Health.* Boston: South End Press.
Dressler, William W.
  1990   "Education, Lifestyle, and Arterial Blood Pressure." *Journal of Psycho-
         somatic Research* 34(5):515–523.
Durkheim, Emile
  1951   *Suicide, a Study in Sociology,* trans. John A. Spaulding and George
         Simpson. Glencoe, IL: Free Press.

Dwyer, Ellen
    1984   "A Historical Perspective." In *Sex Roles and Psychopathology,* ed. Cathy
             Spatz Widom, pp. 19–48. New York: Plenum Press.
Eckenrode, John and Susan Gore
    1981   "Stressful Events and Social Supports." In *Social Networks and Social
             Support,* ed. Benjamin H. Gottlieb, pp. 43–67. Beverly Hills, CA: Sage
             Publications.
Ehlers, Tracy Bachrach
    1990   *Silent Looms: Women and Production in a Guatemalan Town.* Boulder,
             CO: Westview Press.
Ehrenreich, Barbara and Deirdre English
    1979   *For Her Own Good: 150 Years of the Experts' Advice to Women.* Garden
             City, NY: Anchor Press/Doubleday.
Eisenberg, Leon
    1977   "Disease and Illness: Distinctions Between Professional and Popular
             Ideas of Sickness." *Culture, Medicine and Psychiatry* 1(1):9–23.
Elshtain, Jean Bethke
    1981   *Public Man, Private Woman: Women in Social and Political Thought.*
             Princeton, NJ: Princeton University Press.
Engel, George L.
    1977   "The Need for a New Medical Model: A Challenge for Biomedicine."
             Science 196:129–136.
Favret-Saada, Jeanne
    1980   *Deadly Words: Witchcraft in the Bocage,* trans. Catherine Cullen. New
             York: Cambridge University Press.
    1990   "About Participation." *Culture, Medicine and Psychiatry* 14(2):189–200.
Finkler, Kaja
    1974   *Estudio Comparativo de la Economia de Dos Comunidades de México.*
             SepIni 23. Mexico City: Instituto Nacional Indigenista.
    1981   "A Comparative Study of Health Seekers: Or, Why Do Some People
             Go to Doctors Rather Than to Spiritualist Healers?" *Medical Anthro-
             pology* 5:383–424.
    1983   "Dissident Sectarian Movements, the Catholic Church and Social
             Class in Mexico." *Comparative Studies in Society and History: An Inter-
             national Quarterly* 25(2):277–305.
    1985a "Symptomatic Differences Between the Sexes in Rural Mexico." *Cul-
             ture, Medicine and Psychiatry* 9(1):27–57.
    1985b *Spiritualist Healers in Mexico.* South Hadley, MA: Bergin and Garvey.
    1986   "The Social Consequence of Wellness: A View of Healing Outcomes
             from Micro and Macro Perspectives." *International Journal of Health
             Services* 16(4):627–642.
    1989a Review of *A Mexican Elite Family* by Larissa Adler Lomnitz and
             Marisol Perez-Liaauer. *American Ethnologist* 16:597–598.
    1989b "The University of Nerves." In *Gender, Health, and Illness: The Case of
             Nerves,* ed. Dona L. Davis and Setha M. Low, pp. 79–87. New York:
             Hemisphere.

1991   *Physicians at Work, Patients in Pain: Biomedical Practice and Patient Response in Mexico.* Boulder, CO: Westview Press.

Flax, Jane

1991   *Thinking Fragments: Psychoanalysis, Feminism, and Postmodernism in the Contemporary West.* Berkeley: University of California Press.

Forgacs, David and Geoffrey Nowell-Smith, eds.

1985   *Antonio Gramsci: Selections from Cultural Writings.* Cambridge, MA: Howard University Press.

Foster, George McClelland and Barbara Gallatin Anderson

1978   *Medical Anthropology.* New York: John Wiley and Sons.

Foucault, Michel

1980   *The History of Sexuality, Volume I: An Introduction.* New York: Vintage Books.

Franco, Jean

1989   *Plotting Women: Gender and Representation in Mexico.* New York: Columbia University Press.

Freud, Sigmund

1990   *Some Physical Consequences of the Anatomical Distinction Between the Sexes* [1925]. Standard Edition, vol. 19. In *Freud on Women,* ed. Elisabeth Young-Bruehl, pp. 304–314. New York: W. W. Norton.

Friedl, Ernestine

1978   "Society and Sex Roles." In Friedl, *Human Nature,* pp. 186–191. New York: Harcourt, Brace, Jovanovich.

Gadow, Sally

1980   "Body and Self: A Dialectic." *Journal of Medicine and Philosophy* 5:172–185.

Geertz, Clifford

1965   "Religion as a Cultural System." In *Anthropological Approaches to the Study of Religion,* ed. Michael P. Banton, pp. 1–46. Association of Social Anthropologists Monograph 3. London: Tavistock Publications.

1983   "From the Native's Point of View: On the Nature of Anthropological Understanding." In Geertz, *Local Knowledge: Further Essays in Interpretive Anthropology,* pp. 55–70. New York: Basic Books.

Giddens, Anthony

1984   *The Constitution of Society: Outline of the Theory of Structuration.* Berkeley: University of California Press.

Gilligan, Carol

1982   *In a Different Voice: Psychological Theory and Women's Development* Cambridge, MA: Harvard University Press.

1990   "Joining the Resistance: Psychology, Politics, Girls and Women." *Michigan Quarterly Review* 29:501–536.

Good, Byron J. and Mary Jo Delvecchio Good

1981a   "The Semantics of Medical Discourse." In *Sciences and Cultures: Anthropological and Historical Studies of the Sciences,* ed. Everett Mendelsohn and Yehuda Elkana, pp. 177–212. Sociology of the Sciences, vol. 5. Dordrecht: D. Reidel.

1981b "The Meaning of Symptoms: A Cultural Hermeneutic Model for Clinical Practice." In *The Relevance of Social Science for Medicine,* ed. Leon Eisenberg and Arthur Kleinman, pp. 165–196. Dordrecht: D. Reidel.

Gove, Walter R.
1978   "Sex Differences in Mental Illness Among Adult Men and Women: An Evaluation of Four Questions Raised Regarding the Evidence on the Higher Rates of Women." *Social Science and Medicine* 12B:187–198.

Gove, Walter R. and Michael Hughes
1979   "Possible Causes of the Apparent Sex Differences in Physical Health: An Empirical Investigation." *American Sociological Review* 44:126–146.

Groddeck, George
1977   *The Meaning of Illness: Selected Psychoanalytic Writings.* Trans. George Mandler. London: Hogarth Press.

Grosskurth, Phyllis
1991   "The New Psychology of Women." *New York Review of Books,* October, pp. 25–32.

Hahn, Robert A.
1984   "Rethinking 'Illness' and 'Disease.'" *Contributions to Asian Studies* 18:1–23.

Handwerker, W. Penn
1986   "Culture and Reproduction: Exploring Micro/Macro Linkages." In *Culture and Reproduction: An Anthropological Critique of Demographic Transition Theory,* ed. W. Penn Handwerker, pp. 1–28. Boulder, CO: Westview Press.

Harré, Rom
1986   *The Social Construction of Emotions.* New York: Basil Blackwell.

Hawkesworth, Mary E.
1989   "Knowers, Knowing, Known: Feminist Theory and Claims of Truth." In *Feminist Theory in Practice and Process,* ed. Micheline R. Malson et al., pp. 327–351. Chicago: University of Chicago Press.

Helman, Cecil
1984   *Culture, Health, and Illness: An Introduction for Health Professionals.* Bristol: Wright/PSG.

Hemmings, Susan
1985   *A Wealth of Experience: The Lives of Older Women.* London: Pandora Press.

Hinkle, Lawrence E.
1974   "The Effects of Exposure to Culture Change, Social Change and Changes in Interpersonal Relationships on Health." In *Stressful Life Events,* ed. Barbra Snell Dohrenwend and Bruce P. Dohrenwend, pp. 45–72. New York: John Wiley and Sons.

Hinkle, Lawrence E. et al.
1960   "An Examination of the Relation Between Symptoms Disability and Serious Illness in Two Homogeneous Groups of Men and Women." *American Journal of Public Health* 50:1327–1341.

Hoare, Quintin and Geoffrey Nowell Smith, eds. and trans.
  1971   *Selections from the Prison Notebooks of Antonio Gramsci.* New York:
           International Publishers.
Holmes, T. and M. Masuda
  1974   "Life Change and Illness Susceptibility." In *Stressful Life Events, Their
           Nature and Effects,* ed. Barbara Snell Dohrenwend and Bruce P. Doh-
           renwend, pp. 45–72. New York: John Wiley and Sons.
House, James S. et al.
  1988   "Social Relationships and Health." *Science* 241:540–545.
Hubbard, Ruth
  1990   "The Political Nature of 'Human Nature.'" In *Theoretical Perspectives
           on Sexual Difference,* ed. Deborah L. Rhode, pp. 63–73. New Haven,
           CT, and London: Yale University Press.
Hyman, Martin
  1972   "Social Isolation and Performance in Rehabilitation." *Journal of
           Chronic Diseases* 25:85–97.
Ibrahim, Michael A.
  1980   "The Changing Health State of Women." *American Journal of Public
           Health* 70:120–121.
Jack, Dana Crowley
  1991   *Silencing the Self: Women and Depression.* Cambridge, MA: Harvard
           University Press.
Jacobson, David
  1987   "The Cultural Context of Social Support and Support Networks."
           Medical Anthropology Quarterly 1:42–67.
Jelin, Elizabeth, ed.
  1990   *Women and Social Change in Latin America,* trans. J. Ann Zammit and
           Marilyn Thomson. Atlantic Highlands, NJ: Zed Books.
Johnson, Thomas M.
  1987   "Premenstrual Syndrome as a Western Culture-Specific Disorder."
           Culture, Medicine and Psychiatry 11:337–356.
Johnson, Thomas M. and Carolyn F. Sargent
  1990   *Medical Anthropology: A Handbook of Theory and Method.* New York:
           Greenwood Press.
Jordanova, L. J.
  1980   "Natural Facts: A Historical Perspective on Science and Sexuality." In
           Nature, Culture and Gender, ed. Carol P. MacCormack and Marilyn
           Strathern, pp. 46–69. Cambridge: Cambridge University Press.
Kaplan, Berton H., John Cassell, and Susan Gore
  1979   "Social Support and Health." In *Patients, Physicians, and Illness: A
           Sourcebook in Behavioral Science and Health,* ed. E. Gartly Jaco, pp. 102–
           116. New York: Free Press.
Kaufert, Patricia A.
  1982   "Anthropology and the Menopause: The Development of a Theoret-
           ical Framework." *Maturitas* 4(169):181–193.

Kellam, Sheppard G.
1974   "Stressful Life Events and Illness: Research Area in Need of Conceptual Development." In *Stressful Life Events, Their Nature and Effects,* ed. Barbara Snell Dohrenwend and Bruce P. Dohrenwend, pp. 207–214. New York: John Wiley and Sons.

Kirmayer, Laurence J.
1988   "Mind and Body as Metaphors: Hidden Values in Biomedicine." In *Biomedicine Examined,* ed. Margaret Lock and Deborah R. Gordon, pp. 57–93. Dordrecht: Kluwer Academic Publishers.

Kleinman, Arthur
1978   "Concepts and Models for the Comparison of Medical Systems as Cultural Systems." *Social Science and Medicine* 12:85–93.

1980   *Patients and Healers in the Context of Culture: An Exploration of the Borderland Between Anthropology Medicine and Psychiatry,* Berkeley: University of California Press.

1986   *Social Origins of Distress and Disease: Depression, Neurasthenia and Pain in Modern China.* New Haven, CT: Yale University Press.

1988   *The Illness Narratives: Suffering, Healing, and the Human Condition,* New York: Basic Books.

Kleinman, Arthur and Joan Kleinman
1991   "Suffering and Its Professional Transformation: Toward an Ethnography of Interpersonal Experience." *Culture, Medicine and Psychiatry* 15(3):275–301.

Klerman, Gerald L. and J. E. Izen
1977   "The Effects of Bereavement and Grief on Physical Health and General Well-Being." In *Epidemiologic Studies in Psychosomatic Medicine,* ed. Stanislav Kasl and Franz Reichsman, pp. 63–104. Advances in Psychosomatic Medicine, vol. 9. Basel: S. Karger.

Knaster, Meri
1975   "Women in Latin America: The State of Research." *Latin American Research Review* 11(1):3–74.

Kristeva, Julia.
1981   "Women's Time." In *Feminist Theory: A Critique of Ideology,* ed. Nannerl O. Keohane, Michelle Zimbalist Rosaldo, and Barbara C. Gelpi, pp. 31–54. Chicago: University of Chicago Press.

Kuznesof, Elizabeth
1989   "Household and Family Studies." In *Latinas of the Americas: A Source Book,* ed. K. Lynn Stoner, pp. 305–337. New York: Garland Publishing.

Lafaye, Jacques
1974   *Quetzalcóatl and Guadalupe: The Formation of Mexican National Consciousness, 1531–1813.* Chicago: University of Chicago Press.

Landes, R.
1947   *The City of Women.* New York: Macmillan.

Landy, David, ed.
1977   *Culture, Disease, and Healing: Studies in Medical Anthropology.* New York: Macmillan.

Laqueur, Thomas Walter
    1990   *Making Sex: Body and Gender from the Greeks to Freud.* Cambridge, MA: Harvard University Press.

Lavrin, Asunción, ed.
    1987   "Women, the Family and Social Change in Latin America." *World Affairs* 150:109–128.
    1989   *Sexuality and Marriage in Colonial Latin America.* Lincoln: University of Nebraska Press.

Leacock, Eleanor Burke
    1981   *Myths of Male Dominance: Collected Articles on Women Cross-Culturally.* New York: Monthly Review Press.

Leder, Drew
    1985   "Medicine and Paradigms of Embodiment." *Journal of Medicine and Philosophy* 9:29–43.
    1990   *The Absent Body.* Chicago: University of Chicago Press.

Levy, Robert
    1984   "Emotion, Knowing, and Culture." In *Culture Theory: Essays on Mind, Self, and Emotions* ed. Richard A. Shweder and Robert A. LeVine, pp. 214–223. New York and Cambridge: Cambridge University Press.

Lewis, I. M.
    1971   *Ecstatic Religion: An Anthropological Study of Spirit Possession and Shamanism.* Middlesex: Penguin Books.

Lieban, R. W.
    1978   "Sex Differences and Cultural Dimensions of Medical Phenomena in a Philippine Setting." In *Culture and Curing: Anthropological Perspectives on Traditional Beliefs and Practices,* ed. Peter Morley and Roy Wallis, pp. 99–114. London: Peter Owen.

Lock, Margaret
    1986   "Ambiguities of Aging: Japanese Experience and Perceptions of Menopause." *Culture, Medicine and Psychiatry* 10(1):23–46.

Lomnitz, Larissa Adler de and Marisol Pérez-Lizaur
    1987   *A Mexican Elite Family, 1820–1980: Kinship, Class, and Culture.* Princeton, NJ: Princeton University Press.

Low, Setha M.
    1989   "Gender, Emotion, and *Nervios* in Urban Guatemala." In *Gender, Health, and Illness: The Case of Nerves,* ed. Dona L. Davis and Setha M. Low, pp. 23–48. New York: Hemisphere.

Lutz, Catherine A.
    1988   *Unnatural Emotions: Everyday Sentiments on a Micronesian Atoll and Their Challenge to Western Theory.* Chicago: University of Chicago Press.

MacCormack, Carol P. and Marilyn Strathern, eds.
    1980   *Nature, Culture and Gender.* Cambridge: Cambridge University Press.

Macias, A.
    1973   "The Mexican Revolution Was No Revolution for Women." In *History of Latin American Civilization,* vol. 2, ed. L. Hanke, pp. 459–469. Boston: Little, Brown.

MacKinnon, Catharine A.

1982   "Feminism, Marxism, Method, and the State: An Agenda for Theory."
In *Feminist Theory: A Critique of Ideology,* ed. Nannerl O. Keohane et
al., pp. 1–30. Chicago: University of Chicago Press.

1989   *Toward a Feminist Theory of the State.* Cambridge, MA: Harvard University Press.

MacKintosh, Maureen

1981   "The Sexual Division of Labour and the Subordination of Women."
In *Of Marriage and the Market: Women's Subordination in International
Perspective,* ed. Kate Young, Carol Wolkowitz, and Roslyn McCullagh,
pp. 1–15. London: CSE Books.

Maretzki, Thomas W.

1992   "Georg Groddeck's Integrative Massage and Psychotherapy Treat-
ment in Germany." In *Ethnopsychiatry: The Cultural Construction of
Professional and Folk Psychiatries,* ed. Atwood D. Gaines, pp. 379–394.
Albany: State University of New York Press.

Marieskind, Helen I.

1980   "Impact of Technology on Women's Health Care." Chapter 7 in Marieskind, *Women in the Health System: Patients, Providers, and Programs,*
pp. 235–282. St. Louis: C. V. Mosby.

Marks, Elaine and Isabelle de Courtivron

1980   "Introductions." In *New French Feminisms: An Anthology,* ed. Elaine
Marks and Isabelle de Courtivron, pp. 1–9. Amherst: University of
Massachusetts Press.

Martin, Emily

1987   *The Woman in the Body: A Cultural Analysis of Reproduction* Boston:
Beacon Press.

Martin, M. Kay and Barbara Voorhies

1975   *Female of the Species.* New York: Columbia University Press.

McClain, Carole Shepherd

1989   *Women as Healers: Cross-Cultural Perspectives* New Brunswick, NJ:
Rutgers University Press.

McKeown, Thomas

1979   *The Role of Medicine: Dream, Mirage, or Nemesis?* Princeton, NJ:
Princeton University Press.

Mead, George H.

1964   *On Social Psychology: Selected Papers.* Chicago: University of Chicago
Press.

Mechanic, David

1974   "Discussion of Research Programs and Relations Between Stressful
Life Events and Episodes of Physical Illness." In *Stressful Life Events,
Their Nature and Effects* ed. Barbara Snell Dohrenwend and Bruce P.
Dohrenwend, pp. 87–89. New York: John Wiley and Sons.

1978   "Sex, Illness, Illness Behavior, and the Use of Health Services." *Social
Science and Medicine* 12B:207–214.

1979   "Correlates of Physician Utilization: Why Do Major Multivariate Studies of Physician Utilization Find Trivial Psychosocial and Organizational Effects?" *Journal of Health and Social Behavior* 20:387–396.

Meigs, Anna
1990   "Multiple Gender Ideologies and Statuses." In *Beyond the Second Sex: New Directions in the Anthropology of Gender,* ed. Peggy Reeves Sanday and Ruth Gallagher Goodenough, pp. 101–112. Philadelphia: University of Pennsylvania Press.

Mendelsohn, Robert S.
1982   *Male Practice: How Doctors Manipulate Women.* Chicago: Contemporary Books.

Merleau-Ponty, M.
1963   *The Structure of Behavior,* trans. Alden L. Fisher. Boston: Beacon Press.

Morgan, Myfanwy, Donald Patrick, and John L. Charlton
1984   "Social Networks and Psychosocial Support Among Disabled." *People, Social Science and Medicine* 19:489–497.

Morris, David B.
1991   *The Culture of Pain.* Berkeley: University of California Press.

Morse, Janice M. and Joy L. Johnson, eds.
1991   *The Illness Experience: Dimensions of Suffering.* Newbury Park, CA: Sage Publications.

Morsy, Soheir
1978   "Sex Roles, Power and Illness in an Egyptian Village." *American Ethnologist* 5:137–150.

1990   "Political Economy in Medical Anthropology." In *Medical Anthropology: Contemporary Theory and Medicine,* ed. Thomas M. Johnson and Carolyn F. Sargent, pp. 26–46. New York: Praeger.

1991   "Safeguarding Women's Bodies: The White Man's Burden Medicalized." *Medical Anthropology Quarterly* 5:19–23.

Mosse, George L.
1985   *Nationalism and Sexuality: Respectability and Abnormal Sexuality in Modern Europe.* New York: Howard Fertig.

Murphy, H. B. M.
1978   "Historic Changes in the Sex Ratios for Different Disorders." *Social Science and Medicine* 12B:143–149.

Nathanson, Constance A.
1975   "Illness and the Feminine Role: A Theoretical Review." *Social Science and Medicine* 75:57–62.

1979   "Sex, Illness, and Medical Care." In *Health, Illness, and Medicine,* ed. Gary L. Albrecht and Paul C. Higgins, pp. 16–40. Chicago: Rand McNally.

Navarro, Vicente
1974   "The Underdevelopment of Health or the Health of Underdevelopment: An Analysis of the Distribution of Human Health Resources in Latin America." *International Journal of Health Services* 4(1):5–27.

1976   *Medicine Under Capitalism*. New York: Prodist.
Nazzari, Muríel
   1991   *Disappearance of the Dowry: Women, Families, and Social Change in São Paulo, Brazil (1600–1900)*. Stanford, CA: Stanford University Press.
Offen, Karen
   1990   "Feminism and Sexual Difference in Historical Perspective." In *Theoretical Perspectives on Sexual Difference,* ed. Deborah L. Rhode, pp. 13–20. New Haven, CT, and London: Yale University Press.
O'Nell, Carl W. and Henry A. Selby
   1968   "Sex Differences in the Incidence of *Susto* in Two Zapotec Pueblos: An Analysis of the Relationships Between Sex Roles, Expectations and a Folk Illness." *Ethnology* 7:95–105.
Ortiz, Sylvia
   1977   *Espiritualismo en Mexico.* Cuadernos de Trabajo. no. 20. Mexico City: Instituto Nacional de Antropologia y Historia.
Ortner, Sherry B.
   1974   "Is Female to Male as Nature Is to Culture?" In *Woman, Culture, and Society,* ed. Michelle Zimbalist Rosaldo and Louise Lamphere, pp. 67–87. Stanford, CA: Stanford University Press.
Osherson, Samuel and Lorna Amara Singham
   1981   "The Machine Metaphor in Medicine." In *Social Contexts of Health, Illness, and Patient Care,* ed. Elliot G. Mishler et al., pp. 218–249. London: Cambridge University Press.
Pandolfi, Mariella.
   1990   "Boundaries Inside the Body: Women's Sufferings in Southern Peasant Italy." *Culture, Medicine and Psychiatry* 14:255–274.
Pan American Health Organization
   1990   *Health Conditions in the Americas: Health of Women*. World Health Organization Publication 524. Washington, DC: WHO.
Parker, Richard G.
   1991   *Bodies, Pleasures, and Passions: Sexual Culture in Contemporary Brazil.* Boston: Beacon Press.
Parvey, Constance F.
   1974   "The Theology and Leadership of Women in the New Testament." In *Religion and Sexism: Images of Woman in the Jewish and Christian Traditions,* ed. Rosemary Radford Ruether, pp. 117–149. New York: Simon and Schuster.
Patai, Daphne
   1988   *Brazilian Women Speak: Contemporary Life Stories.* New Brunswick, NJ: Rutgers University Press.
Patrick, Donald
   1982   *The Longitudinal Disability Interview Survey: Phase II Report.* London: Department of Community Medicine, United Medical Schools of Guy's and St. Thomas's Hospitals.

Paul, Lois

1974   "The Mastery of Work and the Mystery of Sex in a Guatemalan Village." In *Woman, Culture, and Society,* ed. Michelle Zimbalist Rosaldo and Louise Lamphere, pp. 281–299. Stanford, CA: Stanford University Press.

Paykel, L.S.

1974a   "Recent Life Events and Clinical Depression." In *Life Stress and Illness,* ed. E. K. Eric Gunderson and Richard H. Rahe, pp. 134–163. Springfield, IL: Charles C. Thomas.

1974b   "Life Stress and Psychiatric Disorder: Applications of the Clinical Approach." In *Stressful Life Events, Their Nature and Effects,* ed. Barbara Snell Dohrenwend and Bruce P. Dohrenwend, pp. 135–150. New York: John Wiley and Sons.

1979   "Recent Life Events in the Development of the Depressive Disorders." In *The Psychobiology of the Depressive Disorders,* ed. Richard A. Depue, pp. 245–262. New York: Academic Press.

Paz, Octavio

1961   *The Labyrinth of Solitude.* New York: Grove Press.

Personal Narratives Group

1989   *Interpreting Women's Lives: Feminist Theory and Personal Narratives.* Bloomington: Indiana University Press.

Pescatello, Ann M.

1972   "The Female in Ibero-America: An Essay on Research Bibliography and Research Directions." *Latin American Research Review* 7(2):1–17.

1976   *Power and Pain: The Female in Iberian Families, Societies, and Cultures.* Westport, CT: Greenwood Press.

Phillips, Lynne

1990   "Rural Women in Latin America: Directions for Future Research." *Latin American Research Review* 25(3):89–107.

Rabkin, Judith G. and Elmer L. Struening

1976   "Life Events, Stress and Illness." *Science* 194:1013–1020.

Reiter, Rayna R.

1975   "Men and Women in the South of France: Public and Private Domains." In *Toward an Anthropology of Women,* ed. Rayna R. Reiter, pp. 252–282. New York: Monthly Review Press.

Rhode, Deborah L.

1990   "Theoretical Perspectives on Sexual Difference." In *Theoretical Perspectives on Sexual Difference,* ed. Deborah L. Rhode, pp. 1–9. New Haven, CT: Yale University Press.

Riessman, Catherine Kohler

1989   "Life Events, Meaning, and Narrative: The Case of Infidelity and Divorce." *Social Science and Medicine* 29(6):743–751.

Romanucci-Ross, Lola, Daniel E. Moerman, Lawrence R. Tancredi, et al.

1983   *The Anthropology of Medicine: From Culture to Method.* South Hadley, MA: Bergin and Garvey.

Rosaldo, Michelle Zimbalist
  1974   "Woman, Culture, and Society: A Theoretical Overview." In *Woman, Culture, and Society,* ed. Michelle Zimbalist Rosaldo and Louise Lamphere, pp. 17–42. Stanford, CA: Stanford University Press.
  1984   "Toward an Anthropology of Self and Feeling." In *Culture Theory: Essays on Mind, Self, and Emotion,* ed. Richard A. Shweder and Robert A. LeVine, pp. 139–157. New York and Cambridge: Cambridge University Press.
Rosenberg, Charles E.
  1974   "The Bitter Fruit: Heredity, Disease, and Social Thought in Nineteenth Century America." *Perspectives in American History* 8:189–235.
Rosenfield, Sarah
  1980   "Sex Differences in Depression: Do Women Always Have a Higher Rate?" *Journal of Health and Social Behavior* 21:33–42.
Roskies, Ethel
  1978   "Sex, Culture and Illness: An Overview." *Social Science and Medicine* 12B:139–141.
Rubel, Arthur J., Carl W. O'Nell, and Rolando Collado-Ardón
  1991   *Susto, a Folk Illness.* Berkeley: University of California Press.
Rubin, Lillian Breslow
  1976   *Worlds of Pain: Life in the Working-Class Family.* New York: Basic Books.
Russett, Cynthia Eagle
  1989   *Sexual Science: The Victorian Construction of Womanhood.* Cambridge, MA: Harvard University Press.
Sacks, Karen
  1974   "Engels Revisited: Women, the Organization of Production, and Private Property." In *Woman, Culture, and Society,* ed. Michelle Zimbalist Rosaldo and Louise Lamphere, pp. 207–222. Stanford, CA: Stanford University Press.
Sanday, Peggy Reeves
  1974   "Female Status in the Public Domain." In *Woman, Culture, and Society,* ed. Michelle Zimbalist Rosaldo and Louise Lamphere, pp. 189–206. Stanford, CA: Stanford University Press.
  1981   *Female Power and Male Dominance: On the Origins of Sexual Inequality.* Cambridge: Cambridge University Press.
Sayers, Janet
  1982   *Biological Politics: Feminist and Anti-Feminist Perspectives.* New York: Tavistock.
Scarry, Elaine
  1985   *The Body in Pain: The Making and Unmaking of the World.* New York: Oxford University Press.
Schütz, Alfred
  1967   "Phenomenology and the Social Sciences." In *Phenomenology: The Philosophy of Edmund Husserl and Its Interpretation,* ed. Joseph J. Kockelmans, pp. 450–472. Garden City, NY: Doubleday.

Secretaria de Salud
  1990   *La Salud de la Mujer en Mexico:* Dirección General de Salud Materno
          Infantil Program Nacional "Mujer, Salud, y Desarrollo." Mexico City:
          Secretaria de Salud.
Selye, Hans
  1978   *The Stress of Life.* New York: McGraw-Hill.
Sheehan, Elizabeth
  1981   "Victorian Clitoridectomy: Isaac Baker Brown and His Harmless
          Operative Procedure." *Medical Anthropology Newsletter* 12:9–15.
Shorter, Edward
  1992   *From Paralysis to Fatigue: A History of Psychosomatic Illness in the Modern
          Era.* New York: The Free.
Shweder, Richard A.
  1985   "Menstrual Pollution, Soul Loss, and the Comparative Study of Emo-
          tions." In *Culture and Depression: Studies in the Anthropology and Cross-
          Cultural Psychiatry of Affect and Disorder,* ed. Arthur Kleinman and
          Byron Good, pp. 182–215. Berkeley: University of California Press.
Slade, D. L.
  1973   "Marital Status and Sexual Identity: The Position of Women in Mexi-
          can Peasant Society." In *International Congress of Anthropological and
          Ethnological Sciences,* ed. R. Rohrlich-Leavitt, pp. 129–148. Chicago:
          University of Chicago Press.
Smith-Rosenberg, Carroll
  1985   *Disorderly Conduct: Visions of Gender in Victorian America.* New York:
          Alfred A. Knopf.
Solomon, Robert C.
  1984   "Getting Angry." In *Culture Theory: Essays on Mind, Self, and Emotion,*
          ed. Richard A. Shweder and Robert A. LeVine, pp. 238–254. New
          York and Cambridge: Cambridge University Press.
Stevens, Evelyn
  1973   "Marianismo: The Other Face of Machismo in Latin America. In
          Female and Male in Latin America, ed. Ann Pescatello, pp. 89–102.
          Pittsburgh: University of Pittsburgh Press.
Stolcke, Verena
  1981   "Women's Labours: The Naturalization of Social Inequality and
          Women's Subordination." In *Of Marriage and the Market: Women's
          Subordination in International Perspective,* ed. Kate Young, Carol Wol-
          kowitz, and Roslyn McCullagh, pp. 30–48. London: CSE Books.
Stoll, David
  1990   *Is Latin America Turning Protestant?* Berkeley: University of California
          Press.
Stoner, K. Lynn
  1989   *Latinas of the Americas: A Source Book.* New York: Garland.
Strathern, Marilyn, ed.
  1987   *Dealing with Inequality: Analyzing Gender Relations in Melanesia and
          Beyond.* Cambridge: Cambridge University Press.

1988   *The Gender of the Gift: Problems with Women and Problems with Society in Melanesia.* Berkeley: University of California Press.

Taussig, Michael T.
1980   "Reification and the Consciousness of the Patient." *Social Science and Medicine* 14B:3–13.

Tavris, Carol
1982   *Anger: The Misunderstood Emotion.* New York: Simon and Schuster.

Taylor, William B.
1979   *Drinking, Homicide, and Rebellion in Colonial Mexican Villages.* Stanford, CA: Stanford University Press.

Tirado, Thomas C.
1991   *Celsa's World: Conversations with a Mexican Peasant Woman.* Special Studies no. 27. Tempe: Arizona State University Center for Latin American Studies.

Tomes, Nancy
1990   "Historical Perspectives on Women and Mental Illness." In *Women, Health, and Medicine in America: A Historical Handbook,* ed. Rima D. Apple, pp. 143–171. New York: Garland.

Tong, Rosemarie.
1989   *Feminist Thought: A Comprehensive Introduction.* Boulder, CO, and San Francisco: Westview Press.

Touraine, Alain
1988   *The Return of the Actor: An Essay in Sociology.* Minneapolis: University of Minnesota Press.

Travis, Cheryl Brown
1988   *Women and Health Psychology: Biomedical Issues.* Hillsdale, NJ: Lawrence Erlbaum Associates.

Tuckett, David
1976   *An Introduction to Medical Sociology.* London: Tavistock Publications.

Turner, Bryan
1984   *The Body and Society: Explorations in Social Theory.* New York: Basil Blackwell.

Tutino, John
1983   "Power, Class, and Family: Men and Women in the Mexican Elite, 1750–1810." *The Americas* 39:359–381.

Verbrugge, Lois M.
1978   "Sex and Gender in Health and Medicine." *Social Science and Medicine* 12:329–333.
1990   "Pathways of Health and Death." In *Women, Health, and Medicine in America: A Historical Handbook,* ed. Rima D. Apple, pp. 41–79. New York: Garland.

Virchov, Rudolf
1958   *Disease, Life, and Man.* Stanford, CA: Stanford University Press.

Waitzkin, Howard
1983   *The Second Sickness: Contradictions of Capitalist Health Care.* New York: Free Press.

Warren, Kay B. and C. Bourque

    1991   "Women, Technology, and International Development Ideologies: Analyzing Feminist Voices." In *Gender at the Crossroads of Knowledge: Feminist Anthropology in the Post-modern Era,* ed. Micaela di Leonardo, pp. 278–311. Berkeley: University of California Press.

Watson, Lawrence C. and Maria-Barbara Watson-Franke

    1985   *Interpreting Life Histories: An Anthropological Inquiry.* New Brunswick, NJ: Rutgers University Press.

Weissman, M. M. and G. L. Klerman.

    1977   "Sex Differences and the Epidemiology of Depression." *Archives of General Psychiatry* 34:98–112.

Weller, Robert H. and Leon F. Bouvier

    1981   *Population.* New York: St. Martin's Press.

Widom, Cathy Spatz, ed.

    1984   *Sex Roles and Psychopathology.* New York and London: Plenum Press.

Willems, Emílio

    1975   *Latin American Culture: An Anthropological Synthesis.* New York: Harper and Row.

Wolf, Eric

    1958   "The Virgin of Guadalupe: A Mexican National Symbol." *Journal of American Folklore* 71:34–39.

Yanagisako, Sylvia J. and Jane F. Collier

    1990   "The Mode of Reproduction in Anthropology." In *Theoretical Perspectives on Sexual Difference,* ed. Deborah L. Rhode, pp. 131–144. New Haven, CT: Yale University Press.

Young, Allan

    1982   "The Anthropologies of Illness and Sickness." In *Annual Review of Anthropology.* 11:257–285.

    1983   "Rethinking Ideology." *International Journal of Health Services* 13:203–219.

Young, James Clay

    1981   *Medical Choice in a Mexican Village.* New Brunswick, NJ: Rutgers University Press.

Young-Bruehl, Elisabeth

    1990   *Freud on Women: A Reader.* New York: W. W. Norton.

Zavella, Patricia

    1991   "*Mujeres* in Factories: Race and Class Perspectives on Women, Work, and Family." In *Gender at the Crossroads of Knowledge: Feminist Anthropology in the Postmodern Era,* ed. Micaela di Leonardo, pp. 312–336. Berkeley: University of California Press.

Zborowski, Mark

    1952   "Cultural Components in Response to Pain." *Journal of Social Issues* 8:16–30.

Glossary of Spanish Words and Phrases

Chemical names for medications listed in the chapter notes are translated there from their listings in the Mexican *Diccionario de Especialidades Farmaceuticas,* 33rd edition.

aguantando: gerund of *aguantar,* "to bear, endure"; suggests that the person is making the best of a bad situation. The theme of "enduring" recurs consistently in the women's narratives.

aguanto: first person present tense of *aguantar*; see *aguantando.*

anginas: pain in the throat in general and the tonsils in particular.

asustado/asustada: in a state of fright, having suffered a *susto.*

bien conchudo/conchuda: refers to someone who is lazy or who takes advantage of a situation.

boca del estómago: "mouth of the stomach"; the area around the diaphragm between the lower front ribs and the upper abdomen.

cabrón/cabróna: in the sense used by Juana, refers to someone who is "stupid" or an "idiot."

casa chica: "a little house"; usually refers to a man's second household established with a mistress.

cerebro: the occipital-medullar region of the head, down to the neck muscle.

chantajear: to blackmail; in the sense used by Margarita, refers to emotional blackmail or manipulation.

chingada (or *chingona*): a violated woman, one who is fucked.

cintura: pain in the waist or lower back; associated by women with pain in the ovaries.

comadre: female ritual relative.

como debe de ser: the way things ought to be.

compadre: ritual relative.

cuarentena: the forty days a woman is supposed to rest after giving birth.

empacho: bolus or lump attached to the stomach, traditionally believed to be experienced by children.

envídia: envy; almost always suggests maleficence or witchcraft.

gran chingón: motherfucker.

hacer concha: "to make a shell"; intentionally to ignore a situation, usually an unpleasant one.

la mala vida: a situation when a man treats his wife badly, abuses her physically, and fails to support her.

loquito: diminutive of *loco,* a crazy person. The use of the diminutive removes the "sting" and stigma from the designation.

madre soltera: common designation for a single mother.

mi hija: my daughter; usually addressed to female children, also used as a term of endearment by a father or lover.

mi reina: my queen, a term used by mothers to daughters or as a term of endearment.

negro: dark, black.

niño popis: a spoiled young person from the upper classes.

ovarios: pain in the ovaries, or fallen womb, a typical symptom often reported by women referring to pain in the abdominal region.

por las dos leyes: "by the two laws"; refers to being married in both a civil and a religious ceremony.

presión (or *presión alta y baja*): high and low blood pressure, or just "pressure," is characterized by a wide variety of symptoms that incorporate the heart, eyes, head, and chest with faintness or feelings of dizziness and tiredness. It occurs when one feels either crestfallen or agitated and angry.

pulmón: "lungs"; used to refer to pain in the upper back.

(lo) que vale es la honra: honor is the most important thing in life.

savila: aloe.

señora: a mature woman; also used to refer to a folk healer, not infrequently a woman who knows how to perform witchcraft.

se sienten más: haughty, arrogant, people who consider themselves better than everyone else.

susto: a fright; often identified as a cause of sickness.

tengo confianza: "I have (*tener*) trust"; usually refers to a person who is not family. To have trust in a person suggests a close relationship outside the family.

tú: informal, intimate, or less respectful second person form of address.

uno vale menos: refers to the loss of one's worth as a person.

usted: formal, honorific second person form of address.

vecindad: city tenement house, usually consisting of numerous one- or two-room apartments constructed around an open courtyard.

Index

This book has been set in Linotron Galliard. Galliard was designed for Mergenthaler in 1978 by Matthew Carter. Galliard retains many of the features of a sixteenth-century typeface cut by Robert Granjon but has some modifications that give it a more contemporary look.

Printed on acid-free paper.